PREFACE.

The question may, with great propriety, be asked, "Why publish another book on a subject which has been ably and thoroughly discussed by so many authors, as the *Evidences of Christianity?*" Perhaps the author will not be able to give a satisfactory answer to this question. An eminent divine says, "The multitude of old books affords no argument against the publication of new ones; since new ones will be read when old ones are neglected, and almost all mankind are in this respect *Athenians.*" To this it may be added, that, though there are a great many good books, there are more bad ones than good; therefore, as bad ones are constantly multiplying, so should the good ones. And though this book may not be so good as others heretofore published, yet I have reason to think it will be read, because the Christian public have always heretofore favored me with their attention when I have asked it. But I have one reason more to give·—Some lessons on the subjects embraced in this book, prefixed to my Scripture Questions, Vol III., have excited considerable interest where they have been studied, and there has seemed to be a call for something from me to accompany them.

On a subject which has been so often discussed as the *Evidences of Christianity*, it could not be expected that there would be much original thought in such a work as this; and considering that there are so many works, prepared with great labor and care, already on the shelves of the bookseller, the propriety of sending forth one possessing so little *thoroughness* as this, may be questioned; but the very *thoroughness* of most of the works which have been written on this subject, renders them in a measure unsuitable for the common reader. They are all important to the *student*; but the author does not write for students. Most of these works present such a mass of matter, that the common mind cannot grasp it, and see at one view the force of the evidence presented; or else they are so much epitomized as to be unreadable. The object of the writer has been, in the following pages, so to classify and condense the evidence, that the whole force of each particular kind might be seen at one view. He is aware that the number of his *pillars* might have been multiplied; for there are several of the points noticed under some of these divisions, which might each constitute an independent series of

THE
FOUR PILLARS:

OR THE
TRUTH OF CHRISTIANITY DEMONSTRATED,

IN

Four Distinct and Independent Series of Proofs:

TOGETHER WITH AN EXPLANATION OF THE

TYPES AND PROPHECIES

CONCERNING

THE MESSIAH.

BY HARVEY NEWCOMB.

WIPF & STOCK · Eugene, Oregon

Wipf and Stock Publishers
199 W 8th Ave, Suite 3
Eugene, OR 97401

The Four Pillars
Or the Truth of Christianity Demonstrated
in Four Distinct and Independent Series of Proofs:
Together with an Explanation of the Types
and Prophecies Concerning the Messiah
By Newcomb, Harvey
Softcover ISBN-13: 978-1-7252-9915-3
Hardcover ISBN-13: 978-1-7252-9916-0
eBook ISBN-13: 978-1-7252-9917-7
Publication date 2/1/2021
Previously published by Seth Goldsmith
and Crocker & Brewster, 1842

This edition is a scanned facsimile of
the original edition published in 1842.

proofs; but it might be doubted whether the edifice would be strengthened by it. The author has endeavored, also, to render the work *practical*, so as to have it a book to be *read* as well as *studied*.

As to the *Types and Prophecies concerning the Messiah*,—works on these subjects are not so common as those on Evidences; and yet, they furnish an important species of evidence. They are likewise rich in instruction upon the way of salvation; and there is great need of their being better understood, preparatory to the study of the New Testament.

Those who study my "Scripture Questions, Vol. III., will find this volume better adapted to the "Introductory Lessons," as a help, than any other one that I have seen. But I hope the schools will not confine themselves to this, but will obtain other books also. I have learned with pleasure that those "Introductory Lessons" have been the occasion of calling forth a series of lectures on the subjects contained in them from many pastors. I hope the publication of this volume will not prevent other pastors from doing the same. I have by no means exhausted the subject; but have left vast treasures untouched.

In collecting materials, I have not thought it necessary, in general, to quote the author specifically from whom facts have been gathered. I have had before me the following works, gleaning from one and another such parts as suited my purpose:—*Horne's*

Introduction; Paley's, Wilson's, Alexander's, McIlvaine's, and *Chalmers's Evidences; Beecher on Skepticism; Keith* and *Kett on the Prophecies; Keith's Demonstration of Truth; Reinhard's Plan; McEwen on Types, the Notes of the most approved Commentators on the Bible;* and several smaller works.

CONTENTS.

	Page
Preface,	iii
Introduction,	1

CHAPTER I.

FIRST PILLAR.

Necessity of Religion. Christianity the only true,	5
Atheism—fruits of,	6
Paganism—defined,	9
Furnishes no suitable object of affection and worship,	9
No pure code of morals,	10
Gives no rational account of the origin and future destiny of man,	10
Transcendentalism,	10
Makes no satisfactory and certain provision for the pardon of sin,	11
Islamism—its doctrines,	13
A caricature of Christianity,	15
Its defects—doctrine of rewards and punishments,	15
Does not satisfy the wants of the human soul,	16
Makes no provision for the expiation and pardon of sin,	16
Presents unworthy views of the world to come,	16
No provision for the renovation of human character,	17
No pure code of morals,	17
Deism or Natural Religion,	18
Includes all who deny the grand essentials of Christianity,	19
Mr. Parker's ordination sermon,	19
Deficient in making no provision for the pardon of sin,	20
No provision for the reformation of sinners,	21
Nothing to inspire devotion,	21
No pure code of morals	23

viii CONTENTS.

Gives no satisfactory information as to the origin of all things, the object of man's existence, and his future destiny, ... 25
Christianity, ... 27
It gives a rational account of the origin of all things, of the object of man's existence, and of his relations and duties to God, ... 27
Furnishes a perfect code of morals, . . . 28
Accounts for the fact of man's present state, . . 29
Makes provision for the pardon of sin, . . 29
Makes provision for thorough reformation of character, 30
Takes hold of the heart, and inspires devotion, . 30
Practical Remarks, ... 33

CHAPTER II.

SECOND PILLAR.

External Evidence, ... 40
Inspiration defined, ... 40
Unitarian views of inspiration, ... 41
Views of Transcendentalists similar, . . . 42
Orthodox views defended, ... 44
Truth of the Scriptures inseparable from their plenary inspiration, ... 48
The New Testament testifies to the inspiration of the Old, ... 49
Quakers and Transcendentalists, . . . 49
Authenticity of the books of the New Testament, . 51
Genuineness of existing copies, ... 60
Their inspiration, ... 63
Practical Remarks, ... 73
Bible to be received with submission, . . . 73
Obligation of all to believe and obey it, . . . 74
Unbelief will not diminish obligation to obey, . 75
A dreadful doom awaits those who read or hear, and obey not, ... 76
Obligation of gratitude for evidence of the truth of the Bible, ... 77

CHAPTER III.

THIRD PILLAR.

Internal Evidence, ... 78
General evidence apparent to the student of the Bible, showing it to be the production of a Supreme Intelligence, ... 78

CONTENTS.

What the Bible teaches concerning God, essential to the Supreme Being,	82
The Scriptures reveal things which could not be otherwise known,	83
They reveal truths above the conception of finite beings,	84
They contain a rational account of the origin of all things,	86
They account, in a rational and satisfactory manner, for the present character and condition of man,	86
The Bible proved a revelation from God by the agreement of its parts,	88
The writers of the Bible profess to speak by inspiration,	90
The majesty of its style,	91
Perfection of its code of morals,	91
The account it gives of Christ, and his plan of salvation,	92
Preservation of the Scriptures, evidence of their divinity,	97
The Bible speaks to the heart and conscience,	98
Conclusion and summary of the argument,	99
Why men do not believe—dislike of the truth,	101
Practical Remarks,	103

CHAPTER IV.

FOURTH PILLAR.

Evidence from the fulfilment of Prophecy,	105
Preliminary remarks,	105
Authenticity of the Pentateuch,	106
Curses, after the fall, compared with facts,	106
Predictions of Noah concerning his sons,	108
Ishmael,	109
Of Isaac concerning his sons,	112
Concerning the children of Israel,	112
Practical Remarks,	123
Awful warning against apostacy,	123

CHAPTER IV.

Fourth Pillar—continued,	128
Comparison of prophecies with accounts of travellers,	128
Respecting Palestine,	129
Concerning the Philistines,	133
The Ammonites,	134
The Edomites,	135
Nineveh,	148
Tyre,	149

CONTENTS.

Babylon,	150
Daniel's prophecy,	155
Destruction of Jerusalem,	166
The seven churches of Asia,	170
Peter's prophecy concerning scoffers and false teachers,	179
Paul, concerning the judicial blindness of those who receive not the truth,	179
John, concerning apostacies,	180
Conclusion,	180

Practical Remarks.

Instability and emptiness of human greatness,	182
Solemn warning to nations that forget God,	183
Folly of those who think God too merciful to punish sinners forever in hell,	183
Certainty of the promises and threatenings of the Bible,	184

CHAPTER V.

Predictions concerning the Messiah,	186
Introductory remarks,	186
Intimation given immediately after the fall,	188
Promises to the patriarchs,	191
Job's prediction of the Redeemer,	192
Prophecies concerning the birth of Christ,	193
Concerning the nation, tribe, or family, of whom Christ should come,	195
Concerning the time of his coming,	196
Prediction of Moses to the children of Israel,	204
Concerning the Spirit of God resting on Christ,	204
Correspondence of Christ's *works* with those predicted of the Messiah,	207
Prophecies concerning the *ministry* of Christ,	207
Concerning his conduct in regard to the applause of men,	209
Concerning his character as a sufferer,	210
Concerning the character of his enemies,	212
Concerning the treatment of him by the people,	212
Concerning his trial and condemnation,	213
Concerning his being delivered up to his enemies,	214
Concerning the conduct of his disciples when he was arrested,	215
Concerning his conduct before Pilate,	215
Concerning his treatment on the cross,	215
Concerning his resurrection and ascension,	217
Concerning the object of his death,	219

Practical Remarks.

The fulfilment of these prophecies proves the divine inspiration of both the Old and New Testaments,	220
These predictions show that the great design of the Bible is to reveal Christ,	220
The whole gospel, as understood by evangelical Christians, revealed in the prophecy of Daniel,	221
Stupidity of those who reject the gospel,	223
No salvation for those who reject Christ,	224
The kingdom of Christ will triumph over all opposition,	224
Piety of Christ to be imitated,	225
Christ an object of love,	229

CHAPTER VI.

On the Types,	232
Introductory remarks,	232
Definition of a type,	233
Adam, a type of Christ,	235
Bloody sacrifices,	237
Noah's ark,	242
Practical Remarks,	243
Great principle on which the scheme of the gospel is founded,	243
True idea of Atonement,	245
No acceptable worship except through Christ,	246
Forsaking all for Christ, illustrated by Abraham's example,	247
Love of God,	248
Exhortation to sinners,	249

CHAPTER VII.

Types—continued,	251
Melchizedek,	251
Isaac and Ishmael,	252
Moses a type of Christ,	253
Moses' vail,	254
Redemption of the children of Israel from Egypt,	255
David a type of Christ,	257
Burial and resurrection of Christ,	257
The leprosy and ceremony of cleansing,	257
Practical Remarks,	258
Why so many Christians live in slavish fear,	258

No salvation by Moses, ... 260
Necessity of a Mediator, ... 261
Why it is so difficult for the impenitent to understand the Gospel, ... 262
The condition of sinners, ... 263
Illustration of Christian experience, ... 266
Nature and necessity of faith illustrated, . . . 269
Dreadful nature of unbelief, ... 271
Conclusion of the whole, ... 273

APPENDIX.

A.

Facts showing the antiquity and authenticity of the Bible, ... 277
Antiquity of the Old Testament, . . . 277
Genuineness of the Old Testament, . . . 278
Facts corroborative of the Scripture narratives, . 279
Agreement of profane history with the New Testament, ... 291
Testimonies of the adversaries of Christianity. . 294

B.

Inspiration, ... 297

INTRODUCTION.

1 Peter, iii. 15.

Be ready always to give an answer to every one that asketh you a reason of the hope that is in you, with meekness and fear.

The Christian religion is not a blind superstition, depending on the implicit faith of its adherents in certain dogmas proposed by its teachers to be received on their authority; but every article of its faith is substantiated by the most unquestionable evidence. A good and substantial reason may be given for every truth which challenges the belief of men. Hence, the apostle exhorts the Christians of his day to be ready always to give a reason of the hope that was in them, that the religion they professed might commend itself to the reason and conscience, both of opposers and revilers, and also, of sincere inquirers after the truth. With them, this was an easy matter. They could say, "Our hope is founded on the fact that Jesus Christ died on the cross to save us from our sins, and rose again for our justification; and that he hath ascended up on high, and now sitteth on the right hand of God, to make intercession for us. These facts we have received from his apostles, who were eye-witnesses to these things; and they have attested the truth of what they say, by the miracles which they have wrought before our eyes. We have also experienced, in our own souls, the saving power of the religion of Jesus."

The obligation to be always ready to give a reason of the hope that is in us, is no less binding on us at the present day; though the evidence to establish the facts and doctrines on which we rely is more remote, and requires more effort on our part to understand it, so as to give a reason for our hope that will convince the inquirer and confound the gainsayer.

It is proper, also, in this connection, to remark on the *manner* in which this reason of our hope is to be given. We are not to treat all inquiries and objections superciliously, or with contempt; nor to settle the matter simply by saying *we know;* but we are to render a good reason for our hope, and that in a good spirit—"with meekness and fear." If we treat opposers with harshness or contempt, they will be confirmed in their unbelief, and say that we are conscious of the want of evidence, and therefore refuse to reason the matter. But, if we treat them kindly and answer them judiciously, we may lead them to investigate, and perhaps, by the spirit we manifest, prove the superiority of our faith.

The truth of Christianity is substantiated by at least four distinct and independent series of proofs; either of which is, by itself, sufficient to establish its authenticity and divine authority, in the view of any unprejudiced mind. These are contained in the fol-

INTRODUCTION.

lowing propositions, each of which I propose to prove by itself·

I Man needs, and must have, some sort of religion: Christianity is the only system that is adapted to the necessities of man's moral nature: therefore, Christianity must be the only true religion.

II. The authenticity of the Holy Scriptures, contained in the Old and New Testament, as a revelation from God, is clearly established by *external* evidence.

III. The Bible contains, within itself, the most conclusive evidence of its divine origin.

IV. The Bible contains prophecies which have been fulfilled, and which are fulfilling; and the fulfilment of these prophecies demonstrates the fact of the divine inspiration of the Bible.

These constitute so many *Pillars*, either of which would alone support the sacred edifice. And here is one of those sublime wonders which cluster around the Christian religion. Here is a building supported by four pillars, each independent of the other, and yet all standing so exactly in the centre, that, if either one, or all but one were taken away, the balance would still be so exactly preserved, that there would be no shaking of the edifice nor sinking of the foundations.

THE

FOUR PILLARS, &c

CHAPTER I.

THE FIRST PILLAR.—*Man needs and must have some sort of Religion: Christianity is the only System of Religion that is adapted to the Necessities of Man's Moral Nature: therefore, Christianity must be the only true Religion.*

There is, inherent in the nature of man, a sense of moral obligation and accountability, which instinctively calls for a knowledge of his origin, present relations and duties, and future destiny. The proof of this is found both in his own consciousness, and in the fact that there never was known to exist a nation or tribe that was wholly destitute of some form of religion. It has, indeed, been said, that some barbarous tribes have been discovered, that had no ideas of religion whatever; but, a closer examination has proved the contrary; and that this opinion should have gained credence with travellers is accounted for, by the fact that most barbarous tribes are very reserved and private about their sacred things. The existence of this principle in man is also proved from the fact that professed atheists have never been able to drive all ideas of religion from the minds of the common people, nor even from their own minds in the hour of peril. Such men have been known to fall on their knees, in a storm at sea, and cry out to the God whose existence they had denied, to save them; and the death-bed of Voltaire, as well as other distinguished men of this class, is said to have been a scene of remorse, despair, and indescribable horror. If we could conceive it possible to banish all religion from the earth, we could hardly form any conception of what would be the sate of things. There would be an entire removal of all restraint; and universal anarchy, confusion, and bloodshed, would prevail, till the whole race of man would be extinct. The experiment was tried a short time in France; and if it had been pursued much longer, it would have depopulated the nation. And this experiment was tried under every advantage of learning, philosophy, and refinement. Says a distinguished writer, "The National Assembly of France, in the commencement of the revolution, appointed a committee to inquire and report whether there were or ought to be a God; and the committee reported that there could be no liberty on earth, while there was believed to be a God in heaven; and that there is no God; and that death is an eternal sleep. The assembly adopted the report, abolished the Sabbath, burnt the Bible, instituted the *decade*, or week of ten days, and ordained the worship of the goddess of Liberty, in the person of a vile woman. But, the consequences were too terrible to be endured: it converted the most polished nation of Europe into a nation of fiends and furies, and the theatre of voluptuous refinement into a stall of blood." "What is it to kill a man?" said one of these atheistic philosophers, while the work of death was going on, and the blood was flowing from the guillotine as from an inexhaustible fountain. "Only to change the direction of a few ounces of blood; and so in the progress of the revolution which they contrived and let out upon the world, they changed in about five millions of instances, a few ounces of blood."* "Atheism," says another, "has no bond of union for its professors; no basis of mutual confidence. It breeds suspicion, and consequently hatred, in every breast; and it is actuated by a selfishness which utterly disregards all the bonds of nature, of gratitude, and of friendship. To an atheist, fear becomes the ruling passion. Conscious of his own want of virtue, honor, and humanity, he naturally views his fellows in the same light, and is ready to put them out of the way as soon as they appear, in any degree, to become obstacles to the accomplishment of his plans. Hence, the bloody actors in this tragedy, after glutting their revenge by shedding the blood of innocent Christians, turned their murderous weapons against each other." "Between atheism and superstition there is this great difference, that

---

* Dr. Beecher's Lectures on Skepticism, pp. 80, 83.

while the latter sanctions some crimes, the former opens the flood-gates to all. The one restrains partiality, the other removes all restraint from vice.—Every kind of religion presents some terrors to evil doers; atheism promises complete impunity, and stamps virtue itself with the character of folly."*

During the reign of terror in France, when no one was secure of his head for a single hour, it is said that a company of the nobility were sitting together in trembling and breathless anxiety, not knowing the moment when they might be summoned to the guillotine;—an accomplished lady, who had been drawn into the prevailing atheism by a gentleman present, approached him, and broke the sombre silence that pervaded the assembly, with these emphatic words, Monsieur,—GIVE ME BACK MY GOD!"

All the various forms of religion existing now, or that have existed in the world, are comprised under four denominations, namely, *Paganism, Mohammedanism, Deism, and Christianity*. I do not reckon Judaism among these, because in its original form it is a part of the true religion, and identified with christianity. And so, if we enter into a minute examination of all minor sects, we shall see that they will all find their place, in classification among these four.

We will now enter upon a brief examination of these systems, in order to see how far they severally furnish what is required by the necessities of man's moral nature. And,

I. As to *Paganism*. It may seem strange that a

---

* Alexander's Evidences, pp. 24, 26.

moment should be spent upon the inquiry, whether this is such a religion as we need; yet, there are those among us, who maintain that it is good enough for the heathen, and that there is no need of sending them the gospel; but, if it is good enough for them, it is good enough for us.

Paganism comprises all the forms of idolatry which prevail, or which have prevailed among the heathen. It would be impossible, in this place, to enter into an extended description of what is included under this term. Perhaps, however, we cannot form a better idea of Paganism, than by considering its objects of worship. These are innumerable, including good and evil spirits; the sun, moon, and stars; the earth, the air, the ocean; thunder and lightning; meteors; minerals; stones; iron; silver; gold; plants; leeks; onions; trees and forests; wheat and corn; fishes; insects; reptiles; birds; four-footed beasts, as the bull-dog, cat, wolf, baboon, lion, crocodile, hog, rats, mice, porcupine; departed heroes; as well as all the faculties and passions of men; and universal nature. In the modern Paganism of the East, the number of gods adored amounts to many millions.

It will be seen at once that the religious principle, of which we have spoken as being inherent in the soul of man, can find no scope for its exercise, when such are the objects of adoration. There is nothing in them worthy of love or devout admiration—nothing to excite pious feeling—nothing to inspire confidence. On the contrary, many of them are objects of contempt; and where any moral character has been attributed to their gods, it has been of the most hateful and disgusting description. There is, therefore, in Paganism no one supreme object on which the soul of man can fix, as an object of delightful contemplation, complacent desire, and devout affection.

Another grand defect of heathenism is, that it furnishes no pure code of morals. It cannot be expected that their code of morals will be any better than that of their gods; and hence we find that the practical fruits of Paganism have always corresponded to the description given in the first chapter of Romans.

Still another defect, and which shows most conclusively, its failure to meet the moral necessities of man, is, that it gives no rational account of the origin of his being, or his future destiny. The great majority of Pagan nations believe in the transmigration of souls; or the passage of souls at death from one body to another. Hence, all is dark concerning the past, and a painful uncertainty hangs over the future. The Pagan has no idea of his origin immediately from the hand of a beneficent Creator; and for aught he knows, his soul may have inhabited the body of a swine or a reptile; and then, as to the rewards of the righteous, and the hopes of heaven, in comparison with the prospects of the wicked, it is only the privilege, perhaps, of entering the body of a horse or some other noble animal, in preference to a mouse or a reptile. Others are left by their religion entirely in doubt as to the immortality of the soul; and others still, have no prospect set before them, but that of annihilation, or of absorption into the essence of the Deity; an idea, however, which seems to be reviving among us, under the form of transcendentalism; though I do not presume to speak with confidence on this subject, for I confess that I am unable to understand the views of this school. They are too subtile, ærial, and mystical for my apprehension, and therefore it would not be strange if I should misapprehend them. But if, as I understand them to say, the soul of man is essentially a part of God, when it leaves the body it must return again to the divine essence, lose its separate existence, and be precisely what it was before it existed in the human body; so that we are likely, for aught I see, to have a sect of Hindoos among ourselves.

But, another defect in Pagan systems of religion is, that they make no such certain provision for the pardon of sin, as to give relief to the conscience burdened with guilt. For the knowledge of human depravity, and a sense of sin, are almost universal with the heathen. They also feel the necessity of some sort of satisfaction being rendered to their gods for sin. But, their views of the kind of expiation that will be acceptable to the Deity are very vague and indefinite. They have some notion, however, that the victim sacrificed must bear some proportion in value to the person sinning; and hence the origin of human sacrifices, which have prevailed, to a greater or less extent, perhaps, among all heathen nations. Self-inflicted tortures, also of every variety and form, are resorted to for the same purpose; and yet there remains a painful uncertainty whether any of these will procure the pardon of their sins. An affecting illustration of the failure of all the expedients and rites of

Paganism, to satisfy the demands of a guilty conscience, is found in a fact related by the missionary Swartz:—"A man on the Malabar coast had inquired of various devotees and priests how he might make atonement for his sins; and he was directed to drive iron spikes, somewhat blunted, through his sandals, and on them to place his naked feet, and walk to a certain place, a distance of nearly five hundred miles. If, through loss of blood, or weakness of body, he was unable to proceed, he was obliged to wait for healing and strength. He undertook the journey; and while he halted under a large shade tree, where the gospel was sometimes preached, one of the missionaries came and preached in his hearing from these words: "The blood of Jesus Christ cleanseth from all sin." While he was preaching, the man rose up, threw off his torturing sandals, and cried out aloud, "*This is what I want;*" and he became a living witness of the truth of that passage of scripture, and also of the insufficiency of heathenism to administer to the moral necessities of the soul that is panting after immortality.

Another case, no less affecting, occurred on the coast of Africa. An English sailor, in conversation with one of the natives, found him troubled on account of his sins, and told him that he must go to the "Christian's God, who paid the debt." This was all, however, which the sailor could tell him. He had heard of Christ as being our surety; and that was all which he knew. But this seemed to be the very thing of which the man felt his perishing need. It took full possession of his soul. He went on board the ship, and wrought his passage to England. There, in one of the large towns, I believe either in London or Liverpool, he went about the streets, inquiring of every one he met, for the "Christian's God, who paid the debt." But the people thought him crazy. However, at length he met with a clergyman, who was struck and interested with his inquiry, and took him home, heard his story, and instructed him more perfectly in the way of life ; and no sooner did he learn the way of salvation through a crucified Redeemer, than he most heartily and cordially embraced it. Such facts as these most forcibly illustrate the great truth, that there is, in the breast of a sinner, a conscious need of some form of expiation for sin, that shall satisfy divine justice, and restore him to the favor of God. Paganism is the religion of more than five hundred millions of our race.

II. The system of religion which next claims our attention, is Mohammedism, so called from Mohammed or Mahomet, its founder. This is in some respects superior to Paganism, because it contains some proportion of truth ; but it is a strange commingling of truth with the most monstrous absurdities. It may be instructive to dwell a few moments on its doctrines ; and this indeed is necessary to our inquiry, whether it is adapted to the moral necessities of man. The Mohammedans have correct ideas of the nature and attributes of God, but reject the doctrine of the Trinity. They abhor idolatry, but place Mohammed, their prophet, next to God. Their ideas of creation, also, agree with the Scripture account, from which they were doubtless derived. They believe that there are two recording angels in heaven, one standing on the right hand of God, and the other on the left, who keep account of all the actions of men, both good and bad ; that, at death, two angels will inquire of the departed spirit who was his Lord and Prophet ; that those who shall be able to say that God was their only Lord, and Mohammed their prophet, will find a great light in their graves, and shall rest in glory ; but those who cannot so answer these questions, shall be kept in darkness till the day of judgment ; that, at the end of the world, after the last trumpet shall have sounded, all things will turn to nothing again, and God only shall remain in existence ; but afterwards, all creatures will be raised again to life, and gathered together for judgment ; that then, God, accompanied by Mohammed, will judge all mankind ; and that Mohammed will intercede for his followers All the works of men, they say, will be weighed in scales, the good against the bad ; and then, all will be permitted to take vengeance on those that have injured them ; and this will be done by taking away a portion of the good works of the one who has done an injury, and giving them to the injured party ; but if the good works are exhausted, a part of the sins of the injured will be placed to the account of the injurer. Those whose good works outweigh their bad, shall immediately enter into paradise ; while those whose bad actions outweigh their good, shall be cast into hell. Those whose good and bad deeds are equal, shall remain in the middle, between paradise and hell, without enjoying happiness or enduring misery ; but all of them who are Mohammedans shall be released from this confinement, at the second inter-

MOHAMMEDISM 15

cession of Mohammed; but the time they shall be confined there will not be less than 900 years, nor more than 7,000. The Mohammedan hell is corporeal, and the description they give of the torments to be endured there, is too horrible to be repeated. Over this, they say there is placed a sharp bridge, as long as the world and as high in proportion, but not wider than a single thread of a spider's web; and this overhung on both sides with briers and thorns. Over this all mankind must pass. The good Mohammedans will pass swifter than lightning. But the wicked, and those who do not believe in Mohammed, will slip and fall headlong into hell-fire. Their ideas of heaven are, that it is a place of sensual pleasure. It is painted out in the most extravagant colors which imagination could invent, but free from all the pain, distress and bitterness of soul, which follow the excessive indulgence of animal appetites and passions in this life. This is the religion of 120,000,000 of our race.

It will be at once perceived that this is but a caricature of Christianity, leaving out those doctrines and facts which are essential to the system, and retaining only such as could be metamorphosed to suit the purposes of the Impostor.

This system fails to meet the moral necessities of man, in several important particulars:

1. Its doctrine of rewards and punishments is founded on erroneous principles. It gives a mercantile character to the relations between man and his Creator; as though we could bring God under obligation to us by our good works, while we become indebted to him by our evil deeds; and thus set off the one against the other. Whereas God, by virtue

of the claim he has upon us as our Creator, and as the Supreme Ruler of the universe, is justly entitled to perfect obedience from us ; and our disobedience, being a violation of our obligations to him in certain particulars, can never be cancelled by performing our obligations in other particulars. Having, therefore, once sinned, we could not expiate our sin by perfect obedience all the rest of our lives. But,

2. If this doctrine were founded on correct principles, it would not satisfy, in this respect, the wants of the human soul. Who would be able to keep an exact account of all his actions, and weigh the good and bad in an even handed balance, so as to know what to calculate upon as his future destiny ? Hence the soul must always be under the most fearful apprehensions as to the future ; for, though the intercessions of the prophet may avail at last to deliver the soul from hell, yet what ground of comfort or consolation is there in the idea of deliverance from hell, after suffering the most excruciating torments for nine hundred or seven thousand years ? Yet, it is to be admitted that this is as comforting a system as that of the *Restorationists*, who rest their hopes of salvation on the prospect of the termination of a limited period of future punishment.

3. This system makes no provision for expiation, or the pardon of sin. Even the intercession of Mohammed does not avail for this ; but sin must be balanced by good works, or else punished in hell, even in the case of the faithful. So that, the great thing, the need of which the soul feels most intensely of all, is entirely absent from this system.

4. It presents unworthy views of the world to

come. What satisfaction can the soul that is panting after immortality derive from the idea of a sensual paradise? All our ideas of wretchedness, and misery, and moral debasement, are connected with sensual indulgence. What, then, has the soul to expect from Mohammed's paradise?

5. There is no provision in this system for the renovation of the human character. It admits that man is sinful, and yet makes no provision for regeneration. No change of character was required by its author, in those who embraced it, but only a change of profession; and from the character of its heaven, no change of character would need to be required of those who enter there. They may go there with the same passions, the same desires, and the same dispositions which they have here; and hence the idea of perfect happiness and freedom from pain and suffering, must be an illusion of the fancy; for these are inseparable from the indulgence of the dispositions and propensities of fallen humanity.

6. Finally, Mohammedism is deficient in giving to man a pure code of morals. Its good works consist of formal prayers, alms, fasting, and pilgrimages; while it encourages a sanguinary, revengeful spirit, and permits polygamy and slaveholding among the faithful. Its practical effects are opposed to all advancement in human society; and the whole system is unfriendly to human liberty. Wherever it has prevailed, it has desolated the fairest portions of the earth, and brought the people under the iron hand of despotism. It interposes an effectual barrier against all improvement. A striking illustration of this is found in the conduct

of the successor of Mohammed in the conquest of Egypt. Coming to the great library of Alexandria, where all the learning of antiquity was deposited, it became a question what should be done with it. The caliph settled the matter with this summary reason: "If the books are contrary to the Koran, they ought to be destroyed; or if not, they are unnecessary, for the Koran is sufficient—let them be burnt." And, to give some idea of the sacrifice that was made to this barbarous spirit, it is sufficient to say that the manuscripts served for fuel to heat the public baths for six months. Such has ever been the spirit of this religion. And where it prevails, the ruins of civilized and cultivated society, which existed before them, remain; but the people are at the same point of elevation, or, rather, below the point where they were a thousand years ago.

III. We now come to the system which is set up in enlightened, civilized lands, in opposition to Christianity. This is denominated *Deism*, or *Natural Religion*. Its leading doctrine, from which its name is derived, is a belief in a Supreme Intelligence. But, among those who properly come under this denomination, there are various shades of belief. They may be classed as follows: 1. Those who admit the existence of a Supreme Being, but deny that he concerns himself with the affairs of men; 2. Those who admit not only the being, but the Providence of God; but allow no difference between moral good and evil, and deny that God takes any notice of our moral conduct; 3. Such as believe in the natural attributes of God, and his all-governing Providence; yet deny the immortality of the soul, or any future state; 4. Such as admit the existence of God, his Providence, and the obligations of natural religion; but so far only as these are discoverable by the light of nature, without any divine revelation; and 5. To these may be added all, who, though they admit that there is some truth in the Bible, yet deny that it is inspired in such a sense that its declarations can be relied upon as divine authority; and hence, deny also those doctrines which are essential to the system of religion taught therein; as the doctrine of human depravity, the Deity and atonement of Christ, the deity and office of the Holy Spirit, regeneration, and kindred doctrines. Though some who belong to this class may claim the Christian name, yet they have no title to it, and no right to appropriate it to themselves, inasmuch as they deny all that is peculiar to Christianity. If any one supposes that I do them injustice by classing them with Deists, I will quote from a sermon preached at the ordination of one of their ministers, an explanation of what the preacher considers the Christian creed. Speaking of Christianity, he says, " The only creed it lays down, is the great truth that springs up spontaneously in the holy heart—THERE IS A GOD."* If this be not a Deistical creed, I know not what can be called such. The very name of *Deist* is derived from this main article of their creed, that "*there is a God.*" This is, indeed, a true creed; but it does not, by any means, teach all that is necessary for man to know. It does not teach even the very first principles of Christianity.

---

* " A Discourse on the Transient and Permanent in Christianity, &c., by Theodore Parker, Minister of the Second Church, Roxbury."

DEFECTS OF DEISM.

1. The grand defect of Deism is, that it makes no provision for the pardon of sin. It has no Saviour—no expiation for sin—no atonement. Indeed, it is not settled among its advocates, whether man is a sinner or not; or whether he is accountable to any higher power. Some Deists admit that man is a sinner, and maintain that sin may be pardoned on repentance. But how did they make this discovery? Without a revelation, I see not how it is possible for us to know whether God will pardon sin on any terms. Who is authorized to speak for him? Which of his works teaches us that he will pardon sin? Do we learn it from any of the natural laws of the universe, which he has established? Which of these laws have we known to be suspended for the convenience of man? If the stone begins to roll down the precipice, will it stop or turn aside because a man is below? Does God hold up his rain because one man's harvest is exposed? Will he call back his thunderbolt because a man is in its way? The most natural conclusion to be drawn from what we can see of God's works, and of his providential government, is, that he *will not* pardon sin; and this agrees with all our ideas of justice. Our sense of justice is injured when we see a notorious criminal escape the punishment of the law, and left at large to prey upon society; and what knowledge can we derive from nature to show that retributive justice is not also essential to the divine government? I think it is clear, then, that the fact that God will pardon sin, and the way in which he

will pardon it, are what we can know in no other way, than by a revelation from God himself. It appears, then, that Deism, in all its forms, is deficient in the grand point which of all others it is most necessary for man to know.

2. Deism is not only deficient in not making provision for the pardon of sin, but also, in not making provision for the reformation of sinners. It has no motives to present for repentance beyond those which should have operated to restrain and prevent sin. It makes no provision for regeneration, nor for divine aid in reformation.

3. There is nothing in the system to take hold of the religious principle in man, and inspire devotion. It views God at a distance, as not taking interest enough in man to reveal himself, and make known his will to him. It does not present him as a near object of affection ; and furnishes no proof that he is pleased with our acts of homage and devotion. The most natural conclusion to the mind of a sinner would be, that God views him with abhorrence, and that his devotions will only provoke the divine indignation. Deism proves nothing to the contrary ; nor can the placability of God, and his delight in the homage of his fallen creatures be known, except by a revelation from himself. After the experiment with Atheism had failed in France, another experiment was tried with pure Deism. A society was formed, called *Theophilanthropists*, or *lovers of God and man*, for the worship of God upon the pure principles of natural religion. It was patronized by distinguished men, and enjoyed the favor of government ; and permission was

given for them to use the churches, of which they had eighteen or twenty in Paris alone. Their creed was simple, consisting of two articles, the existence of God, and the immortality of the soul ; and their moral system embraced two great principles, love to God and love to man ; which, however, must have been borrowed from Christianity. Their worship consisted of prayers and hymns of praise, and they had a manual of worship and a liturgy. Music, vocal and instrumental, were employed. Lectures also were delivered. " Great efforts were made to have this worship generally introduced throughout France ; and the views of the society even extended to foreign countries. Their manual was sent into all parts of the country by the minister of the interior free of expense. Never did a society enjoy greater advantages at its commencement." But it entirely failed to take hold upon the mass of the people. At first, large audiences attended ; but they were mostly spectators ; and after the novelty was over, they dwindled away, so that, instead of filling twenty churches, they occupied but four ; and, in a little while, being prohibited the use of the churches, the society became extinct. " The chief reason of this was the want of a devotional spirit. There was nothing to interest the feelings of the heart. Their orators might be men of learning, and they might produce good moral discourses, but they were not men of piety, and not always men of pure morals. Their hymns were said to be well composed, and their music good ; but their musicians were hired from the theatre. They found it impossible to raise, in some of their societies, a sum which any Christian congregation, even the poorest, would have collected in a single day. One of their societies petitioned government to grant them relief from a debt of not more than forty dollars, stating that their annual income did not exceed twenty dollars."* There were other difficulties which they encountered, but these are sufficient to show that there is nothing in Deism to take hold of the heart, and secure an interest in public worship. The same thing is now going on in those congregations among us, which have rejected the essential and saving truths of the gospel, and settled down upon a cold system of refined Deism. A few of the older people attend from the habits which were formed under a different system ; but it has little power over the young ; and many, even of the older people, have ceased their attendance, and become habitual neglecters of public worship ; so that the congregations are fast dwindling away, and will soon follow the example of their brethren, the Theophilanthropists of France. And probably this event will be greatly accelerated, when the funds collected by our Puritan fathers for the support of a pure gospel shall have been exhausted.

4. Another defect in this system is, that it does not furnish a pure code of morals, and therefore fails to secure even a good moral character in its ablest advocates. Among those who profess to adopt the system of natural religion, there is a very great diversity of sentiment as to what is right, and what is wrong, some even maintaining that there is no difference between right and wrong, except so far as custom and the opin-

---

* Alexander's Evidences, pp. 36—39.

ions of men are concerned; and others making it all consist in sincerity of purpose, whatever may be the character of the action. Besides this, the system fails to provide adequate motives for doing right, or sanctions and penalties against wrong doing. It need not surprise us, then, to learn, that it has not secured a good moral character even to its ablest advocates. Lord Bolingbroke resolves all morality into self-love as its first principle and final centre. In the details of his morality, he is equally lax; and his bad temper and dissipated habits but too unhappily confirmed the bad tendency of his principles. When Thomas Paine had completed the first part of his Age of Reason, he submitted it to Dr. Franklin before its publication. The Doctor advised him not to publish it, on the ground of the bad moral tendency of the doctrines it inculcated; assuring the author that, though it might have no bad effect upon his own morals, supposing his philosophy might be a safeguard against it, yet, that it would be dangerous to the morals of the common people. Dr. Franklin was an acute observer of men and things, and he knew how to calculate the results of causes. The sequel has more than proved the correctness of his opinion; for not only have Deistical principles proved most disastrous to the morals of the people who have embraced them, but the great philosopher himself, whom Franklin supposed to be proof against his own principles, fell a deplorable victim to their influence; himself a dreadful witness against the influence of his doctrines. "He had written the first part of his Age of Reason, and committed it for publication to Joel Barlow, in this country. The second part was published in 1795, after he had been an actor in the early scenes of the French revolution. At this time, he was habitually drunk. He returned to America in October, 1802, bringing with him as a companion the wife of a French bookseller, having separated from his second wife. He died at New York, in 1809, in contempt and misery. His disgusting vices, his intemperance and profligacy, made him an outcast from all respectable society. He is represented as irritable, vain, cowardly, filthy, envious, malignant, dishonest, and drunken "—a personification of his own principles. Yet, we are left to infer, from the language of Franklin, in giving his advice, that, when he first began to propagate his Deistical sentiments, he was a man of good moral character. Nor need we go far to find examples of similar degeneracy of morals, from the same cause.

5. Once more,—Deism gives no satisfactory information as to the origin of all things, the object of man's existence, or his future destiny. Nothing can be certainly known, in regard to these most important matters, except by a revelation from heaven; and such a revelation Deism rejects. All is therefore left as matter of conjecture and painful uncertainty. The human soul instinctively craves this knowledge; and it is reasonable to suppose that a beneficent Creator, having given this desire, as part and parcel of our being, would not leave it to prey upon itself, but would satisfy it with the knowledge it craves; especially as this knowledge is essential to an understanding of our duty to Him. The painful uncertainty of which I have spoken was felt by the ancient philosophers, who had

3

rejected the heathen mythology, and yet were destitute of a revelation, being left to the guidance of natural religion. Cicero, in arguing in favor of the immortality of the soul, says he speaks not "in the character of the Pythian Apollo, that all he says shall pass for certain and established; but as a man from the probable many pursuing probabilities by conjecture. For I have," continues he, "no means of passing beyond what may have the resemblance of truth." And, in regard to the condition of the soul after death, he says, "There are, who think no departure takes place, but that the soul and body fall together, and the soul is extinguished with the body. Of those who think the soul to depart, some think it dissipated immediately; others, to remain a long time; others, forever. Moreover, as to what the soul itself is, or where or whence, there is great variety of opinions." After discussing a number of the prevailing opinions on the subject, he says, "The opinions of the rest afford a hope that souls, when they have left the body, may arrive in heaven as their proper home;" and he makes his auditor say, "I wish it fact; and then, if it be not, *yet I wish to be made to believe it*." And, in regard to Plato's reasoning, in favor of the soul's immortality, "I know not how, while I read, I assent; when I lay the book down, and begin to reflect with myself upon the soul's immortality, *all that* assent slides away." Such is the painful uncertainty of the human mind in regard both to its own nature and origin, and to every thing future, when destitute of a divine revelation on which it may depend for certainty, in endeavoring to ascertain the truth. This Deism,

CHRISTIANITY. 27

or natural religion, does not furnish ; but leaves the mind a prey to these distressing uncertainties.

We have now examined three of the four systems of religion which prevail among mankind ; and it appears, if we admit all that they claim, they entirely fail of meeting the moral necessities of man. It now only remains to examine Christianity in the same light ; and to inquire, whether, admitting what it claims to be, it provides for the necessities of man's moral nature. We have seen that Atheism will not do for us. We must have some religion. We have examined Paganism, Mohammedism, and Deism, and find them all insufficient to meet the cravings of an immortal mind, and the necessities of dependent beings in a state of probation. And now, if Christianity fails us, what shall we do ? We shall, indeed, be in a pitiable condition. But I shall undertake to show that Christianity does entirely and perfectly meet the moral necessities of man. And,

1. It gives a rational account of the origin of all things ; of the object of man's existence ; of his relations and duty to God ; and of his future destiny ; and this, on the authority of a revelation from the only Being who could impart this information. This last point, however, I am not about, in this place, to prove ; for as we have done with the other systems, we are now to judge of the adaptedness of Christianity to meet the moral necessities of man, by what it professes to be.

What could be more sublime and worthy the credence of man, than the account which the Bible gives of the origin of all things ? "In the beginning, God created the heavens and the earth!" This, surely, must, if believed, satisfy the desires of the human soul; and why should we not believe it? And, then, what more worthy object of man's existence can be imagined, than what is taught in the Bible : that God created him to manifest forth his glory, and to impart enjoyment to him—the enjoyment of numberless benefits in this world, and a participation in his own glory in the world to come. And what more satisfactory account could be given of the relations of man to God, than that he is entirely dependent for all things upon the Being who brought him into existence? or, of his duty to God, than that he is bound to love him supremely, with all his heart, and mind, and strength, and above all other objects? And, what more worthy of God, as to his future destiny, than that, originally continuing in the state of holiness, he was to enjoy an eternal state of spiritual blessedness, in communion with God, and in the society of holy beings ; and that, having sinned, a provision has been made, by an act of free grace, for his experiencing a renovation of nature, and being reinstated in the favor of God ; or, as a punishment for disobedience and impenitence, to be forever banished from his presence, and shut out from the enjoyment of his favor? Is not information like this worthy of a revelation from God? And does it not satisfy the cravings of immortal desire in the human soul?

2. The religion of the Bible furnishes a perfect code of morals, with adequate motives and sanctions. In the ten commandments, every thing wrong is for

bidden, and every thing that ought to be done is required. This is brought into a very small compass, by a classification of offences and duties, and forbidding or requiring the highest of each class. A close examination of them, in this light, will show that there is not the slightest defect in them; and that perfect obedience to them would secure a perfect state of society, like that which exists in heaven. The same may be said, also, of the two great moral principles laid down by our Saviour, requiring supreme love to our Creator, and equal love to our fellow men. And these moral duties are provided with adequate sanctions and motives. Eternal death is threatened as the punishment of disobedience, and eternal life is promised to obedience; and then, to meet the case of the penitent transgressor, the law of love, and the promise of pardon, are brought in to take hold of his heart, and reform his character and life. Is not here a perfect code of morals, adapted to the case of man?

3. Christianity, or the religion of the Bible, explains how man came to be in the wretched, fallen condition in which he finds himself. It carries him back to his primeval state, when he came pure and holy from the hand of his Maker; and traces back his depravity to the first act of disobedience, and shows his relations to the head of his race, as necessary to the social state, by which all mankind became involved in the consequences of his transgression. This is what no other system does; and it is what could not be learned but by a direct revelation from God himself.

4. It makes adequate provision for the pardon of sin, and the restoration of the penitent sinner to the

favor of God. And this it does in a way which commends itself to the human understanding and heart, and relieves entirely the difficulty arising from the apparent collision of the attributes of justice and mercy. It provides a full and sufficient expiation for sin, in the sufferings and death of the Son of God, substituted for the sinner ; and it makes this available to all mankind, upon the simple and easy terms of repentance and faith. And, when received, it satisfies the burdened conscience, and gives peace to the troubled soul. This is peculiar to the Christian system. Other systems have, indeed, their modes of expiation, but their sacrifices are not of sufficient value for the redemption of the soul ; and they lack, also, the sanction of the word of God, to render it certain that they will be accepted of him.

5. Christianity, also, makes provision for a radical and thorough reformation of character. It furnishes the special divine influence upon the heart in regeneration, changing the dispositions of the soul, and setting aright the springs of action. This is entirely peculiar to Christianity. Regeneration does not enter into the idea of any other system. It is even ridiculed by those who assume the name of Christians, while they deny its peculiar doctrines. But this is the secret of its transforming power. And this accounts for the wonderful changes it makes in the characters of men, often very suddenly. The gospel of Jesus Christ secures the accompanying influences of the Holy Spirit to render it efficacious upon the hearts of men.

6. Christianity takes hold on the heart, and inspires a devotional spirit. Hence, when the gospel is

preached in its purity, it secures a regular attendance upon public worship. The reason is, it is addressed to the heart. It is peculiarly a religion of the affections. Though it deals much in doctrines, and discusses and teaches strong truths, yet they are all such as come home to the business and bosoms of men— truths in which every man, woman, and child has a direct personal interest. It is entirely unlike the cold speculations of philosophy or abstract morality. It appeals to the heart; and it presents objects to the affections worthy of their highest exercise. It also wakes up intellect, and elevates the whole character of man. It likewise improves his social condition. By subduing evil passions, and cultivating the mild and tender affections, it softens, refines, and elevates the social character. To what other cause can be attributed the superior social condition of those countries where Christianity prevails, and that, just in proportion to its purity ? And I may add, also, of those towns, neighborhoods and families, where its transforming power is most deeply felt. What portions of the earth ever presented a population equal in their social condition to Scotland and New England ? And, where was ever a population so thoroughly under the influence of the Christian religion, as Scotland since the reformation, and New England in its early history ? And where was ever a people found of more energy and activity of intellect ? Why is it that the canvass of New England has whitened every sea, and her commerce entered every port in the world ? And why is it, that the enterprize of her sons has reached every town and village in this land ? And why, that their ingenuity has given birth to those inventions by which the elements and all the powers of nature are made to contribute to the service of man ? I can answer these inquiries in no other way than by attributing these results to the impulse which Christianity has given to the intellectual powers of the population which has come under its influence. It wakes up thought; it furnishes themes of contemplation ; it excites inquiry, and leads to investigation. And, the intellect thus aroused, will not confine itself simply to religious subjects ; nor will the influence be confined to those who have heartily and cordially embraced the religion of Christ, but the whole community will feel the impulse. There is nothing more striking in the contrast between Christian and heathen lands, than in this particular. The heathen are generally noted for their stupidity and dulness of intellect. But, when Christianity enters a heathen land, it wakes up intellect, and gives birth to learning and enterprize. But I cannot longer dwell on this part of the subject.

The conclusion to which I arrive, from the considerations which have been presented, is, that Christianity is perfectly and exactly adapted to the condition and moral necessities of man ; and *therefore*, that it must be of divine origin. We have seen that man has invented other systems, and that they have all failed of meeting these ends. When, therefore, we have discovered one which does exactly meet them, it is a reasonable conclusion that it is not of man, but of God. It is plain, also, that to devise and develope such a system is entirely beyond the power of man. None could know how so perfectly to adapt a system of religion to the nature, condition and wants of any being, but He who created him. Besides, there is a perfection in Christianity, which appertains not to the works of imperfect men. It is complete in its plan, and perfect in its details. Who but God could produce such a system ?

PRACTICAL REMARKS.

1. I have doubtless had the testimony of those of my readers who profess to have experienced the saving power of Christianity, to the truth of what I have written. Yet, have you thought of the conclusions which must follow from these premises ? If the foregoing reasonings and conclusions are correct, it must follow that Evangelical Protestant Christianity is the only religion which is adapted to the wants of mankind, and that it must prevail universally, or the world will never be raised from its present degraded condition. You believe, on the authority of God's word, that all mankind are to come under the influence of Christianity ; and that this is to be accomplished by the blessing of God upon the instrumentalities employed by the church ; and that this blessing is to be bestowed in answer to prayer. Now, let us look this matter in the face, and see what we have to do. Including heathen, Mohammedans, Jews and Catholics, all of whom must be converted or lost, we have six or eight hundred millions who are yet to be evangelized—taught the true principles of the gospel, and led to embrace them. And who is to do it ? The number of nominal Pro-

testants in the world, is only about sixty or seventy millions ; and of these, perhaps not more than ten or fifteen millions can be reckoned as truly converted. This brings us to the appalling conclusion that not more than one in sixty, eighty, or a hundred of the human race have at the present time, any well grounded hope of being saved. If this work were entirely of man, we might despair of the world ever being converted. But God is able to do it. And, such is the diffusive spirit of Christianity, that every one that is converted, becomes an instrument of converting others ; and thus, the more it extends, the more its power is increased, and that in an increasing ratio ; so that a little calculation will show that a general and continued outpouring of the Holy Spirit would soon accomplish the work. But this can never be done in our day, unless there is a mighty waking up among the people of God, both as to the employment of means, and as to prayer for the descent of the Holy Spirit. And, if we live on as we now do, at least sixty persons must perish, to every one of us, and that *during our lives and through our neglect.* This we are forced to believe, in order to be consistent with our professions ; but, if we felt its force, I am persuaded we should make a new consecration, not only of ourselves, but of our time, talents, and possessions to the Lord. What other object of pursuit in this world is worth naming in comparison with the conversion of the world to God ? And yet, how few are there, who do not put it the very lowest in the scale of their pursuits ? O that the Lord would pour out his Spirit upon us, and wake us up to just views, and feelings, and action upon this momentous subject !

But this is not all. Let us come nearer home. The population of this country is about sixteen millions. But of these, not more than about two millions, or, at the farthest, not more than two and a half millions, even profess to have embraced the gospel that is made known and proclaimed to them continually. Six or eight persons to one in this highly favored country remain, according to the conclusions to which we are compelled to come, to be converted or lost. If we look around, can we find, on an average, more than one to six or eight, who even profess to have a hope of eternal life founded on the Lord Jesus Christ, with the renewing and sanctifying grace of the Holy Spirit ? Yet, there are large tracts of country, in our new settlements, where a sermon is not heard for many weeks, and there is scarcely spiritual salt enough to preserve the population from moral putrefaction. If the result of individual and associated effort and prayer in our churches, continues to be what it now is, when will the case be improved ? And what will become of the six or eight yet unconverted, to the one that has hope ? And what will become of the churches when their present members shall be called to their rest ? And then, where will their children be ? And what, in these circumstances, ought we to do ? And what will my readers do ? Will they take these questions to their closets, and, on their knees, ask the Lord to make known to them what they ought to do, and to give them strength to perform it ? One solemn conviction is fastened upon my mind by this subject, that, unless this land is blessed with revivals of religion more powerful, more extensive, and of longer continuance than any we have ever yet experienced, the great mass of the present generation, both in this land and the heathen world, must be lost. Nor do I see how to avoid a similar conclusion in regard to any particular place, where the church goes on, from year to year, without revivals,—that, unless the Spirit of God is poured out with greater power, and extent, and continuance, the same result must follow in regard to the greater part of those in the midst of whom we are living. And, I think the fact that the Spirit of God is not so poured out among us, ought to lead every one of us to inquire whether there may not be in us, individually and personally, some hindrance to this blessed work. The work of examination is an individual work. When the Jews put the leaven out of their houses, before the passover, every family searched their own house—no one felt himself responsible for the old leaven that might remain in the house of his neighbor; but he was bound to see that there was no leaven in his own house. So let us do each one for himself.

2. Another class to whom this subject addresses itself, are the *skeptical*, the *doubting*, and the *indifferent*. And, I would address you emphatically in the language of Joshua to the children of Israel: " How long halt ye between two opinions ?" And, in the language of Elijah: " Choose ye this day whom ye will serve !" You have the alternatives presented before you—examine them, and make your choice; and make it in view of eternal consequences. Here is

Atheism, which degrades you to a level with the brutes, and makes you the creature of a day, with no higher object than to eat, and drink, and die—will you choose this? Here is *Paganism,* with its gods many, and lords many—will you choose this, and daub your faces with ashes, and bow down to a senseless block, and call it your god? Or, will you choose the religion of the false prophet, and rest your hopes of a heaven of sensual delights upon the word of a man who proved the divine authority of his mission by the story that he rode one night upon an ass, in company with the angel Gabriel, from Mecca to Jerusalem, and from Jerusalem to the seventh heaven? Or, will you take *Deism,* and content yourself, like the heathen philosopher, to float in a sea of doubt and uncertainty, from the probable many, pursuing probabilities by conjecture, having no means of passing beyond what may have the resemblance of truth? Is this a pleasant path to walk in? Does it give ease, and comfort, and delight to your soul, when you know not what may be beneath your feet—whether an elysian paradise, or a burning volcano? and but one thing is quite certain to you, and that is, that very soon the ground will open beneath your feet, and let you know, by experience, the best or the worst. Will you choose this? For, let me solemnly advertise you, that there is nothing on which you can stand between this and the evangelical system of truth revealed in the Bible, embracing the doctrines of atonement, regeneration, and the eternal punishment of the wicked. No man in his senses can honestly and sincerely set down to the study of the Bible, as a book addressed to the common understanding of mankind, and find any other system of truth in it. And, I think I have shown that this system of truth is just what your soul needs. And now, again I solemnly put the question,—which will you choose?

3. Finally,—There is one class more whom I would seriously and tenderly address. I mean those who regularly and constantly sit under the sound of the gospel, and admit its truths, and yet never heartily and cordially embrace them—who acknowledge that the system of religion taught in the Bible is just what they need, and that they must perish without it, and yet never lay it seriously at heart, and settle their hopes upon this only sure foundation—but go on, with their eyes wide open, with the full prospect of perdition before them. There is nothing more painful to the heart of a Christian who feels for the souls of men. We labor hard with the skeptical and unbelieving, hoping that, if we can but convince them of the truth of Christianity, they will certainly embrace it. Indeed, I seriously question, whether any one who has tried the experiment of floating in the sea of error and doubt, will ever be convinced of the truth of Christianity, without embracing it. But here you are, seriously convinced that all the doctrines set forth in the Bible are true—perhaps you have never doubted them—you believe that you are a sinner in the sight of God—that you deserve to be sent to hell—that Christ died to save you from your sins—that he is now inviting and entreating you to come to him—that you may come if you will—that you must be born again, or you can never see the kingdom of God—that a world of eternal joy and felicity, and a world of

eternal wretchedness and misery are spread out before you, as the result of your action in reference to these truths—and yet, all this exerts no living power over you, but you live on from week to week, as though there were, in your view, no God, no heaven, no hell. And yet, you seem to pay serious attention to the word, and to be interested to know the truth. I must say that I am astonished—amazed. And I am sure, if you could look up and behold a bright vision of angels looking down at the scene, the amazement they would express in their looks, and gestures, and language, would be indescribable; for they know the meaning of eternity, and heaven, and hell. Yes! and you, dear friends, will very soon know their solemn reality. May God give you to see and know your true interest, and to embrace the salvation offered in the gospel, that when you come to see and know the realities of eternity, they may be joyous and not grievous to your souls. O, defer not this momentous subject, but see to it now that your foundation rests on the Rock of Ages.

CHAPTER II.

THE SECOND PILLAR.—*The Authenticity of the Holy Scriptures contained in the Old and New Testament, as a Revelation from God, is clearly established by External Evidence.*

PRELIMINARY REMARKS.

1. It is necessary to define what we mean, when we say that the Scriptures are a Divine revelation; because there are various views on this point, some of which make a revelation, after all, of very little consequence, because they are so loose as not to render it an infallible guide.

It is not necessary that we should enter into an examination of the various theories which have been advanced concerning inspiration, by those who have received the Scriptures as containing an infallible revelation of God's will to man. They are worthy of a separate examination; but, in this place, they would only tend to confusion. It is important, however, to understand clearly the difference between the views of inspiration entertained by Orthodox Christians, and those held by the rejecters of the fundamental doctrines of Christianity. This will explain the ease with which the latter are accustomed to dispose of many truths plainly and clearly taught in the Holy Scriptures. Dr. Priestly, who was one of the Fathers of Unitarianism, "denies that the Scriptures were written by a particular divine inspiration; and asserts that the writers, though men of the greatest probity, were fallible, and have actually committed mistakes in their narratives and reasonings." And, in this sentiment, he has been followed by the mass of Unitarian writers.*

---

* The following quotations are made, as a specimen of what may be found in the works of accredited Unitarian writers:

EUROPEAN UNITARIAN WRITERS

PRIESTLY.—" The writers of the books of Scripture were men, and therefore fallible "

" Like other historians, they were liable to *mistakes*, with respect to things of small moment."

" Not that I consider the books of Scripture as *inspired* "

" Paul often reasons inconclusively "

" As it is not pretended that there are any miracles adapted to prove that Christ made and supports the world, I do not see that we are under obligation to believe it merely because it was an opinion held by an apostle "

BELSHAM.—" The Scriptures are not themselves the word of God, neither do they ever assume that title."

WAKEFIELD —" I believe, no more than Thomas Paine, that the sun and moon, either in the apparent or philosophical acceptation of the phrase, stood still at the command of Joshua."

EVANSON —" The Evangelical histories contain gross and irreconcileable contradictions "

IMPROVED VERSION OF THE NEW TESTAMENT; *published and recommended by American Unitarians.*—" The account of the miraculous conception of Jesus was probably *the*

The modern Transcendental views of inspiration, which have made so much noise of late, differ substantially very little from those of Dr. Priestly, and other Unitarian writers, from his day to the present. I will quote from a recent publication of this new school,* that the reader may see how far they agree with those of Dr. Priestly, already mentioned. Speaking of the Books of the Old Testament, and the faith of Christians in their infallible inspiration, this writer says,—

"But modern criticism is fast breaking to pieces

---

fiction of some early Gentile convert, who hoped, by elevating the dignity of the founder, to abate the popular prejudice against the sect."

AMERICAN WRITERS.

CHRISTIAN EXAMINER —"There was a time in the dark ages, when it was maintained, we cannot say believed, for the proposition does not admit of being believed, that the whole Bible, including the historical books of the Old Testament, was a revelation."

"His reasoning (the writer of Hebrews) cannot be regarded as of any force, by an intelligent reader of the present day."

"The words of Christ were reported from memory by the Evangelists, and not always with perfect accuracy."

These are only a specimen of what may be found scattered through this work in a great variety of forms, as well as in other Unitarian works; all of which go to show that the sentiments expressed in the South Boston Ordination Sermon, concerning inspiration, are *not a new developement* of Unitarianism, but the same form that it had from the beginning, with, perhaps, the difference hinted by the author himself, that he comes out with it openly before the people, while others may confine it to the study, and to learned discussions.

* Mr. Parker's Ordination Sermon.

this idol, which men have made out of the Scriptures. It has shown . . . . . that their authors, wise as they sometimes were, pious as we feel often their spirit to have been, *had only that inspiration which is common to other men, equally pious and wise;* that they were by no means infallible; but were mistaken in facts and reasoning; and uttered predictions which time has not fulfilled." " The history of opinions on the New Testament," he continues, " is quite similar. It has been assumed at the outset, it would seem with no sufficient reason, without the smallest pretence on its writers' part, that all of its authors were infallibly and miraculously inspired, so that they could commit no error of doctrine or fact. Men have been bid to close their eyes at the obvious difference between Luke and John; the serious disagreement between Paul and Peter."

The writer goes on at considerable length in this strain, and even intimates that Christ himself was mistaken in predicting his second coming. His ideas of revelation, if I understand him, are the same in regard to the truths of religion, as to the truths of science; for he puts the sacred writers on a level with the discoverers of the principles and facts of natural science.

But such a revelation as this would be no revelation at all. It does not meet the moral necessities of man. It gives him no authority to which he can appeal as a standard of truth, and of right and wrong. It leaves him still upon the boundless ocean of conjecture, without oar or rudder, or any beacon to direct his course. It is not a whit better than that Deism or natural religion, which denies all revelation. But, a revelation, to meet the wants of man, must be a direct communication of the divine will, imparting a knowledge of those facts and doctrines which it is necessary for us to know, which can be appealed to as of divine authority. Nothing else will satisfy the mind of man. It is reasonable to expect such a revelation from a beneficent being to his dependent creatures. And, though the writer last quoted says that "the current notions respecting the inspiration of the Bible have no foundation in the Bible itself;" and triumphantly asks, "which evangelist, which apostle of the New Testament, what prophet or psalmist of the Old Testament, ever claims infallible authority for himself or for others?" Yet, this is precisely what they claim for themselves and for each other ; and if they were honest men, and spoke the truth, it must follow that they were in such .a sense inspired that God spake by them, so that what they wrote is the infallible word of God. This will appear,

(1.) From the direct assertions of the writers themselves. Moses himself represents that God spake to him face to face, and communicated to him his will. Joshua asserts in the beginning of his book, that the Lord spake to him. Samuel gives an account of the manner in which the Lord first revealed himself to him, and represents that this was continued, so that the people resorted to him to *hear the word of the Lord*. David said, "*The Spirit of the Lord spake by me, and his word was in my tongue.*" And every one of the prophetical books except Daniel, and that is partly historical, begins with the direct announcement of the inspiration of the author, and generally in this simple form,—the word of the Lord came to such a prophet; thus professing not only to speak *in the name of the Lord*, but to speak the words which came to him from God by direct inspiration. The same is true, also, of the New Testament. Though the writers of the gospel narratives nowhere expressly claim this inspiration; yet it is implied in the promise of the Saviour, recorded by John, that, when the spirit of truth should come, he would guide them into all truth; that he should teach them all things, and bring all things to their remembrance, whatsoever he had said unto them;* and Luke's narrative of the Acts of the Apostles gives a particular account of the descent of the Holy Spirit, and the inspiration of the apostles and though Mark and Luke were not apostles, yet we have no evidence that this inspiration was then confined to the twelve apostles; and we know, moreover, that both these evangelists were the companions of inspired apostles, the one of Paul, and the other of Peter, under whose superintendence they must have prepared their narratives. Paul repeatedly declares the fact of his own inspiration. In his epistle to the Galatians, he says, respecting the gospel which he preached, " I neither received it of man, neither was I taught it, but by the revelation of Jesus Christ." The same assertion he repeats in his epistle to the Ephesians; and in his first epistle to the Corinthians, he declares that even the *words* of his gospel were dictated by the Holy Spirit—" Which things," says he, " also we speak, not in the words which man's wisdom teacheth, but

---

* John 14 : 26 ; 16 · 13.

which the Holy Ghost teacheth." How strange that, with all these declarations before him, any man should presume to assert that the sacred writers make no claim to infallible divine inspiration ! But,

(2.) The sacred writers not only claim this for themselves, but for each other. The writer alluded to, again asks, "Did Christ ever demand that men should assent to the doctrines of the Old Testament, credit its stories, and take its poems for histories ?" To this it may be replied, that, in all his ministry, he *assumes*, and *takes for granted* the fact of the divine inspiration of the Old Testament Scriptures. He appeals to them, and so do the evangelists, continually in this expressive form : "It is written"—implying that what he referred to as being written was of unquestioned authority. He does not, indeed, assert their inspiration in so many words ; for that was unnecessary, when the fact was not disputed. Again, he refers the Jews to their own Scriptures, as testifying of himself. No one can attentively and candidly examine these frequent appeals of Christ to the Scriptures then existing, without the fullest conviction that he regarded them as the word of God. But there is one place in which he distinctly recognizes the several parts of the Old Testament Scriptures, thus showing that he regarded all the books then included in the Jewish canon, (which are the same as those now included in the Old Testament) as being of divine authority. After the resurrection, as recorded by Luke, he declares "that all things must be fulfilled which were written in the *law of Moses*, and in the *prophets*, and in the *Psalms* concerning me."* Now, it is well known that the Jewish Scriptures were divided into three parts; the first containing the five books of Moses; the second, comprehending Joshua, Judges, Samuel, Kings, and Isaiah, Jeremiah, Ezekiel, and the twelve smaller prophets; the third, comprehended the Psalms, Proverbs, Job, Solomon's Song, Ruth, Lamentations, Ecclesiastes, Esther, Daniel, Ezra, Nehemiah, and the two books of Chronicles. This division was in use long before the time of Christ, and the Jews were in the habit of referring to the first, under the titles *law* and *Moses*; the second was called *the Prophets*; and the third *David*, or *the Psalms* or *holy writings*. And to these several divisions our Saviour evidently alludes under the terms *the law of Moses*, the *Prophets*, and the *Psalms*; thus giving his sanction to the received canon of the Jewish Scriptures.

The apostles, also, in their epistles, constantly appeal to the Scriptures that were received and acknowledged by the Jews, as of divine authority. They also say, when referring to them, "It is written;" they call them *the word of God*; and Paul says expressly that they were given by inspiration of God; and Peter declares that the prophecy came not, in old time, by the will of man, but holy men of God spake as they were moved by the Holy Ghost;† thus indicating the manner in which this inspiration was given—by the Holy Ghost moving upon the minds of the writers, and di-

---

* Luke 24 . 44
† 2 Timothy, 3 : 15, 16. 2 Peter, 1 . 19—21.

recting them how and what to write. Peter likewise recognizes the epistles of Paul as belonging to the sacred Scriptures, speaking of them in connection with the *other* Scriptures, showing that he regarded them of equal authority.*

I have only quoted a small portion of the testimonies to the Old Testament contained in the New, nor of the assumptions of divine inspiration on the part of the New Testament writers. If these are not sufficient to satisfy the mind of the reader, a personal examination cannot fail to do so. I should not have dwelt so long on this subject, but for the fact that it is a fundamental point, and one that is disputed; the views which I have been combatting being openly advocated and preached among us by those who profess to be Christian ministers—views which would destroy the foundation of our hopes, and leave us destitute of any certain standard of faith and practice.

The Scriptural idea of inspiration then, is, that the sacred writers were under such an influence of the Spirit of God, that what they wrote is truly and properly the word of God, communicated to mankind through them.

2. My second preliminary remark is founded on the foregoing; and it is this,—that the question of the truth of the Scriptures cannot be separated from that of their divine inspiration; for, if they are not inspired they cannot be true, because they profess to be inspired. The Scriptures contain the narrative of facts and the statement of doctrines, which the writers

---

* 2 Peter, 3 : 15, 16.

profess to have received by divine revelation; and these facts and doctrines are of such a nature that they could not be mistaken concerning them. Therefore, if we prove that the writers were honest men, and entitled to credit for their veracity, we prove their inspiration.

3. If we prove the authenticity and genuineness of the New Testament, we also prove the same concerning the Old; as it has already been shown that the inspiration of all the books of the Old Testament is established by the writers of the New. And this may be narrowed down still more; for, if we prove the truth of Luke's gospel, we have this point conclusively established. It is true, however, that the books of the Old Testament are capable of being authenticated by separate and independent evidence; but the object in this place is, to narrow down and simplify the argument, so that its force may be more clearly seen.

4. There are some sects who hold that inspiration is common to all men; and that any one, by improving the light that is in him, may receive directly from God all the revelation that he needs. This is the doctrine of the Quakers, and of some other sects; and if I understand them, it is the doctrine of the Transcendentalists; though, perhaps, in a modified form, with less of anything supernatural in their ideas of inspiration. But this does not appear to be consonant with the plans of divine wisdom. It does not appear from the works of God, or from anything we know of his operations, that he ever makes a useless expenditure of energy or power. So obvious is this fact, that it

has passed into a proverb—"There is nothing made in vain." But, a particular revelation to every individual of the human race would be, if I may so speak, an extravagant expenditure of power, when one revelation, well authenticated, would answer equally as well. Yet one written revelation, well authenticated, is better than a particular revelation to every individual would be. This the apostle Peter intimates, when, after referring to the vision which he saw on the Mount of Transfiguration, he says, alluding to the written word, "We have a more sure word of prophecy." There never were so many false prophets and impostors as during the time when the revelation was given; and if inspiration were continued, it would give advantage to Satan to deceive men with false visions, and for men to deceive one another with pretended prophecies; while the mind of man would in a great measure be deprived of its freedom of action, and motives for investigating the truth.

The next inquiry is,—how a revelation from God could be authenticated, so as to commend itself to the people to whom it was immediately given. That God could so communicate information to the mind of a human being as to make it perfectly sure and certain to the individual himself that it was a divine revelation, cannot be doubted by any one who regards God as the Almighty Creator of man. But the word of the man to whom it was communicated might not be sufficient to satisfy the minds of others. It is necessary, therefore, that some visible sign should be given to prove his divine mission; and that this should be given in such a manner that there could be no mistake or possibility of deception.

5. But, after a revelation has been so given, in order to render it available, for the use of subsequent generations, it must come down to them accompanied by such proof of its genuineness and authenticity, as cannot be disputed.

Having prepared the way, by these preliminary observations, we will proceed to examine the evidence by which the several books of the New Testament are authenticated as a revelation from God; bearing in mind, that if we prove that these books are true, they must be what they profess to be, a revelation from God; and that, if they are a revelation from God, the books of the Old Testament are likewise. And, let me here also remark, that the difficulty lies not in the want of evidence, but in selecting from the mass of evidence that which may be condensed and brought before the mind of the reader, within a reasonable compass.

I. The first question to be determined is,—how do we know that the several books of the New Testament were written by the persons whose names they bear; and that these persons lived in the age attributed to them, and were the disciples of Christ? This will appear,

1. From the impossibility of their having been forged, and imposed as authentic, either upon the age in which they profess to have been written, or upon any subsequent age. Would it be possible now for any person to forge and palm off upon this community,

a book bearing the name of John Quincy Adams, as author, when not only the friends of the professed author, but the very person himself is living to contradict it ? Or, on the supposition that no such person existed, as those to whom these books are ascribed, could the community have been imposed upon, and made to believe that there were such persons, and that they had written such books ? Especially, as they profess to relate facts of such a nature as could not fail to obtain public notoriety, and in which the authors themselves are said to have borne a conspicuous part.

But, could they have been imposed on a subsequent age, with any less difficulty ? This supposes one or the other of two facts, either that Christianity existed before, or that it derived its origin from the forgery of these books in an age subsequent to that in which they profess to have been written. If we suppose the former, it involves the absurd idea that a community or sect of people could be made to believe that they had been for ages in possession of these books, containing a history of the origin of their religion, when they had not ; or, if we suppose the latter, we must believe a position equally absurd, that the community, at a certain time, were made to believe that a certain sect had existed for ages, in various parts of the world, maintaining public worship, with certain established rites and ordinances, and that the history of this sect had been interwoven for centuries with the history of the world, when no such facts had existed. Such a thing would be as impossible as it would be now to impose upon this community Marshall's Life of Washington as an authentic history, on the supposition that no such man as Washington ever lived, and that no such event as the American revolution ever occurred. But,

2. We are not left to this negative testimony alone. We have an unbroken chain of testimony, from the present generation back to the apostolic age, proving beyond the possibility of contradiction, the authenticity of the New Testament; and this proof extends to all the books included in the New Testament; and to no other works of the same age. These books are quoted or alluded to by a series of writers, who may be followed up in unbroken succession, from the present time to the days of the apostles. But, as no one will doubt this fact in later ages, it is unnecessary here to commence an examination lower down than the fourth century; and if any should inquire how we can know the fact of their having been thus quoted or alluded to, fourteen hundred years ago, the answer is at hand. Manuscript copies of the writings alluded to, written in or near the ages when the authors lived, have come down to us, are preserved in many public and private libraries, both in this country and in Europe; and they have been carefully examined, and extracts made from them and published, by learned men, who would not hazard their reputation by publishing false extracts, when the original manuscripts are in the possession of the public, so that their errors could easily be detected. These books we have in our possession; and we have the means, by reference to the original manuscripts, to determine whether the extracts published are genuine.

But, besides innumerable quotations, from various writers, we have no less than ten distinct and formal catalogues of the several books of the New Testament, which were extant in the fourth century, all of which agree with the list of the New Testament books now received. In the year 397, a provincial council assembled at Carthage, composed of forty-four bishops, of which Augustine was a member. One of the acts of this council reads thus . " It is ordained that nothing beside the canonical scriptures be read in the church under the name of the divine scriptures ;" and then proceeds to enumerate the canonical books, agreeing precisely with our books, and no more. In a book written by Augustine, also, there is a similar catalogue, concerning which he says, " In these books, those who fear God seek his will." A short time before this date, Rufinus published a book, in which he gives a catalogue of both the Old and New Testament books, agreeing exactly with ours, " which," he remarks, " we find, by the monuments of the fathers, to have been delivered by the churches as inspired by the Holy Ghost."

There are also several other writers of this period, whom I have not space to quote. In the year 350, also, " Epiphanius, bishop of Constantia, on the island of Cyprus," wrote against heresies, and gave a list of the books of the New Testament agreeing exactly with ours. Passing by several other writers of this century, we come to Eusebius, the author of a history of the church, who wrote about the year 315, and who mentions all our present books, as belonging to the canon of Scripture.

We will now pass to the third century, where we find the celebrated Origen, who flourished about the year 230, of whom Jerome says that he was the greatest doctor of the churches since the apostles' days,—that he had the Scriptures by heart, and labored day and night in studying and explaining them. He was esteemed as one of the most learned men of his age, both by Christians and heathens. He lived within a hundred years of the death of the Apostle John; so near the time of the publication of the books of the New Testament, that he must have had the means of knowing their origin and authors. He speaks of all the books of the New Testament, and of no others, as belonging to the sacred canon. The writings of four others, bishops of the third century, also contain large extracts from every book of the New Testament, quoted as Scripture.

In the second century, we meet with Tertullian, a native of Carthage, who was born about fifty years after the death of the Apostle John. His works contain quotations from all the books of the New Testament, except four of the short epistles; and the omission to quote from these is no proof that he did not receive them, as these quotations are incidental, without any design of giving a complete catalogue. Concerning these quotations Dr. Lardner observes, that " There are more and larger quotations of the small volume of the New Testament in this one Christian author, than of all the works of Cicero, in the writers of all characters for several ages;" and the same is true with regard to Irenæus and Clement, both writers of the second century. And, there is reason to believe that, in the time of Tertullian, the original epistles, in the handwriting of the apostles, were in the possession of the churches to which they had been sent ; for he tells those to whom he was writing that, if they would visit the apostolical churches, they might see the very chairs in which the apostles sat, and see their very authentic letters, which, he says, were still read in those churches. But, besides Tertullian, in this century, Melito, bishop of Sardis, wrote a commentary on the book of Revelation, and Tatian composed a harmony of the gospels. These were born about the time of the death of the Apostle John. But, beside these, we have Justin Martyr, who was ten years old at the death of the Apostle John. He was, before his conversion, learned in all the philosophy of the Greeks. His works, some of which have come down to us, contain numerous quotations from, and allusions to, the four gospels, which he represents as containing the " genuine and authentic accounts of Jesus and of his doctrines." The same is true, also, in relation to the Acts and the greater part of the Epistles. The book of Revelation is said expressly, by him, to have been written by " John, one of the apostles." But, still higher up, we have the testimony of Papias, bishop of Hierapolis, in Asia, who was a hearer of John, and a disciple of Polycarp, who was John's pupil. He says, " If at any time I met with one who had conversed with the elders, I inquired after the sayings of the elders : what Andrew or what Peter said ; or what Philip, Thomas, or James had said ; what John or Matthew, or what any other of the disciples of the Lord were wont to say." This was very natural ; and it seems to bring us back to the apostolic age ; for we should doubtless have said the same, if we had been there. This writer gives a very valuable testimony to the gospels of Matthew and Mark, and the first epistles of Peter and John. He also alludes to the Acts and Revelation.

But, we have testimony even from the age in which the apostles lived. There are five writers, who were personally acquainted with the apostles, and who quote or allude to almost every book of the New Testament. These are, Barnabas, Clement, and Hermas, all of whom are mentioned in the New Testament; and Polycarp and Ignatius, the former a disciple of John, and the latter having enjoyed the privilege of frequent intercourse with the apostles. Their works, though small, contain more than two hundred and twenty quotations or allusions to the sacred volume, which they call " The Sacred Scriptures," " The oracles of the Lord," &c., showing that they regarded them as a revelation from God.*

---

* The following anecdote will serve to show both the extent to which the Scriptures are quoted by the fathers, and also, the remarkable providence by which they have been preserved, during barbarous and apostate ages, and a sure safeguard interposed against their alteration, corruption, or interpolation

The late Rev. Walter Buchanan, of Edinburgh, related that, as he was dining with a literary party, and afterwards spending the evening together, some one of the party proposed the following question " Supposing all the New Testaments in the world had been destroyed at the end of the third century, could their contents have been recovered from the writings of the first three centuries?" No one even guessed at an answer But Lord Hailes, who was one of the party, having in his possession all the writings of those centuries, set himself at work to ascertain the fact; and after two months' close application, he sent to Mr. Buchanan, and informed him of the result, stating that he had marked the quota-

Thus, we have the testimony of the whole church, from the present, back to the apostolic age, that the several books of the New Testament were written by those persons whose names they bear, and in the age to which they are ascribed. Yet, we are not confined to the testimony of Christians alone; although we must regard their testimony as of more value than any other, because they were convinced of its truth, and staked all that was dear to them on their belief in the Christian religion. But,

3. We have the admission of the enemies of Christianity, in relation to the authenticity of these books. They were widely circulated; and in the controversies which arose, they were freely appealed to and quoted, both by Christians and Pagans. The emperor Julian, an apostate from the Christian faith, and a most bitter opposer of Christianity, wrote against it in 361; and he bears testimony to the four gospels and the Acts of the Apostles, as having been the genuine productions of the persons to whom they are ascribed. He has also quoted several of the Epistles, and no where insinuates that the authenticity of any of the books of the New Testament is to be questioned. *Herocles*, who wrote in 103, and *Porphyry*, in 270, both against Christianity; and also, Celsus, who wrote 76 years after the death of the Apostle John, all pro-

---

tions, so that any other person could examine them; and he had actually discovered, quoted in those writings, the whole of the New Testament, except seven or eleven verses, which, he believed, might be found, on further examination. This seems to be something more than a mere accident. The hand of God is to be recognized in it.

ceed in their arguments upon the concession that the Christian Scriptures were the works of the authors to whom they were ascribed. The quotations of the latter are so numerous that they amount almost to an abridgement of the gospel narrative. Yet, though it would have been a great advantage to their arguments, they nowhere breathe a suspicion against the authenticity of these books.

4. There are also several other considerations, which go to show that these books could have been written only in the age, and by the authors to which they are attributed, to which I have room only briefly to allude. Their language and style are in perfect harmony with the character and circumstances of their reputed authors. They were Jews, by birth and education, and Jews were to a great extent the persons to whom they wrote; hence Jewish peculiarities are found broadly stamped upon them all; and the language is a mixture of Hebrew and Greek, such as could have prevailed only in Palestine, before the destruction of Jerusalem, and the dispersion of the Jews. After that, the language of the New Testament ceased to be a living language. And, we find in each of these books the peculiar characteristics of their reputed authors, such as they are represented to be, in the narratives written by each other. There are, also, incidental allusions to the manners and customs of the age, and to facts in the history of the age, such as could not have been correctly made by a writer in any other age, and such as would not have been attempted in a forgery. Such is the allusion to the universal taxing, mentioned in the second chapter

of Luke, which agrees with the accounts stated in profane history.

Thus, though I have given but a very brief outline of the testimony under this head, I think the point is established beyond question, that the several books of which the New Testament is composed, are the productions of the age and of the men to whom they are ascribed; and, at the same time, all the proof adduced under this head goes to show that these books were written by the inspiration of God.

II. The second point to be proved is, that we have the *genuine* writings of these men, and that they have not been altered or corrupted since the age in which they were written. It only requires a little attention to the facts of the case, to show the impossibility of any such alteration or corruption. As soon as these books were published, they were eagerly sought after, and copies were multiplied and carried into distant countries, and preserved as sacred treasures. They were read in families, and expounded in churches. They were made the subject of attack and discussion, between Christians, heretics, and Pagans. In a short time copies were spread over the whole inhabited portion of the world, and they were translated into various different languages. All this took place before the declension of piety, which introduced the superstitions of the Roman and Greek churches. Harmonies, commentaries, and catalogues were carefully made and published. Thus universal notoriety was given to the books. And how could alterations have been made in them? To succeed, they must have been made in all the copies. Could enemies have done it? Would Christians have received them? Could heretics have made them? Would the orthodox have received them? Could the orthodox have made them? Would not the heretics have taken advantage of it, to promote their views? Yet we hear nothing of all this.

But we are not left here to reason from the impossibility of the thing. More than three hundred and fifty ancient manuscript copies of the books of the New Testament have come down to us. These were written in different ages and countries. They have been carefully compared, and found to agree in all essential particulars; though there are just such variations in the reading as might be expected to occur by the mistakes of transcribers, such as the omission or transposition of letters, errors in pointing, &c. But the very worst of these manuscripts, if it were the only copy of the New Testament, would not pervert one Christian doctrine or precept. These manuscripts agree, also, with the numerous quotations contained in the works of early Christian writers.* But, besides this, we have a number of ancient translations, some of which were made as early as the beginning of the second century, which agree substantially with the received text. One of these, the ancient Syriac, the oldest version extant, was not known in Europe till the 16th century; yet, when it came to be compared with the received text, they were found to agree almost exactly, containing no important variation. "So

---

* See note, page 57.

clearly and impressively," says an eminent writer, " has Divine Providence attested the integrity of our beloved Scriptures."

Still, there may be, in many minds, who yield to the force of the foregoing facts and arguments, a question whether the present received English version of the Bible is a faithful translation of the original. But I think a very cursory examination of the facts will satisfy their minds on this score. Before the present translation was made, there were several versions, differing somewhat from each other; and some dissatisfaction was felt with the Bishop's Bible, then in common use. In 1604, King James gave orders that a new translation should be made ; and fifty-four men, preeminently distinguished for learning and piety, were appointed to undertake the work, of whom forty-seven entered upon it. These were divided into six classes, and a distinct portion of the Bible allotted to each class. Every individual of each class translated by himself the whole of the books allotted to them ; after which they met and decided upon the renderings which they would adopt. When it was finished, it was sent to each of the other companies, to be again examined. This was done by one reading the translation aloud, while each of the others held in his hand the original, or some other version, and the reader was interrupted and remarks made, as occasion called for. Thus the present English version is the result of six separate translations, brought into one, by the discussion and critical examination of all difficult points. This translation was first published in 1811; showing that its authors took time to perfect their work. It has since been frequently revised with great care, and many marginal notes added; but no alterations have been made in the text. "It still remains," says Professor Bush, "not only the standard version, but by the unanimous voice of the most competent judges, it is ranked among the very best translations of this or any other book in the world. In point of fidelity, perspicuity, simplicity, energy, and dignity, it doubtless stands unrivalled." It is a sufficient evidence of its essential accuracy, that it has always been received and appealed to by all denominations of evangelical Christians as a standard version; and though many new versions have been made, none of them have ever obtained any considerable currency.

III. Having established the fact that these books were written by the persons to whom they were attributed, at the time they profess to have been written; and that we are in possession of genuine copies of them; the next inquiry is, how we know that they were written by divine inspiration. This will appear from several sources of evidence :—

1. It has already been shown that the question of the truth of the gospel narratives cannot be separated from that of the divine inspiration of their authors, and the divine origin of the Christian religion. They testify to the fact of their own inspiration, and the inspiration of each other. They could not be mistaken as to this fact, because the matters which they profess to have received by inspiration are not mere matters of opinion, but great facts and principles; and these were attested by miracles, wrought publicly, either

by themselves, or before their eyes. According to Luke's narrative of the Acts of the Apostles, all of them wrought miracles, to prove that what they taught was a revelation from heaven. Paul also declares this concerning himself. And these miracles, as well as those wrought by Christ himself, were of such a character that they could not possibly have been mistaken. When the servants poured water into the water pots, at the command of Christ, and drew out wine, there could have been no deception about it, the wine having been declared good by the governor of the feast; who must have been a good judge. And, when a man had been blind or lame from his birth, and was cured by a word from Christ or the Apostles, and was afterwards seen walking about, or when a man had been dead and buried four days, when it was said that he came forth alive at the word of Christ, and continued alive, and was seen and conversed with by the disciples, for some time afterwards; and so, in regard to the resurrection of Christ; it was impossible that they could have been mistaken. Therefore, these writers must either have asserted the truth, both in regard to their own inspiration and the miracles they relate; or else they must have been guilty of asserting what they knew to have been false. It comes then to this,—The writers of the New Testament were impostors, and imposed on mankind a narrative which they knew to be false, or else their narratives are true, and not only true, but given under the sanction of Divine inspiration, being all that it claims to be,—the word of God. But that they are true will appear,

1. From the fact that these writers have shown themselves, by their conduct, to have been honest men. They could not have been deceived in regard to what they have stated; and if they knew it to be false, we find them acting contrary to all that we know of human nature. They asserted these facts, in the face of opposition, obloquy, persecution, and death. They had no earthly object to gain by it. All the governments of the world were opposed to the religion which they propagated. They could not gain honor, but were certain of receiving shame. They had no prospect of securing wealth, but the certain prospect of losing all things. They could not expect to gain the applause and affection of mankind, for the religion they preached was opposed to all the natural feelings, fixed prejudices, and confirmed superstitions of the people. And, on the supposition that they were impostors, and dishonest and false in their statements, they could have had no prospect of advantage beyond this life; so that they must have been acting not only without motive, but directly in opposition to all the motives which usually influence men. We conclude, therefore, that they were honest men, and that they bore witness to the truth.

2. It will appear that these narratives are true, and therefore that they contain a revelation from God, from the fact that the writers could not have made the people believe that they were true, if they had not been. These narratives were published during the lifetime of multitudes who are said to have witnessed the facts stated in them; and at the same time it is proved, not only by the assertions of these writers,

but by the concurrent testimony of all history, that multitudes did believe them, and risk their all upon their truth. Tacitus, a Roman historian, who was himself a Pagan, has attested the existence of Jesus Christ; his public execution under Pontius Pilate; the temporary checks which this gave to the progress of his religion; its revival a short time after his death; and its progress over the land of Judea and the Roman empire. No one pretends to doubt these facts. Yet these facts show that multitudes must have been made to believe the facts attested in these books; and multitudes in the very places where the miraculous events related in them are said to have transpired. But now, suppose some one should publish a book, asserting that, at a certain time, a man who is now living, who was lame from his birth, had been cured of his lameness by two men calling upon him to rise up and walk, could they make any one believe it, if it was not true, while the man himself, and his friends and neighbors, were living? Yet, if the book of Acts is not an authentic narrative, we must believe precisely such an absurdity. And so, also, of the gospel narratives. Suppose a book should now be published, asserting that about thirty years ago, a certain person had been all over this land, followed by great multitudes, many of whom he had healed of diseases of long standing; in many instances giving the names of persons and places; and that, in several instances, giving names and places, he had raised persons from the dead; that at length he himself suffered capital punishment, and after being some days buried, had risen from the dead, and remained forty days on earth, and then ascended into heaven; could the author gain any considerable credence to such a story, if it was not true, since there would be many persons living, in all the places named, who could examine into his statements? No one would for a moment think such a thing possible; yet this is precisely the case with the gospel of Matthew; and the same also is true of the other evangelists, except that a longer time had elapsed before their publication. That these books contain a true narrative of facts, is proved by the fact that they obtained such a currency in the age in which they were published; and that the religion which they taught, in the short space of about thirty years, in the face of every disadvantage, spread over the whole of the Roman empire. The testimony of the same witnesses who wrote these narratives, must have carried conviction with it wherever they went, or they could not, by the simple force of the account they gave, have secured its introduction so extensively, during the short period of their ministry. And, moreover, we cannot account for this in any other way than that in which they account for it themselves,—that God wrought with them, giving power and efficacy to their word. There is nothing like it in the history of other religions. There is nothing like it in the spread of Mohammedism. Mohammed was four years in making nine converts, while Christ had more than five hundred in three years; and in a very short time after his death, more than five thousand. But the religion of Mohammed, although addressed to the natural passions of men, made little progress till he took up arms to propagate it; while the religion of Christ, which opposes all the natural corrupt propensities of men, and was opposed by all the power of the world, yet spread over the whole world, by the force of a power inherent in itself, in the course of about thirty years

We have, likewise, another testimony to the truth of these narratives, by the existence, at the present day, of ordinances and institutions, the origin of which is there stated. Such are the Christian church; the Christian ministry; baptism and the Lord's supper. The existence of these things, at the present time, is a witness of the truth of the account of their original institution.

3. It must be that these narratives are true, because the facts stated in them were not contradicted by the enemies of Christianity, who lived at the time they are said to have occurred. Even the most malignant of the Scribes and Pharisees, though they were constantly watching to detect imposition, were compelled to admit the miracles of Christ; and therefore they ascribed them to Satanic influence. And Josephus, the renowned Jewish historian of that period, passes over these transactions in silence, although the gospel narratives were extant in his day; and his silence shows that he could not contradict them.

4. These books bear all the internal marks of credible testimony. They were written by eight different authors, and yet, while they preserve a variety of manner and style, there is a perfect agreement among them, as to the facts stated, and the doctrines taught. Nor does any one writer contradict himself. One of the strongest marks of the credibility of a witness before a court, is, that his story is consistent with itself.

This is true of each of these writers. Then again, the testimony of several witnesses is strengthened, by their agreement in relating the same story. This advantage we have in the gospel witnesses. Then the testimony of witnesses is corroborated by its agreement with circumstances ; and this we have also. Such are their minute and accurate allusions to the manners and customs of the age in which they wrote ; their agreement, as to historical facts, with other historians, which will appear especially by comparing them with Josephus and other writers of the same period. As an illustration, take the first two verses of the second chapter of Luke, where the period mentioned is designated by mentioning the name of the reigning emperor, and of the governors of the several provinces of Judea and vicinity, of the high priests, and also the taxing and enrolment which took place at that time ; all of which agree perfectly with the facts, as stated in profane history. And there are many more such allusions, which we have not room to state in particular. It appears, then, that these writings bear the internal marks of credible testimony,—having all the usual characteristics of truth.

5. The early writers, whose testimony has been adduced to prove the authenticity of these books, uniformly speak of them as having been given by inspiration, and as being of divine authority. This is apparent in the quotations already given ; and it is every where apparent in these writings. Iræneus, who was born about the year 57, calls them " divine oracles," and " Scriptures of the Lord." He says the gospel was " committed to writing, by the will of God, that

it might be, for time to come, the foundation and pillar of our faith." Origen says, "Christians believe Jesus to be the Son of God, in a sense not to be explained by any but by that Scripture alone, which is inspired by the Holy Ghost; that is, the evangelic and apostolic Scriptures, as also that of the law and the prophets." And similar expressions abound in the writers already alluded to. The books which now form the New Testament were, at a very early period, collected into one volume, and called the "New Testament," or "New Covenant," in distinction from the Old. This fact is established by Tertullian, who was born only fifty years after the death of John, who alludes to these books under the terms of the "New Testament," and the "Gospels and Apostles." These books were, also, at a very early period, read and expounded in the churches, as being of divine authority. The following extract from Justin Martyr, who was born ten years before the death of the Apostle John, gives us an interesting account of primitive worship. In his apology to the emperor, he says : " The memoirs of the apostles or the writings of the prophets are read ; and when the reader has ended, the president, ' that is, the presiding officer of the meeting,' makes a discourse, exhorting to the imitation of so excellent things." This custom must have been, at this time, (which was about the year 140,) notorious and universal. The same thing is spoken of by many other early writers. And this fact shows that they were regarded by the churches generally as the word of God. The same thing is evident, also, from the fact that, during the primitive ages of the church, commentaries were written upon the books of the New Testament; harmonies of them were formed; copies were diligently compared; and translations were made into different languages. These facts show that they were standard books, regarded as of divine authority. The agreement of the ancient church, as to what were the authentic books of the New Testament, is complete; and the various sects of heretics in the earliest centuries, likewise entirely agree on the same point. And it is evident that the greatest care was taken, in the admission of these books into the sacred canon, by those who had the means of knowing what books had received the sanction of the apostles, as given by inspiration. The fathers, in all their writings, and of all ages and countries, appeal to these Scriptures as of infallible authority. At the same time, none of the apocryphal books, of which there are many, were thus received by the primitive church. They were never received as of divine authority, till they were introduced into the sacred canon by the church of Rome, at the council of Trent, in the sixteenth century.

6. There is one proof more of the inspiration and divine authority of the Scriptures, which I think entitled to no small consideration. It is the unbroken and united testimony of the whole Christian church, from the days of the apostles to the present time. To perceive the weight of this testimony, it must be observed that the testimony of every individual Christian, from that day to this, is founded on a personal conviction so strong that it has exerted a controlling influence over his conduct, and led him to stake all

his interests, for time and eternity, on the truth of this conviction. And this conviction has been formed either on a close and careful examination of the evidence which the Scriptures present that they are a revelation from God ; or from experiencing in themselves feelings and emotions corresponding to those described in the Bible, or from both of these combined. Every Christian that ever lived is a witness to the truth and inspiration of the Scriptures ; and multitudes of these witnesses have sealed their testimony with their own blood. Moreover, this host of witnesses has been collected from all classes of society; embracing emperors, kings, philosophers ; learned men ; intelligent citizens ; men of plain common sense ; together with the poor and ignorant ; and even children ; all of whom have found something on which to rest a firm and unshaken belief, which has stood by them both in life and in death. This is a kind of testimony which cannot be furnished for any other religion. It combines outward evidence with that which is practical and experimental ; and, it seems to me, if it stood alone by itself, it would be invulnerable to all attacks. Every Christian, who has experienced the power of the gospel on his own heart, is a living witness that the Bible is the word of God. He has the witness in himself, and it is manifest in his life. He can appeal to his own knowledge, and say, " I speak that I do know, and testify that which I have seen." And oftentimes this is the most powerful testimony that can be brought before the mind of the skeptical and doubting. They cannot fail to see that the humble Christian has something within him of which they are destitute. But when this testimony is multiplied by the whole number of Christians that have ever existed, it is cumulative, powerful, irresistible.

Thus I have given a brief outline of the external evidence of the authenticity and inspiration of the Holy Scriptures. Any one who will examine for himself, will find that I have only glanced at a mass of matter sufficient to fill many volumes. Yet, I think the evidence I have presented must be sufficient to satisfy any candid and unprejudiced mind that the Christian Scriptures, contained in the Old and New Testaments, are a revelation from God; and that they furnish an infallible standard of truth and duty.

PRACTICAL REMARKS.

1. If the foregoing conclusion be correct, the doctrines taught in the Bible ought to be received with meekness and submission, as a little child receives information from a parent; nor should any objection be entertained against them, on the ground of any supposed unreasonableness, which we may think we discover in the doctrines themselves. The only question for us to examine is, *Does the Bible teach them?* If it does, that is the highest reason we could have for believing them. What could make them so reasonable matters of belief as the fact that God has revealed them? Surely, submission to the teachings of Infinite wisdom and knowledge is in the highest de-

gree reasonable; and nothing can be so unreasonable in the creature of a day, as to question the reasonableness of any thing that God has revealed. Want of attention to this fundamental principle, is the source of nearly, if not quite all the error there is in the world. It amounts to this,—the setting up of our own reason above or in opposition to the wisdom of God. Nor can we judge what it would be consistent or reasonable for God to do. He is infinitely above us. We can see but the minutest parts of his administration. For us to sit in judgment on any particular thing which he has revealed concerning his administration, is as absurd as for the fly, on the corner of a splendid edifice, who can see but an inch around, to sit in judgment on the architecture of the whole building. This view of the subject will remove the difficulties usually thrown around the doctrines of the trinity, of election, and of Divine sovereignty.

2. The fact that the Bible is true, imposes the most solemn obligation on all who possess it, to believe and obey it. And to do this, it becomes necessary that they should search it diligently, and with an humble, teachable spirit, in order to understand what it teaches. This furnishes a strong motive to all to engage in the Sabbath school. This institution, by bringing in the social principle, furnishes excitement and stimulus to engage in this duty. It also furnishes facilities for understanding the Scriptures, by bringing together and comparing the views of various individuals on the same points. If the mere improvement of the intellectual powers is alone to be considered, no means can be employed, which will operate so powerfully

upon a whole community as to engage them all in the regular and constant study of such a book as the Bible. The exercise of mind necessary to a critical understanding of its meaning, and to a nice discrimination of its doctrines, is as great a source of mental improvement as that required in the study of the learned languages, or the abstruse sciences. And wherever such a course of study is thoroughly pursued, there will be a wakefulness of intellect, unknown to the ordinary mass of uncultivated minds. Yet this is nothing, when compared with the unspeakable importance of understanding the revealed will of God, on obedience to which depends eternal life or eternal death.

3. Our disbelief of the Bible will not diminish our obligation to obey it. True, we may not, perhaps, be satisfied with the evidence on which it rests its claim to inspiration ; but is God under any obligation to gratify us any farther on this point ? He has furnished us with evidence more extensive, more weighty, more luminous, than he has given us of any other fact in the past history of our race. If we will not receive this testimony, what if he should leave us to our own voluntary ignorance and blindness,—will it not be our own fault and folly ? And will he excuse us, because we shut our eyes to the light which he has held up before us ? What if we should refuse to believe that the sun shines,—would the heavens gather blackness, and the firmament cease to convey light and heat to the earth ? What if we should refuse to believe that water will drown, and fire burn, and rush heedlessly into them,—will our unbelief save us ? What if we

believe there is no hell,—will our unbelief save us from eternal burnings?

4. A dreadful doom awaits those who hear or read the truths revealed in the Holy Scriptures, and yet obey them not. Christ likens such to a man who "built his house upon the sand; and the rain descended and the floods came, and the winds blew, and beat upon that house, and it fell; and great was the fall of it." In that land, the soil is loose and sandy, and the rains come only at particular seasons of the year; but at those seasons, it pours down in torrents, for so long a time as to raise the little streams, which are dry a large part of the season, to impetuous torrents, which come rushing down the sides of the hills with irresistible force; and if a house is built on the sand, its foundation is swept away, and it is dashed in pieces. And such will be the hopes of all, who do not rest upon obedience to the gospel of Jesus Christ, revealed in this blessed book. A more dreadful storm is approaching, and awful indeed will be the fate of those of who have not their foundation fixed upon Christ, the Rock of Ages. Dreadful were the calamities which God brought upon Sodom and Gomorrah and Tyre and Sidon; but more dreadful still the woes denounced upon Chorazin and Bethsaida, because they received not Christ upon his own testimony,—and, on the same principle, our condemnation will be still greater, if we neglect the same gospel. Paul, speaking of the condemnation of the unbelieving Jews, says, "If the word spoken by angels was steadfast, and every transgression received a just recompense of reward, how shall we escape, if we neglect so great

salvation, which at the first began to be spoken by the Lord, and was confirmed unto us by them that heard him ; God also bearing them witness, both with signs and wonders, and with divers miracles and gifts of the Holy Ghost ?" But we have not this only, but the accumulated testimony of more than eighteen hundred years, during which time, in various parts of the world, God has borne witness to the truth, by the outpouring of his Holy Spirit, and the conversion of sinners to himself. How then shall we escape, if we neglect so great salvation !

4. Finally,—How thankful ought we to be, that God has given us such unquestionable evidence of the truth of his Holy Word ; and that he has preserved it pure and uncorrupted, in the midst of the opposition of heathen and infidels, and the corruption and wickedness of its professed friends ; and that he has preserved it in such a manner that the evidence of its genuineness is within our reach. May his goodness lead us all to repent of our past neglect of the sacred oracles, and to a closer and more faithful examination of, and obedience to, the precious truths therein revealed.

CHAPTER III.

THE THIRD PILLAR.—*The Bible contains, within itself, the most conclusive evidence of its divine origin.*

WE argue the existence of God from the works of creation, because they every where bear the impress of a Supreme Intelligence; but the same evidence of the operation of a Supreme Intelligence in the works of creation prove that God created them. By analogy, the same argument will apply to the Bible. The Holy Scriptures, on every page, bear the impress of a Supreme Intelligence. The existence of such a book as the Bible proves that there is a God; for no one but a Divine Being could have produced such a book. But the same evidence of the operation of a Supreme Intelligence, in the production of this book, proves that God is the author of the Bible.

Let us pursue this analogy a little further. The candid student of *geology* finds the earth to be formed according to the dictates of a superior wisdom. The *soil*, which, of all its parts, is most important for the practical use of man, lies on the surface, and is accessible to every one, and its uses capable of being understood and applied by the meanest capacity. But as he proceeds into the earth, he discovers the coarser metals, which are useful for common purposes, in great abundance ; the precious metals, in sufficient quantities to answer the higher purposes of life ; while the jewels and precious stones, which are chiefly for ornament, are very rare. Yet, beyond all this, as he digs into the bowels of the earth, he discovers new wonders at every step of his progress, which excite his curiosity and admiration, but which he is wholly incompetent to explain. So the student of the Bible finds those doctrines and precepts, which are necessary to a knowledge of his duty and the way of salvation, lie on the surface, and apparent to the meanest capacity, when studied with humility and submission. But beyond this he discovers the coarser metals,—the strong truths, the iron and steel, which impart energy and force to the Christian character,— the precious metals, those discoveries which delight and enrapture the soul,—and, farther on, the jewels and precious stones,—the sparkling gems of truth, o surpassing excellence and surprising beauty. But further on still are those deep and unfathomable wonders, which finite minds can only admire and adore.

The same thing is apparent, if we compare the Bible with the heavenly bodies. The *sun* is the most prominent in the heavens ; and its light and heat are vastly more important to the human race than all the discoveries of astronomy. So the doctrine of the *Atonement of Christ* stands out in the Bible like the sun in the heavens ; and this, to the poor soul burdened with guilt, is as important as light and heat to the world. Yet as the closer observation of the heavens has discovered a beautiful system of order and harmony,—a system of worlds revolving round the sun as a common centre ; so the student of the Bible discovers in it a beautiful system of divine truth, revolving in harmonious order around the cross of Christ, as its common centre. And as every increase of the power of the telescope discovers new wonders in the heavens,—new stars, new suns, and new systems, far off in the regions of infinite space ; so at every advance which the biblical student makes, he discovers new wonders and new glories, which alike confound him by their vastness and fill him with delightful adoration.

If we descend to a more minute examination of the works of creation, we are filled with admiration at the wonderful adaptedness of every thing to its particular design, evincing the all-pervading presence of an Infinite Intelligence in their construction. But to the student of the Bible the same thing is equally apparent in that wonderful book. It is emphatically the *Peoples' Book*,—addressed to the commen sense of mankind, consisting of every variety of style and manner, as well as every species of composition, and containing something especially adapted to every class of persons ; and although written in an obscure province of Western Asia, in rude and barbarous ages, among a people of peculiar manners and habits, differing from all other nations, yet equally adapted to every country and every age of the world ; and alike to the earliest developements of the human intellect and the most advanced stages of cultivation. The child, the ser-

THE BIBLE AND CREATION.

vant, the mechanic, the merchant, the husbandman, and the man of science, all find in it something which they can understand and follow, and something to employ the noblest powers of their minds.

Can such a book be the work of a man, or of any number of men? As well might we ask, could a man, or could any combination of human power and skill, stretch forth the heavens as a curtain, fix the sun in its orbit, and sprinkle the sky with countless worlds and systems of worlds? Or, could human power originate this earth, pile up its mountains on high, spread abroad its beautiful valleys, pour forth its broad rivers, and shut up the sea with doors and bars, saying, "hitherto shalt thou come, but no further, and here shall thy proud waves be stayed?" Or could man, by his knowledge and skill, form the beautiful mechanism of animal bodies, and adapt each one, and every part, so nicely to its specific duties? For surely greater skill cannot be necessary to do these things, than to make a book which shall give exact information to the human mind, on just those subjects in relation to which it needs to be informed, and adapt it to all the varied capacities and tastes of men, in all ages and countries of the world. This beautiful world, with all things therein, was the product of six days' labor; but the Bible was the production of nearly fifteen hundred years. If, then, the student of Nature must come to the conclusion that there is a God, who has made all things, the student of the Bible must come to the conclusion that there is a God, who has revealed himself in that blessed book. But this argument reversed proves this book to be the work of God.

Yet there is a difficulty in presenting this subject in such a manner that it can be appreciated by any other than a student of the Bible, or even to describe it at all, in a treatise or a discourse—the same that there is in describing the features of a beautiful countenance, the exquisite combination of colors in the rainbow, the sweet sounds of a fine-toned instrument of music, or the appalling grandeur of a thunder storm at sea— either of which must be *seen* or *heard* to be understood and felt. Yet there are a few prominent points that may be presented; and this I shall now undertake to do. I observe, then,

1. That, what the Scriptures teach *concerning God*, commends itself to the reason and common sense of mankind, as being essential to the Supreme Creator and Governor of the Universe. Such are, the unity and spirituality of the Divine Essence or Nature; the Eternity of his being; and the perfection of all his attributes, constituting, together, a Being of Infinite Perfection. I need not specify the passages which teach these things concerning God. They are familiar to every one that is familiar with the Bible. But it must be apparent to all, that these things are essential to God; and that a being, falling in the least degree short of Infinite Perfection, could not be God. I do not assert that this truth may not be discovered by the light of nature; yet the fact that all nations, destitute of the Scriptures, have lost this knowledge of the true God, and that it has only been preserved in the Holy Scriptures, shows that the sa-

cred record must be a revelation from God. The light of nature has, by reason of sin, become darkness; and all nations, except such as have been in some way enlightened through the influence of the Holy Scriptures, have no adequate ideas of the nature of the true God. The philosophers of Greece, probably, received their ideas of God from the Jewish Scriptures, which, at an early period, were translated into the Greek language; and whatever correct ideas of God the modern Deists may have, they have stolen from the Christian Scriptures.

2. The Scriptures reveal things which could not be known except by revelation from God; and yet, when revealed, these truths commend themselves to the reason and consciences of men. Such are the facts of the resurrection of the body and the immortality of the soul,—facts, which all the light of nature and of science are incompetent to teach, and concerning which, they have never been able to discover any thing more than "probabilities by conjecture." Such, also, is the provision it reveals for securing the integrity of God's government, while it extends pardon to the guilty. The fact, that God can pardon sin, consistently with his justice, could never have been discovered except by a direct revelation from God himself; for no other being could determine this to be possible; and the fact, that this revelation is accompanied by a scheme which preserves the holiness of God and the integrity of his government, is evidence of its divine origin; this scheme being entirely beyond the capacity of any human being to devise.

3. The Scriptures reveal great facts, so entirely incomprehensible in their nature, as to render the conception of them above the capacity of finite beings. Such is the fact that God subsists in a trinity of persons, while the Divine Essence, or Nature of the Godhead, is one and indivisible. It cannot be shown that this is contrary to right reason; yet it is entirely above the province of reason to comprehend it. That the conception of the idea is above human reason, is proved by the fact that it never has been conceived, except as taught by the Scriptures. The heathen have their "gods many and lords many;" but it cannot, I think, be shown that they have ever conceived the idea of one Infinite Supreme Intelligence, subsisting in a mysterious manner, in a plurality of persons. The fact that this is mysterious and incomprehensible, though often brought as an argument against this doctrine, is in fact an argument in its favor, and in favor of the inspiration of the book which teaches it. If the Bible contained no mysterious and incomprehensible things, it would lose much of its claim to our confidence, as a divine revelation. In a revelation from the infinite God to finite creatures, it is reasonable to expect many facts to be stated, the nature of which are beyond the powers of finite minds. But this doctrine is no more incomprehensible than any thing else that is revealed concerning God. Who can comprehend the eternity of God? Let the human mind stretch its utmost length, backward and forward, and what progress can it make towards the apprehension of a Being who never began to be, and who will never cease to exist? **Beyond**

the utmost verge of human thought, there still lie the trackless shores of eternity. And who can understand the self-existence of God? Who can fathom the meaning of that ineffable name, "I am?" What idea can a finite mind form of existence without a cause? What idea can we form of a First Cause,—a cause which is its own cause—while we have never been conversant with any thing but second causes? The very idea of infinity, in its application to any of the attributes of God, is altogether beyond the grasp of a finite mind. Who can tell how God can be present in every place, and have a perfect conception of all things throughout infinite space at the same moment? What idea can we form of power which has no limit but the will of its possessor? And who can fathom the infinite holiness of God? These are divine and glorious mysteries, just such as we might reasonably expect to find in a revelation from the Infinite God. The existence of these sublime mysteries in this revelation also agree with the analogy of God's works, whereby, also, as well as in his word, he has made himself known. The works of creation and providence, from the structure of the smallest insect and the growth of a spire of grass, to the architecture of the heavens and the rolling of the spheres, are full of mysterious and incomprehensible things. We conclude, therefore, that the fact that the Scriptures contain the declaration of facts, the existence of which is neither absurd nor unreasonable, and yet the nature of which is mysterious and incomprehensible, fixes the impress of divinity upon these Scriptures. The very perfection of nature ascribed to God in the Bible, is evidence, also, of its divine origin; for what finite mind could originate the conception of such perfection?

4. It is an evidence of the divine inspiration of the Scriptures, that they contain a rational and consistent account of the origin of all things. This cannot be said of the sacred books of the heathen; or of any theory or conjecture based upon any thing else but the Mosaic account. All the accounts contained in the sacred books or traditions of the heathen, are filled with absurd and ridiculous fables; and yet they approach so near to a caricature of the account which the Bible furnishes, as to corroborate it. On the supposition that this account is true, we should naturally expect tradition would teach just what it does. But I have said this account is consistent and rational. It is consistent with the character of God. According to this account, almighty power is displayed in the creation in a most sublime and glorious manner—"He spake and it was done, he commanded and it stood fast,"—what more worthy of God? The holiness of God is also equally conspicuous; for, according to this account, all things left the hand of their Creator perfectly good. And what idea can be formed of the origin of all things, more rational and consistent with reason?

5. It is evidence of the divine inspiration of the Scriptures, that they account, in a rational and satisfactory manner, for the present character and condition of man. If we were left to infer that man was originally created the same sinful being which he now is, and placed in the same wretched condition, it

would reflect upon the character of the Creator. But the Bible declares that he was originally created holy, with ability to choose between good and evil; and it gives a history of his fall from the estate in which he was created, which is both rational in itself, and consistent with the infinite holiness of God. And this evidence is greatly strengthened by the fact, that the account contained in the Bible is the only one which furnishes a satisfactory explanation of the present character and condition of the human race, and of the world in which we live. Without this account, we should be left, in regard to this matter, in total darkness.

The same may be said, also, of the diversity of languages in the world; and of many other things which exist under the Divine administration, which have perplexed the wisest of men. But for this explanation, we should be at a loss to account for the existence of suffering, under the wise administration of a Supreme, beneficent Being. But in the Bible it is explained in a manner which commends itself to the conscience of every man. Here, suffering is connected with the curse pronounced upon the head of the race, as part of the penalty of disobedience; and we are taught to regard it as the punishment of sin. Yet David was perplexed to discover, that the sufferings and trials of this life come alike upon both the righteous and the wicked. And he could find no explanation of the mystery, till he went into the sanctuary, to inquire of God; and there he learned that this world is a state of trial and probation, and that exact retribution is reserved for another world. This is what the Scriptures teach; and they further explain the mystery, by declaring that the sufferings of the righteous are not retributive punishments, but fatherly corrections, designed for their good.

6. The Bible is proved to be a revelation from God, by the agreement of its parts. This wonderful volume is made up of more than sixty different books, professedly written by more than thirty different authors, at various times, during a period of about fifteen hundred years. And that they were so written, is evident from the fact, that every author has a style peculiar to himself, and every book bears unequivocal marks of the age in which it professes to have been written. For example, the Penteteuch could not have been written after the captivity, because it is in pure Hebrew; but after the dispersion of the Jews among other nations, their language contained a mixture of the languages of the people among whom they sojourned; and so of the other books, every one contains inherent evidence of having been written in the age to which it is ascribed. Yet all the parts of this book completely harmonize. One grand design runs through the whole, as it were a chain to bind it together; and there is the most perfect harmony of sentiment and doctrine throughout the whole. This allegation will bear the most rigid scrutiny; and the more it is examined, the more apparent it will be. All the books of the Bible agree most perfectly in their representations of God, of human character, and of the way of salvation; and, indeed, on every subject upon which a sentiment is advanced. It would not be possible to form a volume, at the present day, by collecting together the same number of books,

written by an equal number of persons belonging to the same religious denomination, without a diversity of opinion. Nor would it be possible to select thirty men, who, without concert, should write a volume of this size, without any clashing of opinion. But here we have a volume written by upwards of thirty different authors, varying in their education and modes of thinking, according to the customs and habits of different ages; written, too, in different languages. To believe that such a number of books could be produced, without concert, by such a number of uninspired men, at such intervals of time, which should maintain such perfect agreement, consistency, and harmony throughout, requires a degree of credulity beyond any thing ever charged upon believers in the Bible. And to believe that these books were forged by an individual, involves the absurdity of believing that one man could write in so many different styles; that he could imitate the shades of variation in a language at different periods of time; counterfeit the peculiarities of different ages; and make all his authors perfectly agree with the characters ascribed to them; and all this, to such perfection as to defy detection. An impostor, to accomplish such an undertaking, must be more than human. We know, indeed, that contradictions are charged upon the Bible; but these apparent contradictions vanish on a close scrutiny, made by one who is willing to receive the truth. They have weight only with the superficial or unwilling student. And there is not only this agreement in all its parts, but a progressive developement of a grand and glorious scheme from the beginning, which could not, by any possibility, have been continued, carried on and consummated, by different individuals, during a period of fifteen hundred years, except by the direction of God. Nor can we select particular portions of the Bible, and say this or that only is to be regarded as the word of God, without marring the beauty and disturbing the harmony of the whole. It would be like striking off a particular continent or sea, and denying it a place as a part of this world; or like striking out one of the planets from the solar system.

7. The writers of the Bible profess to speak by the inspiration of God. This was proved beyond dispute in a former chapter. But if the writers of the Bible were good men, they would not have professed what was not true, especially as they represent God as regarding liars with abhorrence, and expressly declare that the righteous will not lie. It has also been shown that, from the very nature of the case, they could not have been mistaken. But this book could not have been written by bad men, without contradicting all that we know of human nature; because it would be acting against themselves. It represents God as infinitely holy, and unchangeably opposed to sin. It denounces the most terrible threatenings against sinners. It represents the natural feelings of men as opposed to God—at enmity with him. It represents God as angry with the wicked, and in an attitude of threatening and judgment. Its doctrines are directly opposed to the natural feelings of men; yet there is a most perfect agreement between these doctrines and the character of a just and holy God. Moreover, the scheme of reconciliation between God

MAJESTY OF STYLE. 91

and man, proposed in the Bible, is directly opposed to the natural feelings of men; and calculated to humble the pride of their hearts, bring them to renounce all idea of personal merit, and submit themselves, unconditionally, to their offended Sovereign. Can any one believe such an absurdity, as that bad men would write such a book against themselves? There is no book in the world that wicked men hate so much as the Bible; and no book over which they would rejoice more if it were struck out of existence. This is the natural feeling of all men. It follows, then, that the Bible was neither written by good men without inspiration, nor by bad men for wicked purposes; it must, therefore, be the work of God.

8. No one can be conversant with the Bible without perceiving a majesty of style, commanding awe and reverence, which attaches to no other writings. The impression made upon the mind is, that *God is speaking*. The language of the evangelist, when comparing the teaching of Christ with that of the Scribes and Pharisees, applies with equal force to the whole Bible, in comparison with other writings : " He taught them *as one having authority*, and not as the Scribes." This is especially apparent when compared with the Apochryphal writings, the Koran, or the sacred books of the heathen. The Bible speaks as if the right of its Author to command, or to determine what is truth, were unquestioned; and it never once betrays the consciousness of pretension, or the inability of its Author to enforce what it commands.

6. Another internal evidence of the divine origin of the Bible is, the perfection of its code of morals, its

laws, and its institutions. The law of God, whether contemplated in its summary of two great principles, or its ten precepts, is perfect, as I have before remarked, embracing every thing necessary to be forbidden or required. The same may be said of this law which is truly said of its Divine Author,—nothing can be added to it or taken from it. It bears the impress of its Author. It is a transcript of His holy character. And the same may be said of all the institutions of the Bible. The morality of the Bible is as pure as its Author. It requires conformity of heart and life to a perfect law. Whether we compare it with the moral code of the heathen, of Mohammed, of ancient philosophers, or of modern Deists, it differs from them in this one grand feature, that it is perfect and entire, while imperfection cleaves to the best of them.

This argument, also, is capable of a more extensive application. It is true of everything which the Bible teaches, that there is a perfection about it, which can be found in no other book. If, then, a tree is known by its fruit, this book cannot be the production of imperfect men. It must be the work of a perfect being; and God is the only being of whom absolute perfection can be predicated; therefore the Bible is from God.

Another evidence of the divinity of the Scriptures, is the account which they give of Christ, and the benevolent plan which existed in his mind for the benefit of mankind. No one doubts that there was such a person as Jesus Christ; but some believe, or pretend to believe, that he was an impostor and deceiver;

and others set him down as a mere man, but of excellent character and exalted worth. If any were disposed to regard him as a fictitious character, it might be replied that the human mind is incapable, without divine aid, of conceiving and describing such a character. In all the fictions that ever have been written, there is nothing that will bear any comparison with it. In all these descriptions there is an attempt at perfection ; and the writers generally succeed in producing a character in some respects unnatural and above real life ; yet they can never succeed in divesting them entirely of human infirmity and imperfection ; and most generally these are very manifest. But in the character of Jesus, as drawn by the evangelists and apostles, not the slightest imperfection exists ; while his whole character is brought down to real life. But if we suppose him to have been a deceiver and impostor, we have still greater difficulties to encounter. If we admit the account which the evangelists give of him as true, and consider him as acting the part of a deceiver, we find him acting contrary to all the known principles of human nature. A deceiver and impostor must have some personal object to advance ; and such a person will always be found taking the advantage of circumstances, to favor his own selfish purposes. But we find Jesus always acting contrary to this. He pleased not himself. He sought not ease, or the enjoyment of worldly pleasure and comfort. We never find him returning evil for evil, or railing for railing, though constantly the subject of ill-treatment and abuse. If he had been a deceiver he would have coveted the approbation of the rulers, and cherished the good will of the common people. But though every thing was favorable to this he did neither. At this time the whole mind of the Jewish nation was in waiting anxiety and expectation of the coming of the promised Messiah, as a temporal prince, to deliver their nation from the Roman yoke ; yet he never once gave countenance to the prevailing opinion on this subject, but always opposed it. Instead of seeking the favor of the Scribes and Pharisees, the most influential leaders of the nation, he openly and publicly denounced their hypocrisy, avarice, pride, and false doctrines. When one of the rulers came to him by night, and acknowledged their belief that he was a teacher sent from God, instead of embracing this opportunity for strengthening their good opinion of him, he made a solemn declaration, directly opposed to the strong and deeply cherished prejudices of the nation, —that it was necessary for Jews as well as Gentiles, to be born from above, in order to enter into the kingdom of God. When his own countrymen were filled with astonishment at the wisdom and grace with which he addressed them, instead of taking advantage of the popular feeling to raise a party for himself, he foretold their future rejection of him, and by an allusion to the times of Elijah and Elisha, intimated that the blessings of the kingdom of God would be taken from them and given to the Gentiles ; so that the multitude were filled with wrath, and sought to destroy him. On another occasion, when the people were about to take him by force and make him king, he withdrew from them, and hid himself in a desert place, spending his time in communion with God. He never sought public notoriety, but often enjoined secrecy upon those who had been healed by him. Instead of making the terms of discipleship easy, and promising earthly rewards to his followers, he required them to forsake all they had, with no prospect of worldly advantage, but persecution and the loss of all things. Nor did he, like impostors in general, seek to make converts from among the rich; on the contrary, when a rich ruler came to him, he proposed such rigid terms of discipleship as discouraged the young man from attempting to follow him. He was constantly assaulting the national prejudices of the Jews, and advancing sentiments the most repugnant to their national pride. He shrunk from no hardship or self-denial, and sought no higher enjoyment than he found in doing the will of God. He discouraged the worldly expectations of his disciples, and foretold to them his death; and when the officers came to apprehend him, instead of attempting to flee, or offer resistance, he meekly surrendered himself up, only asking that his disciples might be suffered to depart unmolested. All this is directly contrary to the course pursued by ambitious and designing impostors; and certainly proves at least that he was sincere and honest in whatever he professed to be. But if we suppose his disciples have misrepresented him, and made him appear what he was not, in the accounts which they have given, the difficulty is not at all diminished. His disciples were Jews, partaking of all the bigotry and prejudice of their countrymen; and it would be the most unnatural thing in the world for them to think of doing honor to Jesus, by representing him as opposing all the cherished opinions and feelings of their countrymen, and proclaiming the destruction of their nation, and the reception of the hated Gentiles into the favor of God.

But if we admit that Jesus was honest and sincere, and no impostor, we must admit all that he claimed to be; for the claims which he makes to divinity are of such a nature that he could not be mistaken in regard to them. For he claims to be equal with God the Father; and to be in possession of the attributes of omniscience, omnipresence, and omnipotence. When Nathanael came to him, Jesus told him that he had seen him when he was under the figtree, while Nathanael knew that he had not been present; and he expressly declared to Nicodemus that he himself was then in heaven, while conversing with Nicodemus on earth. He also declared to his disciples that all power was given to him, both in heaven and on earth.

Morever the benevolent plan for the benefit of the human race, which existed in the mind of Jesus, proves him to have been a divine being. For the conception of such a plan, and the attempt to execute it, are altogether beyond the scope of the human mind, or the benevolence of the human heart. This plan was nothing less than that of giving a new religion to the whole world, adapted to the circumstances and wants of all the varieties of the human race, and containing in itself the principle of universal renovation of heart and reformation of life. It is an incontestible fact that, among all the heroes, legislators, philosophers, and priests of antiquity, in all ages before Christ, not one of them ever thought of devising a plan for the benefit of others, extending beyond the limits of the particular tribe or nation to which they belonged; and least of all should we expect such a scheme from an unlettered Jew, enclosed as that nation was by an iron band of prejudice and hatred towards all other nations. The very conception of such a plan, and the attempt to execute it, by a person brought up in the most unenlightened portion of Judea, himself destitute of human learning, proves that he must have been either himself a divine person, or endowed with divine inspiration; but as he professes to be divine, his own claim, in such circumstances, must be admitted.

Now if this argument is valid, it proves that the Scriptures are a revelation from God; for as was shown in the last chapter, Jesus testified to the inspiration of the Old Testament, and promised the gift of inspiration to his apostles, to enable them to write the New.

11. Another argument suitable for this place, is the remarkable, if not miraculous preservation of the Holy Scriptures. The Bible is, of all books, most hated by wicked men; yet there has not come down to us another book, bearing the proofs of equal antiquity, by many ages. Moreover, attempts have repeatedly been made, by persecuting kings and priests, to destroy all the copies of the sacred word. And while the Ark of the Covenant, the tables of stone, and the sacred utensils of the Jews, have long since ceased to exist, the Sacred Scriptures have come down to us with incontestible evidence of their genuineness,—a fact which cannot be accounted for except we admit that the special protection of Providence

has preserved them. The fact already stated, respecting the preservation of the New Testament, in the writings of the fathers, applies here with great force.* And the same may be said of their universal diffusion. There is no other book in the world so widely diffused and so extensively read, at the present day, as the Bible. This book has, indeed, become the standard of literature in many languages. There are but two ways in which this can be accounted for, either of which is proof of the divinity of the Scriptures,—one is, the direct providence of God, and the other, such an adaptation to the wants of men in the book itself as to give it universal currency. Probably both these agencies have contributed to the result. Why has not the Koran been universally circulated? It is translated into the English language; but no one buys or reads it, except from mere curiosity. Evidently because it is not such a book as the necessities of man call for.

12. We might proceed with the enumeration of points of this nature, which are familiar to the student of the Bible, almost indefinitely; but we will mention only one more. The Bible speaks to the heart and consciences of men. It is " quick and powerful, and sharper than any two-edged sword, and is a discerner of the thoughts and intents of the heart." It is this which gives the Bible its power in restraining and reforming mankind. It gives such an accurate description of the character and feelings of men, as to produce the conviction that it could only have been

---

* See note, page 57.

written by the direction of Him who searches the hearts and tries the reins of the children of men. But this argument possesses a double power to the mind of one who has experienced the renovating influences of that Spirit which dictated the word of God. He not only sees therein, as in a mirror, his own native character; but he finds there described the very exercises and affections which he every day experiences in the Christian life; thus furnishing a living testimony to its divine authority. He has the witness in himself. This is what Christ alludes to, when he says, " If any man will do his will, he shall know of the doctrine, whether it be of God, or whether I speak of myself." So if any would know whether the Bible is from God, or whether it be of men, let them receive and obey the gospel which it teaches, and they will have the witness in themselves that it is from God.

Thus I have endeavored to present a few of the leading internal evidences of the divine origin and authority of the Holy Scriptures, from which it appears that what the Scriptures teach concerning God commends itself to the reason and common sense of mankind, as being essential to the Supreme Creator and Governor of the universe,—that the Scriptures reveal things which could not be known, except by revelation from God; and yet when revealed, these truths commend themselves to the reason and consciences of men,—that the Scriptures reveal great facts, so entirely incomprehensible in themselves as to render the conception of them above the capacity of finite beings,—that the Scriptures contain a rational and consistent account of the origin of all things, and acccount, in a rational and satisfactory manner, for the present character and condition of man, the diversity of languages in the world, and many things which exist under the divine administration, which have perplexed the wisest of men,—that though the Bible is made up of a great number of different books, written in different ages, and by different authors, and in a great variety of style, yet there is a perfect agreement of doctrine and sentiment throughout, one grand design running through the whole,—that the writers of the Bible profess to speak by inspiration of God ; and unless what they profess was true, they were bad men ; but that bad men could not make such a book as the Bible, and if they could they would not, because they would not write against themselves ; for to do so would be like a house divided against itself,—that there is a majesty of style in the Sacred Scriptures found in no other book,—that the code of morals, laws, and institutions, as well as every thing it teaches, are so perfect as to show that it must have come from a perfect Being,—that the account which the Scriptures give of Christ, and his benevolent plan for the renovation and reformation of the world, bears the impress of divinity,—that the Scriptures have been preserved and diffused in such a manner as to show that they are under the special protection of God's providence,—and, finally, that it speaks to the hearts and consciences of men. Each of these points furnishes a distinct and independent proof that the Bible is a revelation from God ; and all of them together, a series of proofs, strong and impregnable. And yet the diligent and humble student of the Bible will find these proofs constantly accumulating, to strengthen and confirm his faith, as he digs into this mine of sacred treasure.

But it may be asked, if such is the tendency of the study of the Bible, why is it that so many persons deny its divine authority? This question, however, is easily answered. Those who thus reject the Bible, or parts of the Bible, may be divided into three classes. The first never study the Bible with sufficient care to observe these evidences of its divinity. The second determine before hand that they will not believe certain doctrines; and when they study the Bible, and find it full of these very doctrines, which they hate, they are forced to the rejection of the greater part or the whole of the sacred volume. This is particularly the case in regard to the doctrines of *vicarious atonement*, and the *eternal punishment of the wicked*. These doctrines stand out so prominently throughout the whole Bible, that those who are determined not to believe them, are obliged to deny the inspiration of the greater portion of the Scriptures; and this accounts for the downward tendency of those systems which reject these doctrines. There is no alternative but to embrace them, or give up nearly every thing contained in the Bible, except its bare and naked precepts. Such persons are completely under the dominion of prejudice, in the strictest meaning of the term. They have prejudged the case before examination. And is it to be wondered at, that one who disbelieves the doctrine of vicarious atonement, or the atonement for sin, by the substituted sufferings of another,—is it to be wondered at, I say, that such a one should regard the story of Abraham offering up his son as "a thought at which the flesh creeps with horror?" But that story is in perfect harmony with the grand theme which runs through the whole Bible; and to one who believes in this doctrine, it is not only full of meaning, but exceedingly sublime and beautiful. Nor is it strange that one who rejects this doctrine should find the New Testament full of " obvious contradictions and absurdities;" for the New Testament is full of this doctrine.

But there is a third class, who wish the Bible were not true, because they find it a restraint upon their inclinations, continually marring their pleasures. They cannot quietly take their fill of sin, while the word of God thunders its anathemas in their ears. But all these several classes are opposing themselves to God. The first treat his message with neglect and indifference; the second set up their own reason and their own will against the teachings of Infinite Wisdom; and the third say, with the fool, "No God,—no Bible,"—that is, they wish there were none.

These are all to be classed together, as the enemies of God and man. But there is another class, perhaps in many cases the dupes of these, who are to be regarded with commiseration. They have not gone so far as positively to reject the Scriptures; but they are bewildered in the fogs of skepticism; their confidence in the sacred oracles is impaired; they grope in darkness; the Bible is a sealed book to them; their minds have been thrown off their balance by sophistry and false reason, and they cannot appreciate the evidence of its inspiration. They sink in deep mire, where there is no standing ; and every effort they make to extricate themselves but sinks them deeper. We pity them. We commiserate their wretched condition. We pray God to take their feet out of the horrible pit and the miry clay, and set them on a rock. But the best advice we can give them is, *to study the Bible*, with the sincere purpose of ascertaining its meaning ; and if they persevere in so doing they will soon be convinced that it is the word of God. We doubt whether they will pass from the book of Genesis, before this conviction will fasten strongly and irresistibly upon their minds ; and we may hope also, that they will experience, by the power of that Spirit which gave the word, its efficacy in turning them from darkness to light.

PRACTICAL REMARKS.

1. From the character of God, as we have here seen it presented in his word, is to be inferred the infinite obligation which men are under to honor, adore, love, and obey him. His almighty power and majesty are worthy of all honor ; his eternity of being, his omniscience and omnipresence, and his infinite wisdom, render him an object infinitely worthy of adoration ; his infinite holiness is deserving of the highest love ; and his exalted supremacy, our submission and sincere obedience. Whoever, therefore, fails to render to God due honor, adoration, love and

obedience, is guilty of the violation of infinite obligations.

2. From the fact that God has condescended to give us a revelation of his will, may be inferred our obligation to study, believe, and obey it. Some suppose that they are at liberty to believe what they please; and that if they do not believe the Bible, they are released from the obligation to obey it. But God will hold them accountable for their neglect of the revelation which he has made; and great indeed must be the guilt of those who neglect, contemn, or despise a revelation that God has stooped from his high and lofty throne to make to sinful man. And the guilt of such conduct is greatly enhanced by the nature of the revelation itself, it being entirely the offspring of pure benevolence, communicating a knowledge of just those truths which man needs, and pointing out the way in which he may be delivered from his wretched and miserable condition, and made eternally happy. What awful ingratitude,—what baseness,—what deep and dreadful guilt,—thus to requite the condescending love, the infinite mercy of the holy and blessed God!

CHAPTER IV.

Fourth Pillar, in part.—*The Bible contains prophecies, which have been fulfilled, and which are fulfilling; and the fulfilment of these prophecies demonstrates the fact of the Divine inspiration of the Bible.*

PRELIMINARY REMARKS.

When an event is predicted, and so clearly described as to correspond exactly with the event when it transpires; when this prediction is made and published a long time before the event; and when the event transpires in such a manner as to forbid the idea that it was designedly and purposely brought about by the actors therein for the purpose of fulfilling the prophecy; then we have incontestible proof that the prediction was made by Divine revelation; for no human skill or foresight can discover events that are yet future. In the enumeration of prophecies that have been fulfilled, I shall include the threatenings and promises of the Bible; and I shall consider a book of the Bible, written many ages after the one which contains the prediction, as of good authority to show its fulfilment, especially where there is no allusion to the prophecy fulfilled, to give countenance to the suspicion in the mind of the skeptic, that the event was recorded for the express purpose of showing the fulfilment of the prophecy; though this will by no means weaken, but the rather strengthen the evidence in the mind of the believer. Though it has recently been asserted, that the prophecies of the Bible have never been fulfilled; yet the fact is, that the predictions which have been clearly and manifestly fulfilled are so numerous that it is not possible to bring forward any thing more than a few of the most striking, within the compass allotted to this part of the subject, in the present work. The prophecies concerning Christ, will not be noticed in this connection, but taken up separately, in a subsequent chapter.

THE PENTATEUCH.

1. The first prediction which calls for our attention is, the curses pronounced upon our first parents and the serpent, at the fall, compared with facts.* Has not the condition of woman, in all ages and in all countries, corresponded exactly with the description here given? Have not the serpent tribe, the world over, crawled upon the ground and eaten the dust? And has there not always been enmity between man and the serpent, even where this curse was never read? Has there not every where been a curse upon the ground? Has not man always eaten of the fruit of the ground in sorrow? Has it not always, in every age, and in every land, brought

---

* Gen. iii, 14–19.

forth thorns, and thistles, and weeds, spontaneously; while every useful production, for the sustenance of man, has been produced by cultivation, in the sweat of man's face? And has not man always, after a certain period of toil and suffering, returned to the dust from whence he was taken? It may, indeed, be said, that Moses only described the fact as it was known to himself. But Moses wrote in an early age; and his knowledge of the state of things throughout the world, except as derived from inspiration, must have been very limited. His early life was, indeed, spent in the country then most renowned for learning; but commerce had not then brought the different parts of the world into acquaintance with each other; and still, the greater portion of his life had been spent in leading his flocks, or directing the footsteps of his people over the deserts of Arabia. How could he know that the serpent would every where crawl on the ground and lick the dust? That there would every where be enmity between the serpent and man? And that thorns and thistles would grow spontaneously over all the face of the earth? And how can these facts themselves be accounted for, except on the ground that this account is true? Is nature, in other respects, thus uniform in her productions? Will the fig-tree grow in North America, or the vine in Greenland, or the olive and orange trees in Iceland, or the peach in Kamschatka? How is it, then, that no climate or soil is unfitted for the production of the thorn and thistle? And how is it that, when man undertakes to elude the curse, and live in ease and indolence, disease and pain come upon him, and thus fill up his life with sorrow? Can these things be accounted for, in any rational manner, except on the ground of the truth of the Mosaic account?

2. The predictions of Noah concerning his sons, as recorded by Moses, have been literally fulfilled, and are fulfilling to the present day.* A curse was predicted to fall upon Canaan, the son of Ham; and it was declared that he should be a servant of servants unto his brethren; and from the accounts given in Joshua, Judges, and Chronicles, without any reference to this prediction, it appears that the remnants of the tribes of the Canaanites, who were not destroyed by the children of Israel, according to the command of God, were reduced to servitude, and some of them made hewers of wood and drawers of water to the children of Israel.† Others fled from the country and settled in Egypt, where they afterwards fell under the dominion of the Romans, the descendants of Japheth; so that Canaan was, according to the prediction, under bondage to both his brethren at once. And "although the sentence here recorded was to spend itself mainly upon the descendants of Ham, in the line of Canaan, yet it is an historical fact that the curse of servitude has signally fallen upon other branches of his posterity, of which the fate of the African race is a standing evidence; but how far we are at liberty to refer that fact to the effect of Noah's curse, on this occasion, is not clear."‡ It is, however, quite certain that we are not to construe it

---

* Gen. ix, 25–27.
† Josh. ix, 23, 27. Judges i, 28. 2 Chron. ii, 17, 18.
‡ Bush's Notes, Vol. I, p. 163.

NOAH'S PREDICTIONS. 109

into a justification of the act of enslaving our fellow-creatures.

The manner in which Shem is here spoken of,—"Blessed be the Lord God of Shem," indicates a a formal bestowment of the birthright upon Shem, which was taken from Ham. The import of these words is, "that Jehovah, the true God, should, as the God of Shem, be the object of praise, homage, and blessing; that his name, in opposition to idols, should be acknowledged as known and reverenced in the line of this father of the chosen race, and that they, on the other hand, should receive from him tokens of favor and blessing which were not vouchsafed to other people."* This was literally fulfilled in the history of the chosen people of God of old.

Noah also says, "God shall enlarge Japheth,"—which means that God shall increase both the posterity and territories of Japheth; "and this, as a temporal blessing, has been most remarkably fulfilled; for Japheth, who had several more sons than either of his brethren, appears to have been the progenitor or father of more than half the human race. The whole of Europe, and a considerable part of Asia, were originally peopled, and have ever since been occupied," mainly by the offspring of Japheth.

3. Passing by the prophecies concerning the multitude of Abraham's seed, and their possession of the land of Canaan, which were literally fulfilled; we come to that delivered by the angel to Hagar, concerning her son Ishmael, before he was born; and

---

* Bush's Notes, vol. i, p. 165.

spoken not of him as an individual, but as the head of a nation:—"I will multiply thy seed exceedingly, that it shall not be numbered for multitude; and (speaking of Ishmael,) he shall be a wild man; his hand will be against every man, and every man's hand against him; and he shall dwell in the presence of all his brethren."* From Ishmael proceeded the various tribes of Arabs, who have always been a very powerful people. The description above quoted is literally, "he shall be a *wild-ass-man*,—that is, like the wild ass; and the description of the wild ass in Job, agrees exactly with the character which the Arabs have always sustained: "Who hath sent out the wild ass free? or who hath loosed the bonds of the wild ass? Whose house I have made the wilderness, and the barren land his dwellings. He scorneth the multitude of the city, neither regardeth he the crying of the driver. The range of the mountains is his pasture, and he searcheth after every green thing."† So God has sent out the Arabs, the descendants of Ishmael, free, and loosed them from all political restraint. The same wilderness in which he dwelt, three thousand seven hundred years ago, is still their habitation; and in the barren land, where no other human beings could live, they have their dwellings. Like the wild ass, they scorn the city, and have no fixed habitations. When they make depredations on cities, towns, or caravans, they retire into the desert with such precipitancy, that all pursuit is eluded; so that the crying of the driver or pursuer is disregarded. They may be

---

* Gen. xvi, 12.   † Job xxxix, 5–8.

said to have no lands, and yet the range of the mountains is their pasture. They pitch their tents and feed their flocks wherever they please; and they search after every green thing,—are continually looking after prey, and seize every kind of property that comes in their way. It was foretold that their hand should be against every man, and that every man's hand should be against them; and yet that they should dwell in the presence of their brethren, i. e. sustain their independence in the face of all their brethren. They have always sustained the same predatory character, making war upon all who come within their reach; and yet they have never been subdued. Attempts were made by Sesostris, king of Egypt, Cyrus, king of Persia, Pompey, Trajan, and others, to conquer them; but they were never successful.*

Now how can we account for the fact that Moses should give so exact and complete a description of this people, three thousand and seven hundred years ago, on any other supposition than that he was divinely inspired? And how can we account for the fact, that these people have, for so many ages, answered so exactly to this description, always resisting successfully every attempt to civilize them, except on the supposition that God has preserved them in this condition to fulfil his own word, and set the seal of truth upon the five books of Moses? A distinguished writer says, "If there were no other argument to evince the divine origin of the Pentateuch, the account of Ishmael, and the prophecies concerning his descend-

---

* Horne's Int., vol. i, p. 122.

ants, compared with their history and manner of life during a period of nearly four thousand years, would be sufficient. It may, indeed, be pronounced absolutely demonstrative."

4. The next prophecy which I shall notice is that of Isaac concerning his sons. To Jacob he said, "Let people serve thee, and nations bow down to thee : be lord over thy brethren, and let thy mother's sons bow down to thee." In the second book of Samuel, it is mentioned, without any allusion to this prophecy, that David put garrisons throughout all Edom, and they of Edom became David's servants."* But Isaac says, also, to Esau, "It shall come to pass, when thou shalt have the dominion, that thou shalt break his yoke from off thy neck." Now it is related in the same incidental manner as before, in the second book of Kings, after the degeneracy of the kings of Judah, that Edom revolted from the hand of Judah, whose kings were unable any more to bring him into subjection.† Thus, in both cases, literally fulfilling the prophecy of Isaac.

5. Passing over the promises made to Jacob, and the fulfilment of the prediction to Abraham, of the 430 years' affliction of his posterity, including their oppression in Egypt, we come to the promises and threatenings delivered by Moses to the children of Israel. A careful comparison of the promises contained in the 26th chapter of Leviticus and the 28th of Deuteronomy, which were made to the Jews, on

---

* Gen. xxvii, 29. 2 Sam viii, 14.
† C. Gen. xxvii, 40 w. 2 Kings viii, 20–22.

condition of obedience, with the history of the Jews in the days of Joshua and of the good Judges and Kings, will show a literal fulfilment, so exact that the promise is a fair description of the history; and the same may be said of the threatenings, compared with the subsequent history of the Jews, in the days when they departed from the Lord. But as all have the means of making this comparison for themselves, I shall pass on to compare these prophecies with the history of the Jews, as given by the writers of profane history, together with their present condition *

It is wonderful to see the exact correspondence of historical facts, both sacred and profane, with these threatenings. But passing over the former, for want of time, let us come down to the later periods of their history. The Romans destroyed their cities and ravaged their country, and the inhabitants who escaped from the famine, the pestilence, and the sword, were forcibly expelled from Judea; and fled as houseless wanderers into all the surrounding regions. But the fugitive and exiled Jews still clung to their native soil; and about sixty years afterwards, so many of them had returned as to be able, under an impostor, who claimed to be the Messiah, to make a vigorous attempt to re-conquer Judea, to cast off the Roman yoke, and rescue themselves and their country from ruin. This war lasted two years; in which, exclusive of many that died of famine, sickness, and

---

* The reader is requested, before proceeding farther, to read attentively the 26th chapter of Leviticus and the 28th of Deuteronomy

fire, five hundred and eighty thousand Jews are said to have been slain. They were so beset on every side by the Roman soldiers, that very few of them escaped. Fifty of their strong holds were razed to the ground, and their cities sacked and consumed by fire. Judea was laid waste, and left as a desert.

Thus were accomplished the predictions of Isaiah and Jeremiah, who said, "The cities shall be wasted without inhabitant. Every city shall be forsaken, and not a man dwell therein." And in the language of Moses, "They were rooted out of their land in anger, and in wrath, and in great indignation." A public edict of the Emperor Adrian rendered it a capital crime for a Jew to set foot in Jerusalem; and prohibited him from viewing it even at a distance. Heathens, Christians, and Mohammedans have successively possessed Judea; but the children of Israel have alone been denied the possession of it; and whenever any of them have gone to visit the land of their fathers, they have been more cruelly treated than any where else. Thus has the language of Moses been verified,—"The stranger that is within thee shall get up above thee very high, and thou shalt come down very low."

But Moses proceeds and says, "The Lord shall scatter thee among all people, from the one end of the earth even unto the other." And this prediction was repeated, in various forms, and greater particularity, by the later prophets. It has been literally fulfilled. It is fulfilling at this present time. They have been dispersed throughout all nations. There is not a country on the face of the earth where the Jews are unknown. They are found alike in Europe, Asia, America, and Africa. They are citizens of the world, without a country. They abound in Poland, Holland, Russia, and Turkey. In Germany, Spain, Italy, France, and Britain they are more thinly scattered. In Persia, China, and India, according to the prediction, they are few in number among the heathen. They have trod the snows of Siberia and the sands of the burning desert. From Moscow to Lisbon,—from Japan to Britain,—from Borneo to Archangel,—from Hindostan to Honduras, no inhabitant of any nation upon earth, but a Jew alone, would be known in all the intervening regions. And herein is verified another prophecy of Moses, "And yet, for all that, when they be in the land of their enemies, I will not cast them away, neither will I abhor them, to destroy them utterly." No other example is known of any nation preserving its identity through such a series of calamities; and the fact that they are yet preserved as a distinct people, is a standing miracle to verify the word of God. "Kings," says one of their historians, "have often employed the severity of their edicts and the hands of the executioner to destroy them,—the seditious multitude have performed massacres more tragical than the princes. They have, from age to age, run through misery and persecution, and torrents of their own blood. But like the bush of Moses, they have burnt without consuming."

The Emperor Constantine, after suppressing an insurrection, raised by some of the Jews, caused their ears to be cut off, and then dispersed them as fugitives into different countries, where they carried these marks of their suffering and infamy as a terror to their kindred. Justinian abolished their synagogues, prohibited them from entering into caves for their worship, rendered their testimony inadmissible in courts, and deprived them of the natural right of bequeathing their property; and when they resisted such oppression their property was confiscated, and a bloody execution of them followed, so that the historian says, "all the Jews of that country trembled,"—thus employing almost the very words of Moses, "the Lord shall give thee there a trembling heart, and failing of eyes, and sorrow of mind."

In the reign of the tyrant Phocas, a general sedition broke out among them. They were taken captive; many of them maimed; others executed; and all the survivors banished from the city of Rome. Heraclius, unable to satiate his hatred against them, by inflicting a variety of punishments on those who resided within his own diminions, and finally expelling them from his kingdom, stirred up against them a general persecution, from Asia to the farthest extremities of Europe. They fled from country to country, seeking in vain any rest for the sole of their foot. Mohammed, from the very commencement, infused into his followers a hatred of the Jews; and in Mohammedan countries, they have always been persecuted and oppressed. The church of Rome has always treated them as heretics; pronounced excommunication against those who should favor or uphold the Jews against Christians; forbidden Christians to eat or associate with them; prohibited them from holding any offices,—appointed them to be distinguished by a mark, and ordered their children to be taken from them and brought up in monasteries. Hallam, the historian of the middle ages, says, " They were every where the objects of popular insult and oppression,—frequently of a general massacre. A time of festivity to others was often the season of mockery and persecution to them. It was the custom at Toulouse to smite them on the face every Easter. At Beziers they were attacked with stones, from Palm Sunday to Easter. It is almost incredible to what length extortion of money from the Jews was carried; for they evinced a talent of accumulating riches, which kept pace with the exactions of their plunderers. Philip Augustus released all Christians from their debts to the Jews, reserving a fifth part to himself. He afterwards expelled the whole nation from France;" from which country they were seven times banished. They were also expelled from Spain, —one hundred and seventy thousand families departing from that kingdom. In France, many thousands of them were pillaged and massacred. In England, also, they suffered great cruelty and oppression. During the crusades, the whole nation united in their persecution. At York, fifteen hundred Jews were refused all quarter, and, frantic with despair, perished by each other's hands. They were so hated and despised, that some English barons, to gain the favor of the populace, ordered seven hundred Jews to be slaughtered at once, their houses to be plundered, and their synagogue burned. The kings of England often extorted money from them. The extortions of Henry III. were so great, that they petitioned for leave to depart from the kingdom, but even this was denied them. Edward I. seized all their property, and banished them from the kingdom.

For many ages after the dispersion of the Jews, they found no resting place in Europe, Asia, or Africa. They have generally been confined to a particular part of every city, and compelled to wear a particular dress; and in some places shut up at particular hours. In all parts of Persia they are an abject race, and support themselves by driving a peddling trade. They live in a state of great misery; pay a monthly tax to the government; and are not permitted to own or cultivate land. They cannot appear in public, much less to perform their religious ceremonies, without being treated with scorn and contempt. The revenues of the prince of Bohara are derived from a tribute paid by five hundred families of Jews. In Zante they exist in miserable indigence, and are exposed to considerable oppression. In Egypt the Jews are depised and persecuted incessantly. In Arabia they are treated with contempt. Both in Asia and Africa the Jews are astonished, and the natives indignant, at any act of kindness towards this despised people. Till within the last fifty years the burning of a Jew formed the highest delight of the Portuguese. They thronged to behold this triumph of the faith, and the very women shouted with transport as they saw the agonized martyr writhe at the stake. It is but a few years since there was a severe persecution against the Jews in Persia and Germany; and in several of the smaller States of Germany, even to the present day, they are not permitted to sell any goods, even in the common markets. In Russia they are not permitted, on pain of banishment, to offer any goods for sale, nor to reside in any of the cities of the empire, without an express permission from government; and this is given only when their services are required by the government. And those who harbor Jews that are condemned to banishment, are liable to punishment. Thus is verified the prophecy that, in the midst of all these calamities, no man shall save them.

In this prophecy Moses says, " The Lord shall smite thee with madness, and blindness, and astonishment of heart; so that thou shalt be mad for the sight of thine eyes, which thou shalt see." This was true in the siege of Jerusalem by the Chaldeans; but in that by Titus and the Romans, and in the subsequent conduct of the miserable relics of the Jews, says Walter Scott, their infatuation was so evident that every one who reads of their conduct must be convinced that they were given up to judicial blindness and madness, or they never could have been so bent upon their own destruction. While, by their obstinate resistance of the Roman power, without the least prospect of escaping, they ensured their own miseries; by their intestine rage they became the executioners of the wrath of God upon themselves, almost saved their enemies the trouble of destroying them, and absolutely put it out of their power to preserve them. After the destruction of Jerusalem, some of the worst of the Jews took refuge in a castle, where, being closely besieged by the Romans, at the persuasion of their leader, they first murdered their wives and children. Then ten men were chosen by lot to slay the rest. This being done, one of the ten was chosen to kill the other nine, which he did, and then set fire to the place and stabbed himself.

Moses also says, "The Lord shall bring thee into Egypt again with ships;—and there ye shall be sold unto your enemies for bondmen and bondwomen; and no man shall buy you;" meaning that they should be considered too despicable even to purchase for slaves. After the destruction of Jerusalem by Titus, and the desolation of Judea, by Adrian, many of the captives were sent by sea into Egypt, and sold for a vile price, to perform the meanest offices; and many thousands were left to perish for want; for the multitude was so great that purchasers could not be found for them at any price.

Thus it will be seen that, according to the threatenings of Moses, they have been *slain before their enemies; they that hated them have reigned over them; the pride of their power has been broken; the sword has been repeatedly brought against them, to avenge the quarrel of God's covenant; they have eaten the flesh of their sons and daughters, as they did in the famines and sieges recorded in Scripture, and also during the siege of Jerusalem by the Romans; their cities have been laid waste, and their sanctuaries brought to desolation; their land also has been brought to desolation, and strangers dwell therein; they have been scattered among the heathen, and a sword drawn after them; faintness has been sent into their hearts, in the land of their enemies; they have fallen upon one another with the sword; they have perished among the heathen, and the lands of their enemies have eaten them up; and they that have been left of them have pined away in their enemies' lands ; they have become an astonishment, a proverb, and a by-word, among all nations,* for the name *Jew* has long been a proverbial mark of detestation and contempt, among all the nations whither they have been driven,—" You use me like a Jew,—none but a Jew would have done this,—I would not have done so to a Jew,"—these are common expressions in almost every part of the world ; *they have served their enemies in hunger, and in thirst, and in nakedness, with an iron yoke upon their necks ; the Lord has made their plagues wonderful, and the plagues of their seed, even great plagues, and of long continuance ; and among the nations where they have been scattered, they have found no ease, neither has the sole of their foot found rest ; but the Lord has given them a trembling heart, and failing of eyes, and sorrow of mind ; their lives have hung in doubt, and they have had fear day and night, and none assurance of life ; they have been carried into Egypt in ships, and offered for sale as bondmen ; and yet no man would buy them ; and yet, for all this, according to his promise, the Lord has not cast them away and utterly destroyed them, nor broken his covenant with them ; but he still preserves them, a distinct people,*—the only people under heaven that has been preserved under similar circumstances, furnishing a pledge of the certain fulfilment of the prophecies that yet remain to be accomplished in their restoration.

The infidel, Volney, in his travels, has been unconsciously the instrument of fulfilling a part of this prophecy. Moses says, the stranger that shall come from a far land shall say, " Wherefore hath the Lord done this unto this land? What meaneth the heat of his great anger?" Volney, on viewing the ruins of Palestine and the adjacent countries, exclaims almost in the words of Moses, "Great God! from whence proceed such melancholy revolutions? For what cause is the fortune of these countries so strikingly changed? Why are so many cities destroyed? Why is not that ancient population reproduced and perpetuated?"

The condition of the Jews furnishes from age to age a standing miracle, to attest the truth of his word; and the facts that have been presented furnish demonstrative proof of the inspiration of Moses; and of course proves that the first five books of the Bible are a revelation from God; and this is a strong presumptive evidence of the truth and inspiration of the whole Scriptures, as they all constitute the parts of a grand system, the foundation of which was laid in the Mosaic history.

I know it has been asserted that we have no evidence that Moses wrote all these books; and that the facts stated in the first chapter of Genesis are contrary to the discoveries of science. In my second chapter, I think I proved sufficiently the authenticity of all the books of the Bible; and I now deny that there is any contradiction between the discoveries of science and the facts stated in the first chapter of Genesis; but on this point I am not called upon to exhibit proof, in opposition to a bare assertion,—it belongs to those who have made the assertion alluded to, to show wherein these contradictions consist. It does not belong to me to prove a negative; but if it did, I have room in this place only to say that no objections can be valid against the inspiration of a book that contains so many predictions of future events, the evidence of the fulfilment of which is so unanswerable and overwhelming.

PRACTICAL REMARKS.

The facts presented in this chapter furnish an awful warning against apostasy. Moses says it shall be inquired, "Wherefore hath the Lord done thus unto this land? And what meaneth the heat of his great anger?" And that men shall answer and say, "Because they have forsaken the covenant of the Lord God of their fathers." They broke their covenant, forsook the Lord, and rejected the Messiah, the Saviour of the world,—the promise of their fathers. But they did no more than every member of a Christian church does, who violates his covenant vows, forsakes the service of God and the ordinances of his house, and goes back to the service of sin and Satan. Nay, they did no more than is done by every baptized child of Christian parents, who forsakes the covenant of his fathers, refuses to ratify its vows, and grows up in the persevering rejection of the Saviour. And if God spared not his own chosen people, the children of Abraham, Isaac, and Jacob, when they forsook his covenant, and cast off their vows, but pursued them with such awful judgments from generation to generation, do you think that you shall escape, who are guilty of the same sin, under the full blaze of gospel light? Though you may escape temporal calam'ties in this life, you surely will not escape in that day, when the "sinners in Zion shall be afraid, and fearfulness shall surprise the hypocrites." If, then, the apostate Jews shall dwell with devouring fire, apostate Christians must sink down still deeper in eternal burnings. It is a fearful thing to trifle with solemn covenant relations,—lightly to cast off or violate solemn vows,—or to despise or neglect great privileges. We have an awful example of it in the history of the Jews; and yet we are as highly exalted above them in privileges as they were above the heathen. Moreover, it is mentioned as one of the sins which provoked the Lord to cast off his ancient covenant people, that they "rebelled and vexed his Holy Spirit." And we have reason to believe that many churches have been forsaken of God, and left to spiritual desolations no less dreadful, by grieving his Holy Spirit. How often has God come nigh to his people, and, as it were, overshadowed them with a cloud of mercy, and they have not been ready to receive it; and by their opposition, their indifference, their negligence, or their love of ease, they have suffered it to pass by, leaving the garden of the Lord without spiritual rain, desolate and dry. They have "rebelled and vexed his Holy Spirit;" and unless they repent, and humble themselves before God, they have reason to fear that he will turn to be their enemy, and leave them, as he did his people of old, to utter desolation. About forty years ago the Lord poured out his Spirit with mighty power, in an extensive region of the western country. Sinners bowed themselves, and in great numbers submitted to God, and received Jesus as their Saviour. But there was one denomination of Christians,—a denomination, too, which held an orthodox faith,—who opposed this work. They set apart days of fasting and prayer, to mourn on account of its prevalence. It was the opinion of a venerable father in the ministry, who labored much in this work, that they then grieved the Holy Spirit. Since that period the dews of heavenly grace appear to have ceased to distil upon them. They have been left for forty years to a form of godliness, without the power thereof; and they now have all the marks of a people forsaken of the Lord. And who will say that it was not resisting and vexing the Holy Spirit, which caused the Lord to forsake so many of the churches founded by our Pilgrim fathers in our beloved New England, and leave them to the sweeping desolations of error, which have, in many places, extinguished the last flickering ray of piety among them? Who will say that it was not because his people would not prepare his way, when he came among them? And who will say that it was not because those who sat under the sound of the gospel, would not listen to the voice of entreaty and persuasion, and receive the truth and love the Saviour; and that, therefore, the Lord took from them the blessings which they despised? It becomes us to search our own hearts, and see if we have not rebelled against the motions of the Holy Spirit, calling us to prayer and effort for his glory,— whether we have not hindered the revival of his work in time past, and whether we are not now hindering his work. Has he been grieved away from our hearts heretofore ? And will he come again unless we repent, and remove every thing offensive to him, and prepare him a place in our hearts ? And shall it be, that when he comes among us, like Noah's dove, he shall find no rest for the sole of his foot, and shall depart from us, vexed and grieved by our rebellion, unbelief, and hardness of heart ? And what will be the consequence ? We have heard what he did to his ancient people. Terrible, indeed, have been his judgments upon them. But all the earthly calamities which they have endured, are nothing compared with the calamity of being deserted by the Holy Spirit. If the Spirit of God should leave us, when we come to the sanctuary, our hearts will be hard ; we shall be left to barren ordinances,—a deathlike stupor and coldness will come over us ; there will be no impression of the word ; no edification ; no progress in holiness ; no comfort in divine worship ; every interest of Zion will languish ; there will be no increase of the church ; but there will be grievous declension and apostasy ; many will fall and dishonor their profession ; no sinners will be converted ; there will be no conviction, unless in the shape of remorse and fearful foreboding. Our children, who have been baptized and brought under the covenant, will perhaps be left to ruin in this life ; and we may be compelled in bitter anguish, to stand by their bedside, and see them die in their sins, and perish without hope. All our friends and acquaintances,—all these souls around us, will be lost. And, finally, we shall be left to utter desolation. All the piety will die out of the church, as it has out of many old churches around us ; and the institutions which we have fostered with so much care, with the hope of benefitting our children, will be reduced to the same level with those which we have left, because God has deserted them. Yet if we continue to grieve the Holy Spirit, what is to hinder this result ? " For if the word spoken by angels was stedfast, and every transgression and disobedience received a just recompense of reward, how shall we escape, if we neglect so great salvation ; which at the first began to be spoken by the Lord, and was confirmed unto us by them that heard him ; God also bearing them witness, with signs and wonders, and with divers miracles and gifts of the Holy Ghost ?"

CHAPTER V.

THE FOURTH PILLAR, continued.—*Fulfilment of Predictions given by the Prophets, and by Christ and his Apostles.*

To prove that the prophets and apostles were inspired, and that Jesus predicted future events, it is not necessary to show that *all* their predictions have come to pass, because for some of them the time has not yet come ; nor have I space to mention all that have been fulfilled, but shall be able only to present a selection of a few among the many ; and I shall begin with a comparison of the predictions of the prophets, with the accounts of travellers respecting the appearance of things in those places concerning which prophecies have been uttered ; leaving those which relate to the coming of Christ for a separate consideration.

My principal quotations will be from " Volney's Ruins ;" and he, being an infidel writer, will not be suspected of a design to show the fulfilment of the prophecies of the Bible.

Moses says, in reference to the dispersion of the Jews, " The land,—shall enjoy her Sabbaths, while she lieth desolate ;" and Isaiah says, " Your land,

CONCERNING PALESTINE. 129

strangers devour it, and it is desolate as overthrown by strangers."*

Volney says, in his travels in Palestine, " Every day I found in my route, fields abandoned by the plough;" and, in describing it, he calls it "this *desolate* country," using the same word employed by Moses and Isaiah, in their predictions concerning it. He also says that, within two thousand five hundred years, there have been ten invasions, which have introduced into Syria a succession of foreign nations; thus literally fulfilling the prediction that *strangers* should overthrow and devour the land.

Jeremiah says, in reference to the land of Israel, "destruction upon destruction is cried;" Ezekiel says, "Mischief shall come upon mischief;" and Joel says, "A nation is come upon my land, strong and without number."†

Volney says, " Syria became a province of the Roman empire. In the year 636, the Arabian tribes, collected under the banners of Mohammed, seized upon it, and laid it waste. Since that period, it has been torn to pieces by civil wars, wrested from the caliphs by their rebellious governors, taken from them by the Turkmen soldiery, invaded by the European crusaders, retaken by the Mamelukes of Egypt, and ravaged by Tamerlane and his Tartars, till at length it has fallen into the hands of the Ottoman Turks." So that, according to his testimony, destruction upon destruction, and mischief upon mischief, and nations

---

* Lev. xxvi, 43. Is. i, 7.
† Jer. iv, 20. Ezek. vii, 21, 26. Joel i, 6.

strong and without number, have come upon the land.

Ezekiel says the land shall be delivered into the hands of the wicked for a *spoil*, and that the robbers shall enter into it and defile it.* Volney says that when the Ottomans took Syria, they considered it only as the *spoil* of a vanquished enemy, the lives and property of the vanquished belonging to the conquerors; and that the government is far from disproving a system of robbery and plunder.

Ezekiel says, "The holy places shall be defiled;" and Volney says that, in his day, "The holy places were polluted with the monuments of idolatry. The Mosque of Omar now stands on the site of the Temple of Solomon."

It was predicted, both by Jeremiah and Micah, that Zion should be ploughed over like a field.† Gibbon, the infidel historian, says that after the final destruction of the temple by the Romans, a ploughshare was drawn over the consecrated ground, as a sign of perpetual interdiction. And Richardson, in his travels, says that at the time he visited Mount Zion, one part of it supported a crop of barley, while another was undergoing the labor of the plough.

Jeremiah says, "Every one that passeth by the land shall be *astonished*."‡ "So feeble a population, in so excellent a country," says the traveller, "may well excite our *astonishment*." Isaiah says, in his

---

* Ezek. vii, 21, 22.

† Jer xxvi, 18. Mic. iii, 12

‡ Jer. xviii, 16.

prophetic view of the desolation of the land, "The wayfaring man ceaseth."* Volney says, "Nobody travels *alone*. Between town and town there are neither posts nor public conveyances."

Moses says, in the name of the Lord, "And I will make your cities waste, and bring your sanctuaries unto desolation, and I will not smell the savour of your sweet odours." Isaiah says, "The palaces shall be forsaken." Ezekiel says, "I will destroy the remnant of the seacoast." Moses says, "I will make your cities waste;" and Isaiah says "there shall be few men left."† Volney says, "The temples are thrown down; the palaces demolished; the ports filled up; the towns destroyed; and the earth, stripped of its inhabitants, seems a dreary burying place."

Isaiah says, "Because they have transgressed the law, changed the ordinances, broken the everlasting covenant, therefore hath the curse devoured the earth.‡" Dr. Clarke, in his travels, says that "The pure gospel of Christ is almost as little known in the Holy Land as in California or New Holland;" and Volney says, "God has, doubtless, pronounced a secret malediction (or curse) against the earth."

Isaiah, in vision says, "The vine languisheth, and strong drink shall be bitter to them that drink it." Volney says, that in the mountains they do not prune the vines; and travellers agree in pronouncing the

---

* Isa. xxxiii, 8.

† Lev. xxvi, 31. Isa. xxxii, 14; xxiv, 6. Ezek. xxv, 16.

‡ Isa. xxiv, 5, 6, 9.

wine drank in Jerusalem to be the very worst that is to be met with in any country.

Isaiah says again, "All the merry-hearted do sigh. The mirth of tabrets ceaseth; the joy of the harp ceaseth. The noise of them that rejoice endeth, all joy is darkened; the mirth of the land is gone."* Volney says the Arabs, in singing, excel most in the melancholy strain. To hear their plaintive tones, their sighs and sobs, it is almost impossible to refrain from tears. They have no music but vocal, for they neither know nor esteem instrumental music. They have a serious, sad, and melancholy countenance. They rarely laugh; and the gaity of the French seems to them a fit of delirium." Could any description answer more exactly to the prophecy?

Isaiah says again, "Upon the land of my people shall come up thorns and briars; the forts and towers shall be dens forever." Volney says, "The earth produces only briars and wormwood,"—"At every step we met with ruins of towers, dungeons, and castles, frequently inhabited by jackals, owls, and scorpions." The prophet says, "It is a people of no understanding;"† and the traveller says, "The most simple arts are in a state of barbarism; the sciences are totally unknown." The prophet says, "No flesh shall have peace;"‡ and the traveller (Volney) says, "War, famine, and pestilence assail them at every turn."

Ezekiel says, "Thus saith the Lord God, of the inhabitants of Jerusalem and of the land of Israel, they shall eat their bread with carefulness, and drink their

---
* Isa. xxiv, 8, 11. † Isa. xxvii, 11. ‡ Jer. xii, 12.

water with astonishment; that her land may be desolate from all that is therein, because of the *violence* of all them that dwell therein."* Volney says, "The peasants are every where reduced to a little cake of barley, and to onions, lentils, and water." "Dread prevails throughout the villages; and the arbitrary power of the Sultan gives rise to a tyranny which circulates through every class, and which is every where fatal to agriculture, the arts, commerce, and population."

The prophet says, "The cities that are inhabited shall be laid waste,"—The traveller says, "Every day I found in my route villages deserted and cities in ruins."

The prophet Amos says, "The city that went out by a thousand shall leave a hundred."† A traveller says, "A tract from which a hundred individuals draw a scanty subsistence, formerly maintained thousands."

The prophet Micah says, "I will make Samaria as a heap of the field, and as plantings of a vineyard."‡ Maundrell, in his travels, says, in regard to the same place, "This great city is wholly converted into gardens."

The prophet Zephaniah says, in reference to the land of the Philistines, "The seacoast shall be dwellings and cottages for shepherds and folds for flocks;"§

The reader is requested to read the *whole* of the several prophecies concerning Edom, referred to.

* Ezek. xii, 19, 20. † Amos v, 3.
‡ Mi. i, 6. § Zeph. ii, 5, 6.

and Volney, speaking of the plain of the Philistines, along the seacoast, says, "The houses are so many huts. In winter, they and their cattle may be said to live together, the part of the dwelling allotted to themselves being only raised two feet above that in which they lodge their beasts." All the rest of Philistia, he says, is a desert; and this is predicted by the prophet Amos:—"The remnant of the Philistines shall perish."*

Amos also says, "I will send a fire upon Gaza, which shall devour the palaces thereof;" and Volney says that "the ruins of white marble at Gaza prove that it was formerly the abode of luxury and opulence."

The prophets Isaiah and Zechariah predict the destruction of the cedars of Lebanon, and say that the trees that remain shall be so few that a child might write them; and Volney speaks of the remains of the boasted cedars, and says, "there are but four or five of these trees which deserve any notice."

Ezekiel says, in regard to the land of the children of Ammon, "I will stretch out my hand upon thee, I will destroy thee, I will deliver thee for a spoil to the heathen.† Seetzen, in his travels, says, in regard to the same, "All this country, formerly so populous and flourishing, is now changed into a vast desert, abandoned to the wandering Arabs."

The same prophet says concerning Rabbah, the chief city of the Ammonites, "I will make Rabbah a stable for camels, and a crouching place for flocks."‡

---

* Amos i, 8. † Ezek. xxv, 7. ‡ Ezek. xxv, 5.

CONCERNING EDOM. 135

The same traveller says, " We met numbers of Arabs, with their camels. The keepers drive in goats for shelter during the night." Jeremiah says, "Rabbah shall become an heap," and Burckhardt, in his travels, says, " The buildings exposed to the atmosphere are all in decay. The plain is covered with the remains of private buildings."

There is a similar agreement between the prophecies and accounts of travellers respecting the land of Moab ; but I pass them by for want of space. There are also many prophecies concerning Edom, which the same comparison shows to have been exactly fulfilled.

Jeremiah says of Edom, " I will make thee small among the heathen : thy terribleness hath deceived thee, O thou that dwellest in the clefts of the Rock, that holdest the height of the hill ; though thou shouldst make thy nest as high as the eagle, I will bring thee down from thence, saith the Lord. Also, Edom shall be a desolation."* The travellers, Irby and Mangles, say, " The ruins of the city of Petra burst on the view in their full grandeur, shut in on the opposite side by barren, craggy precipices, from which numerous ravines and precipices branch out in all directions ; the sides of the mountains covered with an endless variety of excavated tombs and private dwellings, presented altogether a most singular appearance." Mackmichael says, " The rocks are hollowed out into innumerable chambers, of different dimensions." " Some of them," says Burckhardt, " are so

---

* Jer. xlix, 15, 16, 17.

high, and the sides of the mountain so perpendicular, that it seems impossible to approach the uppermost;" showing that the kings of Edom did, according to the prophet, literally dwell in the clefts of the rock. Isaiah says, in reference to this city, "They shall call the nobles thereof to the kingdom, but none shall be there; and all her princes shall be nothing."* Irby and Mangles say, "There is not a single human being living near it;" and Burckhardt says, "The sepulchres are numerous and magnificent, and great must have been the opulence of a city which could dedicate such a monument to the memory of its rulers." Isaiah says again, "Thorns shall come up in her palaces, nettles, and brambles in the fortresses thereof."* Travellers, (Irby and Mangles and Laborde,) say, "Most of the plants at Petra are thorny. The thorns rise to the same height as the columns; creeping and prickly plants hide the works of man; the thorn or bramble reaches the top of the monuments, grows on the cornices, and conceals the base of the columns." The prophet says, "The cormorant shall possess it." Burckhardt says this bird is found there in immense numbers. The prophet says, "The owl shall dwell in it." Irby and Mangles say, "Eagles, hawks, and owls, were soaring in considerable numbers above our heads, seemingly annoyed at any one approaching their lonely habitation." The prophet says, "The raven (or crow) shall dwell in it." Burckhardt says the fields in the immediate vicinity are frequented by an immense number of crows. The prophet says, "It

---

* Isa. xxxiv, 12, 13.

shall be an habitation for dragons." Volney says the Arabs avoid these ruins, on account of the enormous scorpions with which they swarm.

The exact and literal fulfilment of the following prediction is very remarkable, and worthy of special notice:—Isaiah says concerning Edom, "*None shall pass through it, for ever and ever;*" and Ezekiel says, "*I will cut off from Mount Seir him that passeth out, and him that returneth.*"* Edom, or Idumea, at the time these predictions were uttered, formed the emporium of the commerce of the East; and long after that time, Roman roads were made through that country, from Jerusalem to Akaba, and from Akaba to Moab. The Idumeans were both an opulent and a powerful people; and they flourished hundreds of years after this prophecy was given. At the time of the destruction of Jerusalem the Idumeans were nearly as numerous as the Jews. Yet now it is utterly desolate. Another prediction declares that "every one that goeth by shall be astonished;" intimating, in connection with this, that travellers should *pass by*, but not pass through it. Volney says, "*This country has not* been visited by any traveller; but from the reports of the Arabs, there are, within three days' journey, upwards of thirty ruined towns, *absolutely deserted.*" Burckhardt entered the territories of the Edomites on the northeast; but soon after found himself without protection, in the midst of a desert, where no traveller had ever before been seen; and it was then, he says, the first time that he had ever felt fear,

---

* Isa. xxxiv, 10. Ezek. xxxv, 7.

during his travels in the desert, and his route there was the most dangerous he had ever travelled. Mr. Joliffe, another traveller, speaking of this country, says it is " one of the wildest and most dangerous divisions of Arabia, and that any research in that quarter was impracticable. Cavaliere Fredani attempted to pass through Edom ; but after spending five weeks in fruitless attempts, was compelled to abandon the enterprize. Sir Frederick Henniker made the attempt, having with great difficulty prevailed on guides to accompany him ; but they deceived him, and led him towards the Mediterranean coast, through the desert, to Gaza. Irby and Mangles attempted to approach Idumea, in the direction nearest to Judea, and apparently most accessible. The Turkish authorities, at Constantinople, Damascus, Jerusalem, Jaffa, and Hebron, all refused to afford them any protection. But they provided themselves with horses, arms, and Arab dresses, being eleven in number, including servants and guides. An Arab tribe agreed to protect them to Kerek, but no money would induce them to conduct them to any place within the territory of Edom. Having afterwards obtained the protection of an intrepid Arab chief, with his followers, and having advanced to the borders of Edom, their further progress was suddenly opposed, in the most threatening and determined manner. And in the whole course of their travels, which extended to about three thousand miles, in Thrace, Asia Minor, Cyprus, the desert, Egypt, and in Syria,—they found nowhere such a barrier to their progress, except in a previous abortive attempt to reach Petra from another quarter ; and though they were never better prepared for encountering it, they never elsewhere experienced so formidable an opposition. The Sheikh of Wada Mousa, and his people, swore that they would not suffer them to go forward, and that they should neither drink of their water, nor pass into their territory. The Arab chief, who had espoused their cause, swore "by the faith of a true Mussulman," that they should drink of the water of Wada Mousa, and go whithersoever he pleased to carry them. Several days were passed in entreaties, artifices, and mutual menaces, which were all equally unavailing. The determination and perseverance of the one party of Arabs was equalled by the resistance and obstinacy of the other. Both were constantly acquiring an accession of strength, and actively preparing for combat. The travellers offered to abandon their object, rather than proceed to extremities. They were told that they were fortunate in the protection of the chief who accompanied them, or they never would have returned. The hostile Arabs, who defied them and their protectors to approach, having abandoned their camps, and concentrated their forces, and possessed themselves of passes and heights, sent messengers with a renewal of oaths and protestations *against entering their territory*, declaring that they should be shot like so many dogs; but the chief who accompanied the travellers was resolute, and threatened war, if they were not permitted to proceed. They were at last allowed to proceed; but only a brief space was allowed them for inspecting the ruins, and they could plainly distinguish the opposing party of Arabs, in great numbers, watching them from the heights. Their protector was then dismayed,—he was never at ease, and constantly urged them to depart. Nothing could obtain an extension of the time allotted them, and they returned, leaving much unexplored, and even unable, by any means or possibility, to penetrate a little farther, in order to visit a large temple, which they could distinctly discern. Through Idumea they did not pass. Thus Volney, Burckhardt, Joliffe, Henniker, and Irby and Mangles, not only give their personal testimony to the truth of the fact, which fulfils the prediction, but also adduce a variety of circumstances, which all conspire to prove that Idumea is so beset on every side with danger to the traveller, that *none pass through it*. Even the Arabs of the neighboring regions, whose home is the desert, and whose occupation is wandering, are afraid to enter it, or to conduct any one within its borders. Seetzen did indeed pass through Idumea, and Burckhardt traversed a considerable part of it. But the former met his death not long after the completion of his journey, and the latter never recovered from the hardships and privations which he suffered there, and, some time after, died in consequence, at Cairo; thus verifying that part of prophecy, which says, " *I will cut off from Mount Seir him that passeth out and him that returneth.*"

" *Edom shall be a desolation. From generation to generation it shall lie waste, &c.* Judea, Ammon, and Moab exhibit so abundantly the remains and the means of an exuberant fertility, that the wonder arises in the reflective mind, how the barbarity of man could have so effectually counteracted for so " many genertions" the prodigality of nature. But such is Edom's desolation, that the first sentiment of *astonishment* on the contemplation of it is, how a wide-extended region, now diversified by the strongest features of desert wildness, could ever have been adorned with cities, or tenanted for ages by a powerful and opulent people. Its present aspect would belie its ancient history, were not that history corroborated by " the many vestiges of former cultivation," by the remains of walls and paved roads, and by the ruins of cities still existing in this ruined country.

" The total cessation of its commerce,—the artificial irrigation of its valleys wholly neglected,—the destruction of all the cities, and the continued spoliation of the country by the Arabs while aught remained that they could destroy,—the permanent exposure, for ages, of the soil, unsheltered by its ancient groves, and unprotected by any covering from the scorching rays of the sun,—the unobstructed encroachments of the desert, and of the drifted sands from *the borders of the Red Sea*, the consequent absorption of the water of the springs and streamlets during summer, are causes which have all combined their baneful operation in rendering Edom *most desolate, the desolation of desolations*. Volney's account is sufficiently descriptive of the desolation which now reigns over Idumea ; and the information which Seetzen derived at Jerusalem respecting it, is of similar import. He was told, that " at the distance of two days' journey and a half from Hebron he would find considerable ruins of the ancient city of Abde, and that for all the rest of the journey he would see *no place of habitation ;* he would meet only with a few tribes of wandering Arabs." From the borders of Edom Captains Irby and Mangles beheld a boundless extent of desert view, which they had hardly ever seen equalled for singularity and grandeur. And the following extract, descriptive of what Burckhardt actually witnessed in the different parts of Edom, cannot be more graphically abbreviated than in the words of the prophet. Of its eastern boundary, and of the adjoining part of Arabia Petræa, strictly so called, Burckhardt writes,—' It might with truth be called Petræa, not only on account of its rocky mountains, but also of the elevated plain already described, which is so much covered with stones, especially flints, that it may with great propriety be called a stony desert, although susceptible of culture; in many places it is overgrown with wild herbs, and must once have been thickly inhabited; for the traces of many towns and villages are met with on both sides of the Hadj road, between Maan and Akaba, as well as between Maan and the plains of the Hauran, in which direction are also many springs. At present all this country is a desert, and Maan (Teman) is the only inhabited place in it. *I will stretch out my hand against thee, O Mount Seir, and will make thee most desolate. I will stretch out my hand upon Edom, and will make it desolate from Teman.*'

"In the interior of Idumea, where the ruins of some of its ancient cities are still visible, and in the extensive valley which reaches from the Red to the Dead Sea,—the appearance of which must now be totally and sadly changed from what it was,—' the whole plain presented to the view an expanse of shifting sands, whose surface was broken by innumerable undulations and low hills. The sand appears to have been brought *from the shores of the Red Sea* by the southern winds; and the Arabs told me that the valleys continue to present the same appearance beyond the latitude of Wada Mousa. In some parts of the valley the sand is very deep, and there is not the slightest appearance of a road, or of any work of human art. A few trees grow among the sand-hills, but the depth of sand precludes *all vegetation* of herbage.' *If grape-gatherers come to thee, would they not leave some gleaning of grapes? if thieves by night, they will destroy till they have enough; but I have made Esau* BARE. *Edom shall be a desolate wilderness.* 'On ascending the western plain, on a higher level than that of Arabia, we had before us an immense expanse of dreary country, entirely covered with black flints, with here and there some hilly chain rising from the plain.' *I will stretch out upon Idumea the line of confusion, and the stones of emptiness.*

"Of the remains of ancient cities still exposed to view in different places throughout Idumea, Burckhardt describes 'the ruins of a large town, of which nothing remains but broken walls and heaps of stones; the ruins of several villages in its vicinity; the ruins of an ancient city, consisting of large heaps of hewn blocks of silicious stone; the extensive ruins of Gherandel Arindela, an ancient town of Palestina Tertia.'

"Burckhardt gives a description of no ordinary interest, of the site of an ancient city which he visited, the ruins of which not only attest its ancient splendor, but they 'are entitled to rank among the most curious remains of ancient art.' Though the city be desolate, the monuments of its opulence and power are durable. These are,—a channel on each side of the river for conveying the water to the city,—numerous tombs,—above two hundred and fifty sepulchres, or excavations,—many mausoleums, one, in particular, of colossal dimensions, in perfect preservation, and a work of immense labor, containing a chamber sixteen paces square and above twenty-five feet in height, with a colonnade in front thirty-five feet high, crowned with a pediment highly ornamented, &c.; two large truncated pyramids, and a theatre with all its benches, capable of containing about three thousand spectators, ALL *cut out of the rock.* In some places these sepulchres are excavated one over the other, and the side of the mountain is so perpendicular, that *it seems impossible to approach the uppermost*, no path whatever being visible. 'The ground is covered with heaps of hewn stones, foundations of buildings, fragments of columns, and vestiges of paved streets, all clearly indicating that a large city once existed here. On the left bank of the river is a rising ground, extending westward for nearly three quarters of a mile, entirely covered with similar remains. On the right bank, where the ground is more elevated, ruins of the same description are to be seen. There are also the remains of a palace, and of several temples. In the eastern *cliff* there are upwards of fifty separate sepulchres close to each other.' These are not the symbols of a feeble race, nor of a people that were to perish utterly. But a judgment was denounced against the strongholds of Edom. The prophetic threatening has not proved an empty boast, and it could not have been the word of an uninspired mortal. *I will make thee small among the heathen; thy terribleness hath deceived thee and the pride of thine heart, O thou that dwellest in the clefts of the rock, that holdest the height of the hill; though thou shouldst make thy nest as high as the eagle, I will bring thee down from thence, saith the Lord: also Edom shall be a desolation.*

"The name of this capital, in all the various languages in which it occurs, implies a rock, and as such it is described in the Scriptures, in Strabo and Al Edrissi.

"Captains Irby and Mangles, having, together with Mr. Bankes and Mr. Legh, spent two days in diligently examining them, give a more particular detail of the ruins of Petra than Burckhardt's account supplied; and the more full the description, the more precise and wonderful does the prophecy appear. Near the spot where they awaited the decision of the Arabs, 'the high land was covered upon both its sides, and on its summits, with lines and solid masses of dry wall. The former appeared to be traces of ancient cultivation, the solid ruins seemed to be only the remains of towers for watching in harvest and vintage time. The whole neighborhood of the spot bears similar traces of former industry, all which seemed to indicate the vicinity of a great metropolis.' A narrow and circuitous defile, surrounded on each side by precipitous or perpendicular rocks, varying from four hundred to seven hundred feet in altitude, and forming for two miles, 'a sort of subterranean passage,' opens on the east the way to the ruins of Petra. The rocks, or rather hills, then diverge on either side, and leave an oblong space, where once stood the metropolis of Edom, deceived by its terribleness, where now lies a waste of ruins, encircled on every side, save on the northeast alone, by stupendous cliffs, which still show how the pride and labor of art tried there to vie with the sublimity of nature. Along the borders of these cliffs, detached masses of rock, numerous and lofty, have been wrought into sepulchres, the interior of which is excavated into chambers, while the exterior has been cut from the live rock into the forms of towers, with pilasters, and successive bands of frieze and entablature, wings, recesses, figures of animals, and columns.

"Yet numerous as these are, they form but a part of 'the vast necropolis of Petra.' 'Tombs present themselves, not only in every avenue to the city, and upon every precipice that surrounds it, but even intermixed almost promiscuously with its public and domestic edifices ; the natural features of the defile grew more and more imposing at every step, and the excavations and sculpture more frequent on both sides, till it presented at last a continued street of tombs.' The base of the cliffs wrought out in all the symmetry and regularity of art, with colonnades, and pedestals, and ranges of corridors adhering to the perpendicular surface ; flights of steps chiselled out of the rock ; grottoes in great numbers, 'which are certainly not sepulchral ;' some excavated residences of large dimensions (in one of which is a single chamber sixty feet in length, and of a breadth proportioned ;) many other dwellings of inferior note, particularly abundant in one defile leading to the city, the steep sides of which contain a sort of excavated suburb, accessible by flights of steps; niches, sometimes thirty feet in excavated height, with altars for votive offerings, or with pyramids, columns, or obelisks; a bridge across a chasm now apparently inaccessible; some small pyramids hewn out of the rock on the summit of the heights; horizontal grooves, for the conveyance of water, cut in the face of the rock, and even across the architectural fronts of some of the excavations; and, in short, 'the rocks hollowed out into innumerable chambers of different dimensions, whose entrances are variously, richly, and often fantastically decorated with every imaginable order of architecture,'—all united, not only form one of the most singular scenes that the eye of man ever looked upon, or the imagination painted,—a group of wonders perhaps unparalleled in their kind,—but also give indubitable proof, both that in the land of Edom there was a city where human ingenuity, and energy, and power must have been exerted for many ages, and to so great a degree as to have well entitled it to be noted for its strength or *terribleness*, and that the description given of it by the prophets of Israel was as strictly literal as the prediction respecting it is true. 'The barren state of the country, together with the desolate condition of the city, without a single human being living near it, seem,' in the words of those who were spectators of the scene, 'strongly to verify the judgment denounced against it.' *O thou who dwellest in the clefts of the rock, &c.—Also Edom shall be a desolation, &c.*

"Of all the ruins of Petra, the mausoleums and

sepulchres are among the most remarkable, and they give the clearest indication of ancient and long-continued royalty, and of courtly grandeur. Their immense number corroborates the accounts given of their successive kings and princes by Moses and Strabo; though a period of eighteen hundred years intervened between the dates of their respective records concerning them. The structure of the sepulchres also shows that many of them are of a more recent date. 'Great,' says Burckhardt, 'must have been the opulence of a city which could dedicate such monuments to the memory of its rulers.' But the long line of the kings and of the nobles of Idumea has for ages been cut off; they are without any representative now, without any memorial but the multitude and the magnificence of their unvisited sepulchres. *They shall call the nobles thereof to the kingdom* (or rather they shall call, or summon, the nobles thereof,) *but there shall be no kingdom there, and all her princes shall be nothing.*

"Amid the mausoleums and sepulchres, the remains of temples or palaces, and the multiplicity of tombs, which all form, as it were, the grave of Idumea, where its ancient splendor is interred, there are edifices, the Roman and Grecian architecture of which decides that they were *built* long posterior to the era of the prophets. *They shall build, but I will throw down.*"*

The next one I shall notice is in regard to Nineveh. The prophet Nahum says, "He will make an

---

* Keith.

utter end of the place thereof. I will make thy grave, for thou art vile."* Mr. Buckingham says, with reference to the site of ancient Nineveh, "The mounds show neither bricks, stones, nor other material for building; but are in many places overgrown with grass." The same prophet says, "She is empty, void, and waste;" and Gibbon, the historian, says, "the city, and even the ruins, had long since disappeared; the *vacant space* afforded a spacious field for the operation of the two armies."

The next prediction of which I shall speak is that concerning Tyre; and I wish to call particular attention to this, because the prophecy of Ezekiel concerning Tyre has been recently referred to in a lecture against the Bible, as a specimen of "predictions that never came to pass." Let us now compare the words of the prophet with the language of the traveller, and we shall see how much dependence is to be placed on the assertions of the lecturer. The prophet Ezekiel says, concerning Tyre, "They shall destroy the walls of Tyrus, and break down her towers: I will also scrape her dust from her, and make her like the top of a rock. It shall be a place for the spreading of nets, in the midst of the sea."† Volney says that this proud city is reduced to a miserable village, whose inhabitants live obscurely on the produce of their little ground and a trifling fishery; and Bruce says, in the very words of the prophecy, that the site of this ancient city is a "rock whereon fishers dry their nets." Now, I ask if any man denies that this

---
* Nahum i, 8, 14; ii, 10.   † Ezek. xxvi, 14.

prophecy has been fulfilled, is his word to be relied on for any historical fact?

The same prophet likewise predicts concerning Egypt, that it shall be laid waste by the hand of strangers, and shall be the basest of kingdoms; and history shows that for twenty-three centuries she has been deprived of her natural inhabitants, and left a prey successively to the Persians, Macedonians, Romans, Greeks, Arabs, Georgians, and Turks. For two thousand years it has never had a prince of its own.

The fulfilment of the prophecies concerning Babylon is still more remarkable.* It is a well known

---

* "The lofty terms in which Babylon is described in Scripture, correspond with the accounts of profane writers. It is called by Isaiah, Jeremiah, and Daniel, 'the golden city,' 'the glory of kingdoms,' 'abundant in treasures,' and 'the praise of the whole earth.' Berosus, Herodotus, Strabo, and Diodorus Siculus, some of the most ancient and authentic writers, represent it as 'the most glorious metropolis on which the sun ever shone, and rank it high among the wonders of the ancient world.'" . . . "According to the most authentic accounts that have come down to us, Babylon contained the astonishing space of sixty miles, and was adorned in every part with gardens, palaces, and temples. Around it were extended walls of stupendous height and thickness, composed of large bricks, cemented with bitumen, that by time acquired a solidity harder than stone. One hundred gates of solid brass, commanded the approaches to the city; and two hundred and fifty towers, of vast dimensions and elevations, were placed at equal distances along the walls. The buildings most remarkable for size and magnificence were, the bridge erected over the Euphrates, the spacious palaces of the kings, and the ancient temple of Belus, composed of eight towers, rising one above another, and diminishing in proportion to their prodigious elevation. At a dis-

fact, recorded in profane history, that Babylon was taken by Cyrus, while Belshazzar and his nobles were indulging themselves in a drunken revel; and that Cyrus effected an entrance into the city by turning the course of the river, which passed through the city, and passing under the wall, through the channel of the river. But this same event was most clearly and plainly predicted nearly two centuries previous. More than a century and a half before his birth, Cyrus was called by name, by the prophet Isaiah, and this very event, and the manner of it, predicted. " Thus saith the Lord,—that saith to the deep, Be dry, and I will dry up thy rivers,—thus saith the Lord to his anointed, to Cyrus, whose right hand I have holden, to subdue nations before him; and I will loose the loins of kings, to open before him the two leaved gates,"*— the drying up of her rivers, indicating the manner in which he should effect an entrance into the city. But if the gates of the city, which led from the river to the streets, had been shut, Herodotus says " the Persians would have been shut up in the bed of the river, and taken as in a net, and all destroyed." But Belshazzar, alarmed at the noise, ordered the gates of his pal-

---

tance these edifices had the appearance of lofty mountains They were calculated to brave the fiercest attacks of hostile power, and to withstand the ravages of remote ages." . . . . " Yet this remarkable prophecy was uttered when it was rising to this state of grandeur, when the dominion of its sovereigns was spreading over the surrounding provinces, and power, opulence, and prosperity combined to insure the long continuance of its empire and glory."—*Kelt.*

* Isa. xliv, 27, 28; xlv, 1; xlvii, 11.

ace to be opened, and sent persons to inquire the cause. Thus the Lord *opened before Cyrus the two-leaved gates*. His troops seized the advantage, rushed in and slew the king, and soon gained possession of the city. Thus exactly fulfilling the words of the prophet, "Therefore evil came upon her, she did not know from whence it arose ; mischief fell upon her, and desolation came upon her suddenly, which she did not know. Her young men fell in the streets, and all her men of war were cut off in that day." There is also here a prediction exactly agreeing with the decree of Cyrus for the rebuilding of Jerusalem,—"He is my shepherd, and shall perform all my pleasure, even saying to Jerusalem, ' Thou shalt be built ;' and to the temple, ' Thy foundation shall be laid.' " And in connection with this, I may allude to the prophecy of Jeremiah, of the seventy years captivity. It has been said by the lecturer alluded to, that this prophecy failed ; and that the captivity was only fifty years. But Daniel, who had the writings of Jeremiah, on reading them, and computing the time since the commencement of the captivity, at a certain time, concluded that the period of their captivity was nearly accomplished ; and, therefore, sought unto God, by fasting and prayer, that the promise of restoration might be accomplished ;* and who is best qualified to determine this part, Daniel, who lived at the time, and was himself interested in the event ; or the man who lives at this distance of time, and depends for his means of information upon the chronology of kings

---

* Daniel ix, 2.

and empires, which have long since ceased to exist?

But the predictions concerning the desolations of Chaldea and Babylon are still more striking. Jeremiah says, "A drought is upon her waters, and they shall be dried up;" and he calls it a "wilderness, a dry land, and a desert."* Travellers say that the canals which formerly watered this country, can now only be traced by their decayed banks. Thy are now dry and neglected; and there is an absence of all cultivation. The prophet says, "her cities are a desolation;" and the traveller says, "The ancient cities of Chaldea no longer exist." "Babylon shall become heaps," says the prophet; and travellers say, "Babylon has become a vast succession of mounds, a great mass of ruined heaps, of various sizes." "Cast her up as heaps," says the prophet, "destroy her utterly, let nothing be left of her." And travellers say that the ruins have been dug up, in search of bricks, so that heaps are cast up on the surface, and nothing is left but rubbish and confusion, heaps of earth and fragments of brick. "I will make it pools of water," says the prophet Isaiah; and Mr. Buckingham says, "the ground is sometimes covered with pools of water in the hollows." "Sit thou silent and get thee into darkness," says the prophet,—"A silent and sublime solitude, a silence as profound as the grave," says the traveller. The prophets Isaiah and Jeremiah say, "It shall never be inhabited nor dwelt in from generation to generation." Travellers say, "In

---

* Jer. l, 12, 38—40.

the sixteenth century there was not a house to be seen at Babylon; and in the nineteenth, it is still desolate and tenantless." "Neither shall the Arabian pitch tent there," says the prophet, "neither shall the shepherds make their folds there." Travellers say that the Arabs cannot be prevailed upon to pitch their tents there for a single night, for fear of evil spirits; and that it is the general opinion of all the people of the country, that it is extremely dangerous to be there after nightfall. The prophet says, " Wild beasts of the desert shall be there, and their houses shall be full of doleful creatures, and owls shall dwell there, and dragons in their pleasant places." And travellers say, "There are dens of wild beasts in various parts, which are the retreat of jackalls, hyenas, and other noxious animals; in most of the cavities are numbers of owls; and venomous reptiles are very numerous throughout the ruins." "It shall be *wholly* desolate," says the prophet. " A more complete picture of desolation could not well be imagined," says the traveller. The prophet says, " Bell," i. e. the Temple of Belus, " boweth down." Rich, in his memoir, says, " The loftiest temple ever built is nothing now but the highest heap in Babylon, *bowed* down to little more than the third part of its original height." Isaiah says, Babylon shall be " as a carcass trodden under feet." Volney says, " The ruins of Babylon are trodden under foot of men." Jeremiah says, " Her idols are confounded, her images are broken in pieces;" and travellers say that images of various kinds are found among the ruins. Jeremiah says, " The walls of Babylon shall be utterly broken;"

and travellers agree in saying that not a trace of her walls is to be discovered. And several travellers unite in saying that it was impossible to behold this scene, and not be reminded how exactly the predictions of Isaiah and Jeremiah have been fulfilled, even in the appearance Babylon was doomed to present.

DANIEL'S PROPHECY.

The following condensed historical view of the things noted in the prophecy of Daniel, is taken from Keith on the Fulfilment of the Prophecies, abridged by him from Sir Isaac Newton.

" ' *And now I will show thee the truth. Behold there shall stand up three kings in Persia* (Cambyses, and Darius Hystaspes), *and the fourth* (Xerxes) *shall be far richer than they all; and by his strength through his riches he shall stir up all against the realm of Grecia. And a mighty king* (Alexander the Great) *shall stand up, that shall rule with great dominion, and do according to his will. And when he shall stand up, his kingdom shall be broken, and shall be divided towards the four winds of heaven: and not to his posterity, nor according to his dominion which he ruled: for his kingdom shall be plucked up, even for others besides those.'**

" Soon after the death of Alexander the Great, his kingdom was divided towards the four winds of heaven, but not to his posterity; four of his captains,

---

* Dan. xi, 2, 3, 4.

Ptolemy, Antigonus, Lysimachus, and Cassander, reigned over Egypt, Syria, Thrace, and Greece. The kingdoms of Egypt and of Syria became afterward the most powerful: they subsisted as independent monarchies for a longer period than the other two; and as they were more immediately connected with the land of Judea, which was often reduced to their dominion, they form the subject of the succeeding predictions. Bishop Newton gives even a more copious illustration of the historical facts, which verify the whole of this prophecy, than that which had previously been given by his illustrious predecessor of the same name,—who has rendered that name immortal. He quotes or refers to authorities in every instance: and his dissertation on that part of the prophecy which relates to the kingdoms of Syria and Egypt is wound up in these emphatic words: 'It may be proper to stop here, and reflect a little how particular and circumstantial this prophecy is concerning the kingdoms of Egypt and Syria, from the death of Alexander to the time of Antiochus Epiphanes. There is not so complete and regular a series of their kings,—there is not so concise and comprehensive an account of their affairs to be found in any author of these times. The prophecy is really more perfect than any history. No one historian hath related so many circumstances, and in such exact order of time, as the prophet hath foretold them; so that it was necessary to have recourse to several authors, Greek and Roman, Jewish and Christian; and to collect here something from one, and to collect there something from another, for better explaining and illustrating the great variety of particulars contained in this prophecy.' So close is the coincidence between the prophetic and the real history of the kings of Egypt and of Syria, that Porphyry, one of the earliest opponents of Christianity, labored to prove its extreme accuracy, and alleged from thence that the events must have preceded the prediction. The same argument is equally necessary at the present hour to disprove the subsequent parts of the same prophecy,—though none can urge it now. The last of those facts to which it refers, the accomplishment of which is already past, are unfolded with equal precision and truth as the first,— and the fulfilment of the whole is yet incomplete. The more clearly that the event corresponds to the prediction, instead of being an evidence against the truth, the more conclusive is the demonstration that it is the word of Him who hath the times and the seasons in his own power.

"The subject of the prophecy is represented in these words :—' I am come to make thee understand what shall befall thy people in the latter days ; for the vision is for many days.'* And that which is noted in the Scripture of truth terminates not with the reign of Antiochus. At that very time the Romans extended their conquests towards the East. Macedonia, the seat of the empire of Alexander the Great, became a province of the Roman empire. And the prophecy, faithfully tracing the transition of power, ceases to prolong the history of the kings of Egypt and of Syria, and becomes immediately descriptive of

---

* Daniel x, 14.

the progress of the Roman arms. The very term (*shall stand up*) which previously marked the commencement of the Persian and of the Macedonian power is here repeated, and denotes the commencement of a third era or a new power. The word in the original is the same in each. And *arms* (an epithet sufficiently characteristic of the extensive military power of the Romans) *shall stand up, and they shall pollute the sanctuary of strength, and shall take away the daily sacrifice, and they shall place the abomination that maketh desolate.** All these things, deeply affecting the Jewish state, the Romans did,—and they finally rendered the country of Judea ' desolate of its old inhabitants.' The propagation of Christianity,—the succeeding important events,—is thus represented:—*The people that do know their God shall be strong and do exploits. And they that understand among the people shall instruct many.* The persecutions which they suffered are as significantly described:—*Yet they shall fall by the sword and by flame, by captivity and by spoil many days. Now, when they shall fall, they shall be holpen with a little help, and many shall cleave to them with flatteries.*† And such was Constantine's conversion, and the effect which it produced. No other government but that of the Romans *stood up*,—but the mode of that government was changed. After the days of Constantine, Christianity became gradually more and more corrupted. Previous to that period there had existed no system of dominion analogous to that which afterwards prevailed.

---

* Dan. xi, 31.   † Dan. xi, 32, 33, 34, 35.

The greatest oppressors had never extended their pretensions beyond human power, nor usurped a spiritual tyranny. But in contradiction to every other, the next succeeding form of government, unparalleled in its nature, in the annals of despotism or of delusion, is thus characterized by the prophet:—*And the king* (the ruling power, signifying any government, state or potentate) *shall do according to his will; and he shall exalt himself and magnify himself above every god, and shall speak marvellous things against the God of gods, and shall prosper till the indignation be accomplished.** This description is suited to the history of the Eastern or Western churches,—to the government under the Grecian emperors at Constantinople, or of the popes at Rome. The extent of the Roman empire might justify its application to the latter; but the connexion of the prophecy, as referable to local events, tends to limit it to the former. In either case it is descriptive of that mode of government which prospered so long in the east and in the west,—and which consisted in the impious usurpation of spiritual authority,—in the blasphemous assumption of those attributes which are exclusively divine, and in exalting itself above the laws of God and man. But instead, perhaps, of being confined exclusively to either, it may have been intended to represent, as it does characterize, the spiritual tyranny, and the substitution of the commandments of men for the will of God, which oppressed Christendom for ages, and hid from men the word of God. The prevalence of superstition,

---

* Dan. xi, 36, &c.

the prohibition or discouragement of marriage, and the worship of saints, as characteristic of the same period, and of the same power, are thus prophetically desscribed :—'*Neither shall he regard the God of his fathers nor the desire of women* (or matrimony), *neither shall he regard any god.** But in his estate shall he honour the God of forces*,—MAHUZZIM,—protectors or guardians, a term so applicable to the worship of saints and to the confidence which was reposed in them, that expressions exactly synonymous are often used by many ancient writers in honor of them, —of which Mede and Sir Isaac Newton have adduced a multiplicity of instances. Mahuzzim were the *tutelary saints* of the Greek and Romish churches. The subserviency, which long existed, of spiritual power to temporal aggrandizement, is also noted in the porphecy : *and he shall cause them to rule over many, and shall divide the land for gain.*† And that the principal teachers and propagators of the worship of *Mahuzzim*,—' the bishops, priests, and monks, and religious orders, have been honoured, and reverenced, and esteemed in former ages ; that their authority and jurisdiction have extended over the purses and consciences of men ; that they have been enriched with noble buildings and large endowments, and have had the choicest of the lands appropriated for church lands ;—are points of such notoriety that they require no proof, and will admit of no denial.'

" Having thus described the antichristian power, which prospered so long and prevailed so widely, the

---

* Dan. xi, 37, 38.   † Dan. v, 39.

prophecy next delineates, in less obscure terms, the manner in which that power was to be humbled and overthrown, and introduces a more particular definition of the rise, extent and fall of that kingdom which was to oppress and supplant it in the latter days. *And at the time of the end shall the king of the south push at him.** The Saracens extended their conquests over great part of Asia and of Europe : they penetrated the dominions of the Grecian empire, and partially subdued, though they could not entirely subvert it, nor obtain possession of Constantinople, the capital city. The prediction, however brief, significantly represents their warfare, which was desultory, and their conquest, which was incomplete. And Arabia is situated to the south of Palestine. The Turks, the next and the last invaders of the Grecian empire, were of Scythian extraction, and came from the north. And while a single expression identifies the Saracen invasion,—the irruption of the Turks, being of a more fatal character and more permanent in its effects, is fully described. Every part of the description is most faithful to the facts. Their local situation, the impetuosity of their attack, the organization of their armies, and the success of their arms, form the first part of the prediction respecting them. *And the king of the north shall come against him like a whirlwind, with chariots and with horsemen, and with many ships; and he shall enter into the countries, and shall overflow and pass over.*† Although the Grecian empire withstood the predatory warfare of the Saracens, it

---

* Dan. xi, 40. † Dan. xi, 40.

gave way before the overwhelming forces of the Turks, whose progress was tracked with destruction, and whose coming was indeed like a whirlwind. Chariots and horsemen were to be the distinguishing marks of their armies, though armies, in general, contain the greatest proportion of foot soldiers And, in describing their first invasion of the Grecian territory, Gibbon relates, that 'the myriads of Turkish horse overspread a frontier of six hundred miles from Tauris to Arzeroum, and the blood of one hundred and thirty thousand Christians was a grateful sacrifice to the Arabian prophet. The Turkish armies at first consisted so exclusively of horsemen, that the stoutest of the youths of the captive Christians were afterward taken and trained as a band of infantry, and called janizaries (yengi cheri) or new soldiers.' In apparent contradiction to the nature of their army, they were also to possess many ships. And Gibbon again relates that 'a fleet of two hundred ships was constructed by the hands of the captive Greeks.' But no direct evidence is necessary to prove that many ships must have been requisite for the capture of so many islands, and the destruction of the Venetian naval power, which was once the most celebrated in Europe. ' The words, *shall enter into the countries and overflow and pass over*, give us an exact idea of their *overflowing* the western parts of Asia, and then passing over into Europe.'

" *He shall enter also into the glorious land, and many countries shall be overthrown.** This expres-

---

* Dan. xi, 41.

sion, *the glorious land*, occurs in the previous part of this prophecy (v. 16), and, in both cases, it evidently means the land of Israel; and such the Syriac translation renders it. The Holy Land formed part of the first conquest of the Turks. And *many countries shall be overthrown.** The limits of the Turkish empire embraced the ancient kingdoms of Babylon, Macedon, Thrace, Epirus, Greece, &c., and the many countries over which they ruled. The whole of Syria was also included, with partial exceptions. These very exceptions are specified in the prophecy, though these territories partially intersect the Turkish dominions, and divide one portion of them from another, forming a singular contrast to the general continuity of kingdoms. And while every particular prediction respecting these separate states has been fully verified, their escaping out of the hands of the Turks has been no less marvellously fulfilled. *But these shall escape out of his hand, even Edom and Moab, and the chief of the children of Ammon.*† Mede, Sir Isaac and Bishop Newton, in applying this prophecy to the Turkish empire, could only express, in general terms, that the Arabs possessed these countries, and exacted tribute from the Turks for permitting their caravans to pass through them. But recent travellers, among whom Volney has to be numbered, have unconsciously given the most satisfactory information, demonstrative of the truth of all the minutiæ of the prediction. Volney describes these countries in part,—Burckhardt traversed them all,—and they have since been visited

---

* Dan. xi, 41. † Dan. xi, 41.

by other travellers. Edom and Moab are in possession of the Bedouin (or wandering) Arabs. The Turks have often attempted in vain to subjugate them. The partial escape of Ammon from their dominion is not less discriminating than just. For although that territory lies in the immediate vicinity of the pachalic of Damascus, to which part of it is subjected,—though it be extremely fertile by nature,—though its situation and its soil have thus presented, for several centuries, the strongest temptation to Turkish rapacity,—though they have often attempted to subdue it,—yet no fact could have been more explicitly detailed, or more incidentally communicated, than that the inhabitants of the greater part of that country, particularly what adjoins the ancient but now desolate city of Ammon, 'live in a state of complete independence of the Turks.'

" *He shall stretch forth his hand also upon the countries.** How significantly do these words represent the vast extent of the Turkish empire, which alone has stretched its dominion over many countries of Asia, of Europe, and of Africa. Ill-fated Egypt was not to escape from subjection to such a master. *And the land of Egypt shall not escape; but he shall have power over the treasures of gold and of silver, and over all the precious things of Egypt.*† The Turks have drained Egypt of its wealth, of its gold and of its silver, and of its precious things: and such power have they exercised over them, that the kingdom of the Pharaohs, the land where everlasting pyramids were

---

* Dan. xi, 42. † Dan. xi, 43.

built, despoiled to the utmost, is now one of the poorest, as it has long been the basest of kingdoms. *The Libyans and Ethiopians shall be at his steps.** These form the extremities of the Turkish empire, and were partially subject to its power. 'After the conquest of Egypt, the terror of Selim's victories,' says the historian, 'spreading wide, the kings of Africa, bordering upon Cyrenaica, sent their ambassadors with offers to become his tributaries. Other more remote nations also towards Ethiopia were easily induced to join in amity with the Turks.' Exclusive of Egypt, they still retain the nominal power over other countries of Africa. Such is the prophetic description of the rise and extent of that power which was to possess Judea in the latter days; and it is a precise delineation of the rise and extent of the Turkish empire, to which Judea has been subject for centuries.

"Every succeeding fact, from the time of Cyrus to the present age, gives as sure a confirmation as the voice of an angel could have done, that the things noted in this prophecy are those of the Scripture of truth. History interprets every part of it. It brings a multiplicity of witnesses, if we will listen to their testimony, from a long succession of ages, each arising to testify to its truth. And although the names of the countries be not mentioned, and the prophecy has received a variety of interpretations, yet we apprehend that it presents us, like every spot on earth which was the subject of Scriptural prophecies, with ocular demonstration that there is a God who ruleth among the

---

* Dan. xi, 43.

nations; and that the Christian religion, the purest and the best on earth, has that God for its author."

We come now to the New Testament; and the first prophecy that meets us is that of the destruction of Jerusalem by the Romans, as spoken by our Saviour. To give an adequate idea of this, however, would require a volume. I shall be able only briefly to allude to a few particulars. And I would remark in the outset, that the three evangelists, Matthew, Mark, and Luke,* who record this prophecy, wrote many years before the event, while Jerusalem was standing, and there were no signs of its approaching destruction. John wrote after its destruction; and we see the remarkable delicacy of the inspired authors of the Bible, that he should not even allude to the subject, lest he should seem to conform the prediction to the event. The first sign of the approach of this event, which Jesus gave to his disciples, was the appearance of *false Christs*, which should deceive many. Josephus, the Jewish historian, states that the country was filled with impostors and deceivers, who induced many people to follow them to the wilderness, where they miserably perished.

The next sign he gave them, was " wars and rumors of wars," nation rising against nation. Josephus and other historians relate that, before the destruction of Jerusalem, in consequence of the rebellion of the Jews, the whole of Judea was a scene of war. Josephus says, " every city was divided into two armies." Italy was also convulsed with contentions for the em-

---

* Mat. xxiv; Mark xiii; Luke xxi.

pire, and within two years, four emperors suffered death. "The emperor Caligula commanded the Jews to place his statue in their temple; and in consequence of a positive refusal to comply with so impious a request, he threatened them with an invasion, which was prevented by his death;" producing "rumors of wars;" and still "the end was not yet," according to Christ's words.

Another sign was that there should be famines, pestilences, and earthquakes, in divers places. There were several different famines during the reign of Claudius Cæsar. They continued to be severe for several years, throughout the land of Judah. Pestilence succeeded them. In the same reign there were earthquakes at Rome, Apamea, and Crete. In the reign of Nero, there was an earthquake at Campania, and another in Laodicea; Hierapolis and Colosse were overthrown, and others happened in various places, before the destruction of Jerusalem. Josephus relates that, in Judea, at the beginning of the war, but before Jerusalem was besieged by Titus, there was such an uncommonly tremendous storm of wind, and thunder and lightning, with "a fearful noise of the agitated earth, as portended, in the opinion of many, the greatest evils."

But another sign of the approach of this calamity, given by the Saviour, was the appearance of fearful sights and signs in the heavens. Josephus gives a very particular account of many very terrible appearances in the heavens; as a comet like a flaming sword, waving over Jerusalem, and the appearance of contending armies in the air. "The great gate of the temple," he says, " which twenty men could scarcely shut, and which was made fast with bolts and bars, was seen to open of its own accord, to let in their enemies. At the feast of Pentecost, when the priests went at midnight into the temple, to attend to their service, they first heard a kind of noise, as of a movement from the place, and then a voice, saying, " Let us go hence." Josephus also says that, four years before the war, a man began at the feast of tabernacles to cry in the streets, and wherever he went, " A voice against Jerusalem and the temple ! A voice against all the people ! Wo, wo, unto them." In this manner he continued to cry for about seven years, when suddenly he cried out, " Wo, wo, to myself," when a weapon struck and killed him. " These and many other extraordinary events, excited great consternation among the Jews, and were intimations of their approaching miseries." Tacitus thus describes them:— " Armies seemed to meet in the clouds. Weapons were there seen glittering ; the temple seemed to be in flame, with fire issuing from the clouds ; and a divine voice was heard, that the Deity was quitting the place, and a great motion, as of his departing !" Josephus was a Jew, who never embraced Christianity, and Tacitus a learned Gentile, who hated and vilified it. Christ predicted, also, that his disciples should encounter great persecution ; that some should be offended and apostatize ; and that the gospel must first be published among all nations ; all of which came to pass before the destruction of Jerusalem ; as appears by the facts recorded in Acts, and in both sacred and profane history. He also declared that the

DESTRUCTION OF JERUSALEM. 169

gospel must first be published to all nations, i. e. *to all nations*, in distinction from its being confined to the Jews. This was done soon after Christ's resurrection. It was true, however, that it was actually preached before this event, not only in lesser Asia, Greece, and Italy, but as far northward as Scythia, southward as far as Ethiopia, eastward as Parthia and India, and westward as far as Spain and Britain.

But the last sign he gave them was " the abomination of desolation, spoken of by Daniel the prophet, standing in the Holy Place," and that Jerusalem should be compassed about with armies ; and then he warns his disciples to flee. The images of the emperor, and the eagles that were carried in front of the legions, were regarded with religious abhorrence by the Jews, as they were ranked among the Pagan deities, and reverenced with divine honors. They were, therefore, rightly called the abomination of desolation, since the erection of them within the Holy Place marked the fatal design of the enemy to lay waste the country, and expose it to all the ravages of war ; the Romans having, before this, at the request of the Jews, removed them from their standard. And strange as it may appear, the Roman general did besiege Jerusalem, and then suddenly and unaccountably retire for a little time, so that all the Christians in the city, taking warning by this sign, and in obedience to the instructions of Christ, fled from the city, some to the mountains, and others to the city of Pella, near the Jordan ; so that in the succeeding calamities, according to the prediction, not a hair of their heads did perish.

Finally, he says, " There shall be great tribulation,

such as was not from the beginning of the world to this time,—no, nor ever shall be. There shall be great distress in the land, and wrath upon this people. The particulars of the siege are all related by Josephus, and form a detail of miseries that admit of no exaggeration; and which he repeatedly declares in terms that entirely accord with the language of prophecy, are altogether unequalled in the history of the world. Christ says there shall not be one stone left upon another of the temple; and it was completely demolished, and its foundations raised, by Titus. The Emperor Julian, an apostate from Christianity, in order to falsify the words of Christ, attempted to rebuild the temple; but while making preparations, there were earthquakes, and balls of fire issuing out of the earth, which destroyed their works and killed the workmen, so that they were compelled to desist.

Yet, notwithstanding all these facts, which are familiar to all readers of history, the lecturer to whom I have alluded, intimates that Jesus was mistaken in a prediction contained in the same chapter from which these are taken, and relating to the same event!

THE SEVEN CHURCHES OF ASIA.

The following condensed account of the present state of these churches, compared with the prophecy, is taken from Keith on the Fulfilment of the Prophecies.

"The CHURCH OF EPHESUS, after a commendation of their first works, to which they were commanded to return, were accused of having left their first love, and threatened with the removal of their candlestick out of its place, except they should repent.* Ephesus is situated nearly five miles north of Smyrna. It was the metropolis of Lydia, and a great and opulent city, and (according to Strabo) the greatest emporium of Asia Minor. It was chiefly famous for the temple of Diana, 'whom all Asia worshipped,' which was adorned with one hundred and twenty-seven columns of Parian marble, each of a single shaft, and sixty feet high, and which formed one of the seven wonders of the world. The remains of its magnificent theatre, in which it is said that twenty thousand people could easily have been seated, are yet to be seen.† But 'a few heaps of stones, and some miserable mud cottages, occasionally tenanted by Turks, without one Christian residing there, are all the remains of ancient Ephesus.' It is, as described by different travellers, a solemn and most forlorn spot. The Epistle to the Ephesians is read throughout the world; but there is none in Ephesus to read it now. They left their first love, they returned not to their first works. Their candlestick has been removed out of its place; and the great city of Ephesus is no more.

"The CHURCH OF SMYRNA was approved of as 'rich,' and no judgment was denounced against it. They were warned of a tribulation of ten days (the ten years' persecution by Dioclesian), and were enjoined to be faithful unto death, and they would receive a

---

* Rev. ii, 5. † Acts xix, 29.

crown of life.* And unlike to the fate of the famous city of Ephesus, Smyrna is still a large city, containing nearly one hundred thousand inhabitants, with several Greek churches; and an English and other Christian ministers have resided in it. The light has indeed become dim, but the candlestick has not been wholly removed out of its place.

The CHURCH OF PERGAMOS is commended for holding fast the name of the Lord, and not denying his faith, during a time of persecution, and in the midst of a wicked city. But there were some in it who held doctrines and did deeds which the Lord hated. Against them he was to fight with the sword of his mouth; and all were called to repent. But it is not said, as of Ephesus, that their candlestick would be removed out of its place.† Pergamos is situated to the north of Smyrna, at a distance of nearly sixty-four miles, and 'was formerly the metropolis of Hellespontic Mysia.' It still contains at least fifteen thousand inhabitants, of whom fifteen hundred are Greeks, and two hundred Armenians, each of whom have a church.

"In the CHURCH OF THYATIRA, like that of Pergamos, some tares were soon mingled with the wheat. He who hath eyes like unto a flame of fire discerned both. Yet happily for the souls of the people, more than for the safety of the city, the general character of that church, as it then existed, is thus described:— 'I know thy works, and charity, and service, and faith, and thy patience, and thy works; and the last

---

* Rev. ii, 8–11.   † Rev. ii, 12–16.

to be more than the first.'* But against those, for such there were among them, who had committed fornication, and eaten things sacrificed unto idols, to whom the Lord gave space to repent of their fornication, and they repented not, great tribulation was denounced : and to every one of them was to be given according to their works. These, thus warned while on earth in vain, have long since passed, where all are daily hastening, to the place where no repentance can be found, and no work be done. 'But unto the rest in Thyatira (as many as have not known the depths of Satan), I will put upon you, saith the Lord, none other burden.'† There were those in Thyatira who could save a city. It still exists, while greater cities have fallen. Mr. Hartley, who visited it in 1826, describes it as 'embosomed in cypresses and poplars. The Greeks are said to occupy three hundred houses, and the Armenians thirty. Each of them have a church.'

"The CHURCH OF SARDIS differed from those of Pergamos and Thyatira. They had not denied the faith ; but the Lord had a few things against them, for there were some evil-doers among them, and on those, if they repented not, judgment was to rest. But in Sardis, great though the city was, and founded though the church had been by an apostle, there were only a few names which had not defiled their garments. And to that church the Spirit said, 'I know thy works, that thou hast a name, that thou livest and art dead.' But the Lord is long-suffering, not willing

---

* Rev ii, 19.   † Rev. ii, 24.

that any should perish, but that all should come to repentance. And the church of Sardis was thus warned :—' Be watchful and strengthen the things which remain, that are ready to die, for I have not found thy works perfect before God. Remember, therefore, how thou hast received and heard, and hold fast and repent. If, therefore, thou shalt not watch, I will come on thee as a thief, and thou shalt not know what hour I shall come upon thee.'*

"The state of Sardis now is a token that the warning was given in vain ; and shows that the threatenings of the Lord, when disregarded, become certain judgments. Sardis, the capital of Lydia, was a great and renowned city, where the wealth of Crœsus, its king, was accumulated, and became even a proverb. But now a few wretched mud huts, 'scattered among the ruins,' are the only dwellings in Sardis, and form the lowly home of Turkish herdsmen, who are its only inhabitants. As the seat of a Christian church it has lost,—all it had to lose,—the name. 'No Christians reside on the spot.'

"' And to the angel of the CHURCH IN PHILADELPHIA write, These things saith He that is holy, He that is true, He that hath the key of David, He that openeth and no man shutteth ; and shutteth, and no man openeth ;—I know thy works ; behold I have set before thee an open door, and no man can shut it ; for thou hast a little strength, and hast kept my word, and hast not denied my name. Because thou hast kept the word of my patience, I also will keep thee

---

* Rev. iii, 3, 4.

from the hour of temptation which shall come upon all the world.'* The promises of the Lord are as sure as his threatenings. Philadelphia alone long withstood the power of the Turks, and, in the words of Gibbon, 'at length capitulated with the proudest of the Ottomans. Among the Greek colonies and churches of Asia,' he adds, 'Philadelphia is still erect; a column in a scene of ruins.' 'It is indeed an interesting circumstance, says Mr. Hartley, 'to find Christianity more flourishing here than in many other parts of the Turkish empire: there is still a numerous Christian population: they occupy three hundred houses. Divine service is performed every Sunday, in five churches.' Nor is it less interesting, in these eventful times, and notwithstanding the general degeneracy of the Greek church, to learn that the present bishop of Philadelphia accounts, 'the Bible the only foundation of all religious belief;' and that he admits that 'abuses have entered into the church which former ages might endure, but the present must put them down.' It may well be added, as stated by Mr. Hartley, 'the circumstance that Philadelphia is now called Allah-Shehr, the city of God, when viewed in connexion with the promises made to that church, and especially with that of writing the name of the city of God upon its faithful members, is, to say the least, a singular concurrence.' From the prevailing iniquities of men many a sign has been given how terrible are the judgments of God. But from the fidelity of the church in Philadelphia of old, in keeping his word, a

---

* Rev. iii, 7–10.

name and memorial of his faithfulness has been left on earth, while the higher glories, promised to those that overcame, shall be ratified in heaven ; and towards them, but not them only, shall the glorified Redeemer confirm the truth of his blessed words, ' Him that overcometh will I make a pillar in the temple of my God ;' even as assuredly as Philadelphia, when all else fell around it, ' stood erect,' our enemies themselves being judges, ' a column in a scene of ruins.'

" And unto the angel of the CHURCH of the LAODICEANS write,—These things saith the Amen, the faithful and true witness, the beginning of the creation of God. I know thy works, that thou art neither cold nor hot ; I would that thou wert cold or hot. So then, because thou art lukewarm, and neither cold nor hot, I will spue thee out of my mouth. Because thou sayest, I am rich and increased with goods, and have need of nothing ; and knowest not that thou art wretched and miserable, and poor, and blind, and naked ; I counsel thee to buy of me gold tried in the fire that thou mayest be rich, and white raiment that thou mayest be clothed, and that the shame of thy nakedness do not appear ; and anoint thine eyes with eye-salve that thou mayest see.'* All the other churches were found worthy of some commendation ; and there was some blessing in them all.

" But in what the Spirit said to the church in Laodicea, there was not one word of approval ; it was lukewarm, without exception ; and therefore it was wholly loathed.

---

* Rev. iii, 14, &c.

"Laodicea was the metropolis of the Greater Phrygia; and, as heathen writers attest, it was an extensive and very celebrated city. Instead of then verging to its decline, it arose to its eminence only about the beginning of the Christian era. 'It was the mother-church of sixteen bishoprics.' Its three theatres, and the immense circus, which was capable of containing upwards of thirty thousand spectators, the spacious remains of which (with other ruins buried under ruins) are yet to be seen, give proof of the greatness of its ancient wealth and population, and indicate too strongly that in that city where Christians were rebuked, without exception, for their lukewarmness, there were multitudes who were lovers of pleasure more than lovers of God. The amphitheatre was built after the Apocalypse was written, and the warning of the Spirit had been given to the church of the Laodiceans to be zealous and repent; but whatever they there may have heard or beheld, their hearts would neither have been quickened to a renewed zeal for the service and glory of God, nor turned to a deeper sorrow for sin, and to a repentance not to be repented of. But the fate of Laodicea, though opposite, has been no less marked than that of Philadelphia. There are no sights of grandeur nor scenes of temptation around it now. Its own tragedy may be briefly told. It was lukewarm, and neither cold nor hot; and therefore it was loathsome in the sight of God. It was loved, and rebuked, and chastened in vain. And it has been blotted from the world. It is now as desolate as its inhabitants were destitute of the fear and love of God; and as the church of the Laodiceans was devoid of true faith in the Saviour, and zeal in his service, it is, as described in his travels by Dr. Smith, 'utterly desolated, and without any inhabitant, except wolves, and jackals, and foxes.' It can boast of no human inhabitants, except occasionally when wandering Turkomans pitch their tents in its spacious amphitheatre. The 'finest sculptured fragments' are to be seen at a considerable depth, in excavations which have been made among the ruins. And Colonel Lake observes, 'there are few ancient cities more likely than Laodicea to preserve many curious remains of antiquity beneath the surface of the soil; its opulence, and the earthquakes to which it was subject, rendering it probable that valuable works of art were often there buried beneath the ruins of the public and the private edifices.' A fearful significancy is thus given to the terrific denunciation, 'Because thou art lukewarm, and neither cold nor hot, I will spue thee out of my mouth.'"

There are some very interesting predictions contained in Daniel, in Revelations, and in one of Paul's epistles, relating to the church of Rome; and to the religion of Mohammed; which have been, in a most extraordinary manner fulfilled; and likewise the predictions concerning the diffusion and propagation of the gospel. But a fair representation of them would require a much larger space than is consistent with the design of this work; and I must hasten to the close of this part of the subject. I shall, therefore, only notice two or three other predictions, which are having their accomplishment among ourselves at the present day.

Peter says, "there shall come in the last days scoffers, walking after their own lusts, and saying, Where is the promise of his coming?" And are there not scoffers among us, some of whom walk after their own lusts? Do they not make a mock of experimental religion, and scoff at the threatenings of God against sinners? And do they not say, "Where is the promise of his coming?" or at least pretend that he was mistaken as to the time when he would come.

Again, the same apostle says, "There shall be false teachers among you, who privily shall bring in damnable heresies, even denying the Lord that bought them." And have there not arisen false teachers among us? And did they not privily, in the days of our fathers, while professing to be orthodox, bring in damnable heresies, even denying the Lord that bought them? The apostle also says, "many shall follow their pernicious ways; by reason of whom the way of truth shall be evil spoken of." And is it not so? Do not many follow the pernicious ways of these false teachers? And is not the way of truth evil spoken of?

But again,—the apostle Paul, speaking of those that receive not the love of the truth that they might be saved, says, "God shall send them strong delusions, to believe a lie, that they all might be damned, who believed not the truth, but had pleasure in unrighteousness." Here is a declaration of the awful truth, that, when men reject the truth from hatred of it, and refuse cordially to embrace it, God sends upon them a judicial blindness, so that they are left to embrace and continue in fatal and soul-destroying errors, which at last will drown their souls in perdition. And is it not so? Have we not examples of it among us? How often do we see those who have sat under the sound of the gospel, and whose hearts have been moved upon by the Holy Ghost,—how often do we see them resisting those influences, and rejecting the truth, because they hate it, and cannot submit their hearts to it? And how often does God leave them to embrace some soul-destroying error, to their own damnation?

Once more,—the impenitent often bring up the inconsistent conduct of professors of religion, and the cases of apostasy that occur among them, to prove that there is nothing in religion. But it proves just the contrary. All this is predicted. Christ intimates that there will be many false professors; and John, speaking of such says, "They went out from us, because they were not of us." Christ says also, that because iniquity shall abound, the love of many shall wax cold; and is it not so? Does not iniquity abound? And has not the love of many among us waxed cold? Are not some of us now verifying this prediction? How warm is our love to him that died for us? Does it lead us to live, not to ourselves, but unto him? How much sacrifice of personal interest or feeling does it lead us to make, for the sake of Him and his cause?

It appears from the facts that have been presented in this and the preceding chapter, that the whole Bible, as we have it, was given by inspiration of God. We have shown that prophecies spoken by Moses, Isaiah, Jeremiah, Ezekiel, Joel, Amos, Micah, Zephaniah, Zechariah, Obadiah, and Nahum, have been fulfilled. We might likewise show the same of David and of all the prophets; but think it unnecessary in this place. We have seen also, that prophecies spoken by Jesus Christ, Paul, and Peter, have been fulfilled. We might have shown the same of John. But to prove the truth of the Bible from prophecy, it is not necessary to point out particular predictions that have been fulfilled in every particular book. The Jews had a rule that a man who was acknowledged as a prophet,— whose words had been attested by fulfilment, or by miracles, or signs, or by another acknowledged prophet, was sufficient to attest the inspiration of another prophet. Now we have this testimony in regard to all the parts of the Bible. Jesus Christ was shown to be a prophet, by the testimony of John the Baptist, whose prophetic character was attested by an angel, and acknowledged by the people; Christ has also been shown to be a prophet by the miracles which he wrought, and by the fulfilment of predictions which he uttered. And we have his testimony to the whole of the Old Testament,—" All things which are written in the law of Moses, in the Prophets, and in the Psalms," concerning himself, he says must be fulfilled; thus recognizing these three parts into which the Jewish Scriptures were divided, as of Divine origin; and these comprise all that we now have in the Old Testament. Christ also declared to his apostles that he would impart to them the gift of inspiration, to enable them to write the gospel, and settle the foundation of the Christian church; and this attests the books that were written by them. But as Paul was not one of the original apostles, we have the testimony of Peter to the inspiration of his epistles; and as to the evangelists, Mark and Luke, they were the companions of Peter and Paul, and their gospels are substantially the gospels according to Peter and Paul. We have also the testimony of Paul and Peter, both of whom we have proved to be inspired, by the fulfilment of predictions which they uttered; and they both bear testimony to the inspiration of the Old Testament. So that the argument now presented produces evidence entirely conclusive of the inspiration of the whole Bible, as we have it.

PRACTICAL REMARKS.

This whole subject, and the facts here presented, call for some serious and solemn reflections:

1. The facts here presented show the instability and emptiness of all human greatness. Where are now those mighty empires, those great cities, those splendid palaces, which the ambition of great men once reared to perpetuate their memories? The wild beasts have the dominion; the cities lie waste; the palaces are in ruins; and the names of the men who reared them are lost in the oblivion of ages, while their ashes are not permitted to sleep under the monuments which they erected; but, stolen with sacrilegious hands, they are carried to distant lands, and exposed for gain to the gaze of the curious. And shall any of

us be so foolish as to spend our time and strength to heap up earthly treasures, which shall share the same fate, while we neglect to secure a treasure in heaven, —the true riches which shall never fade away ? Those palaces shall stand forever,—those mansions shall endure through eternal ages,—those pearly gates shall never open to the enemy,—no hostile foot shall ever tread those golden streets. Is it wise, then, to expend our energies here, where, in a few years, the houses which we build will be heaps of ruins, and our names will soon be forgotten ?

2. Here is a solemn warning to those nations which forget God, and refuse to acknowledge his hand in their blessings. It was this which brought down the proud and haughty king of Babylon from his throne, and spread utter desolation over so many kingdoms, which were once among the fairest portions of the earth. And we have reason to fear, that unless we repent of our sins, and acknowledge God in our national capacity, the same forgetfulness of God will bring destruction and desolation upon our own beloved land ; so that her Christian temples will be laid low, her proud cities reduced to heaps of rubbish, the palaces of her merchant princes overthrown, her inhabitants wasted away, and her beautiful fields turned to the silent desolation of dark, impenetrable forests, inhabited only by wild beasts of prey.

3. We learn the folly of those who think God is too merciful to punish sinners forever in hell. Was he too merciful to cast off his own chosen people, on account of their sins, and expose them to calamities indescribable, from generation to generation ? Was he

too merciful to overthrow the splendid city of Tyre, whose merchants were princes, and leave nothing of all their greatness but a bare rock, on which the fishermen spread their nets? Was he too merciful to overthrow Nineveh, that great city, wherein were more than six score thousand persons, that could not discern between their right hand and their left hand, so that now even the place where it stood, cannot be identified? Was he too merciful to overturn Babylon and Edom and Moab, and turn vast countries, thickly peopled, and cultivated as a garden, into a waste howling wilderness? And will he be so merciful to sinners now living under the broad blaze of the Sun of righteousness, who shut their eyes to this glorious light, and turn a deaf ear to the calls of his mercy,—will he be so merciful as not to punish them in eternity, but to take them up to heaven in their sins, to pollute those mansions of unfading glory, reserved in the heavens for them that love him? "Verily I say unto you, it shall be more tolerable, in the day of judgment, for Tyre and Sidon," than for them.

4. We learn the certainty of the fulfilment of all the promises and threatenings of the Bible. "God is not a man, that he should lie; neither the son of man that he should repent: hath he said, and shall he not do it? or hath he spoken, and shall he not make it good?" Let the exact fulfilment of his terrible threatenings against his own ancient people for their disobedience answer. Let the judgments denounced and fulfilled against Moab, Edom, Tyre, and Babylon, answer? And what has he said concerning those who

are living in impenitence and sin? "Cursed is every one that continueth not in all things that are written in the book of the law to do them." "He that believeth not is condemned already, because he hath not believed on the only begotten Son of God. He that believeth not the Son shall not see life, but the wrath of God abideth on him." "God is angry with the wicked every day. If he turn not, he will whet his glittering sword; he hath bent his bow and made it ready. He hath also prepared for him the instruments of death." "For I lift up my hand to heaven and say, I live forever. If I whet my glittering sword, and mine hand take hold on judgment, I will render vengeance to mine enemies, and will reward them that hate me." These are only a few of the multitude of God's threatenings against sinners. And why is it that they are not heeded? Why is it that they go on as careless and indifferent as if there were no judgment, no heaven, no hell? It is, doubtless, because they expect in some way or other to escape. But there is but one condition annexed to these threatenings; and that is, that he turn,—turn from his sins, to seek the Lord,—turn from his unbelief, to the Saviour of sinners. We have seen how exactly and minutely every jot and tittle of his threatenings have been fulfilled against those ancient nations, who refused, upon fair warning, to turn from their sins to the Lord. And no less exactly will be fulfilled upon us the awful threatenings of his word against the impenitent and unbelieving, unless we repent.

CHAPTER V.

FOURTH PILLAR, continued.—*Prophecies concerning Christ, with their fulfilment.*

LUKE XXIV, 24.

"All things must be fulfilled which were written in the law of Moses, and in the Prophets, and in the Psalms, concerning me."

THESE words were spoken by our Saviour, after his resurrection, and just before he ascended up, to sit on the right hand of God, in the heavens. It has been denied, by one who professes great veneration for the character of Jesus Christ, that there were any direct predictions concerning him in the Old Testament; but here it is directly asserted by Jesus himself, that there were predictions concerning him, in each of the three grand divisions of the Old Testament,—the *Law of Moses*, the *Prophets*, and the *Psalms*. Which shall we believe? If I thought Jesus could have been mistaken in so important a matter as this, I could not hold him in such veneration. But believing him, as I do, to be a divine person, I consider it impious to assert, in contradiction to his own declaration, that there are no such predictions concerning him.

It is useful to examine these prophecies, because they constitute an important branch of the evidence on which we rely to prove the authenticity of the Christian religion. Jesus himself deemed it necessary to open the understandings of his disciples to the true meaning of these prophecies, in order to substantiate his claims to the Messiahship. It cannot, therefore, be an unimportant matter for us to examine. It concerns the foundation of our hopes. It is, also, a matter of deep practical interest, because it leads us into a right understanding of the grand design of the coming of Christ, and his sufferings and death.

I therefore request the reader to follow me in an examination of these prophecies and their fulfilment. But before we proceed, I would remark that we have all the materials for conducting such an examination impartially. The Scriptures which contain these prophecies, are sustained by evidence entirely independent of those which contain the account of their fulfilment; and those which contain the account of their fulfilment, are sustained by evidence entirely independent of those which contain the predictions; and here they meet together, and prove each other. The Old Testament, in the hands of Christians, is the same as that in the hands of the Jews. The Jews have such convincing evidence of the divine authority of their Scriptures, that they have never dared to erase these prophecies, though they prove that He whom they crucified is the true Messiah; nor have any of their writers ever disproved, or even denied, the main facts narrated in the New Testament, which show the correspondence between these prophecies and Jesus

Christ. There are prophecies, also, concerning the prevalence of Christianity, the fulfilment of which is recorded in profane history. So, also, some of the prophecies concerning Christ himself, are found to be in accordance with facts recorded in profane history.

With these observations, I proceed to the consideration of these prophecies, and their fulfilment. And I shall include, under this term, the *promises*, as well as direct predictions.

I. The first intimation of a Saviour was graciously given immediately after the fall; and even before the curse was pronounced upon our first parents, that it might not fall so heavily upon them, as to overwhelm them in despair. In pronouncing sentence upon the serpent, the Almighty said, "I will put enmity between thee and the woman, and between thy seed and her seed; it shall bruise thy head, and thou shalt bruise his heel." This has received a literal fulfilment in the enmity which has always existed between the natural seed of the woman and the natural seed of the serpent. But it has a spiritual meaning of far higher import. In the fourth chapter of Galatians, Paul, speaking of the promises made to Abraham and his seed, says, "He saith not, And to seeds, as of many; but as of one, And to thy seed, which is Christ." This gives us a clue to the meaning of *seed*, in the passage under consideration. And as Christ is the spiritual head of his people, this will apply not only to Christ and Satan, but also to their spiritual seed; the wicked being accounted, as our Saviour informs us, the children of the devil, and believers in Christ, the children of God, by virtue of their union with him. Now it is a well known fact, that there has always been enmity between the spiritual seed of the serpent, and the spiritual seed of the woman. The seed of the serpent have always hated and persecuted the seed of the woman. This persecution began with Cain, and has continued ever since. But in this contest, the seed of the woman, through their Divine Head, have always been triumphant; though for a time the children of the evil One have prevailed. When the good seed were in danger of being swallowed up by the violence of the old world, their Divine Head swept off their enemies from the face of the earth, by a flood of waters. So, also, the seed of the woman bruised the serpent's head, in the overthrow of Sodom, as a signal display of his care over the church, to overawe the wicked inhabitants of the land, lest his people in their feebleness should be cut off. Again, he bruised the head of the serpent in the deliverance of his people from the land of Egypt; and likewise in all the signal deliverances which he wrought for them, when their enemies were ready to swallow them up. But this was done most triumphantly, when Christ came into the world to destroy the works of the devil, and triumphed over them on the cross, and in the resurrection. The works of the devil were the introduction of sin and death into the world. Christ has destroyed these works, by atoning for sin, and triumphing over death. Satan bruised his heel, when he assaulted him with temptations and persecutions, and procured his crucifixion. Christ bruised his head when he cast him out of those persons into whom he had entered, thus showing his power over him ; and when he made provision for the deliverance of those whom Satan had led captive at his will. And he will do this completely, when he shall deliver his church from all her enemies, and provide them a secure abode in his kingdom of glory, secure from all the assaults of the Adversary ; while he will cast the serpent and his seed into outer darkness, to be tormented forever and ever.

There is some evidence that the spiritual meaning of this was in a measure understood by our first parents. Adam seems to express his faith in this promise, by the name which he afterwards gave to the woman. He called her *Eve*, which signifies *Life*, " because she was the mother of all living ;" or, as it may be rendered, "*the living One*," alluding to the promised seed, who was to restore that life, which was lost by transgression. Eve also seems to have manifested her faith in the promised Saviour, by the expressions which she made on the birth of Cain and Seth. There appears to be an allusion, in these expressions, to the promised seed. So that there is some ground for the opinion expressed by Pres. Edwards, that Adam and Eve were themselves the first fruits of Christ's redemption. It is true, that the intimations of a Saviour to come, at this early period, were obscure ; and they did not probably give the patriarchs a very definite idea of the way of salvation ; yet enough was revealed to enable them to exercise faith in Him that was to come. And this obscurity is just what we might naturally expect, in the beginning of a revelation that was gradually to unfold itself through successive ages.

II. The next intimation we have of a Saviour, in the form of a prediction or promise, is, in the promises made to the patriarchs, Abraham, Isaac, and Jacob. There were, however, other intimations of the same event, in the form of types ; but of these I purpose to speak separately. This was given more than two thousand years after the first; and it was a little less obscure. The promise is substantially the same, as given at different times to the patriarchs ; and it has reference not to Christ only, but to the spiritual seed, of whom Christ is the head. It is substantially expressed in these words,—" I will be a God unto thee and to thy seed ; and in thy seed shall all the families of the earth be blessed." Although the promise that he would be a God to Abraham's seed refers primarily, and in a restricted sense, to his natural seed ; yet it can have its full accomplishment only in his spiritual seed,—that is to say, all true believers, of whom, according to Paul, he is the spiritual father.* If this promise had reference only to his natural seed, there could be no sense in which it would appear that all the nations of the earth have been blessed in them. But if it is understood as referring to Christ, it is perfectly clear and plain ; for it is through him that the nations of the earth have received all their blessings ; and in the extension and universal prevalence of Christianity, this promise is yet to receive a more perfect and glorious accomplishment.

---

* Rom. iv, 11.

It is to be remarked, as we proceed, that every new promise or prediction, and every new dispensation, brings with it an increase of light. The intimation given indirectly, immediately after the fall, was obscure. This, to Abraham, is direct and plain. Yet nothing was given in detail, but it was left for Abraham's faith to rest upon this simple declaration of God. But as we proceed we shall perceive the obscurity gradually receding, and the light breaking clearer and more clearly upon our vision; until at length it beams forth in perfect day.

III. The next prediction is that of Job. It is uncertain whether Job lived before or after Abraham; but probably he was either cotemporary with Abraham, or that he lived in the next succeeding generation. He says, "I know that my Redeemer liveth, and that he shall stand at the latter day upon the earth: and though, after my skin, worms destroy this body, yet in my flesh shall I see God: whom I shall see for myself, and mine eyes shall behold, and not another." The expression, "at the latter day," evidently points forward to the personal appearance of the Saviour; and his declaration that he should see him in his flesh, seems to allude to the resurrection of his own body. This shows that the patriarchs were justified by faith in a promised Messiah.

But I shall not have space to proceed with a particular consideration of each prediction in its natural order; and must, therefore, make a classification, giving in connection the several predictions which relate to one and the same event. We will consider, then,

PROPHECIES CONCERNING CHRIST.

IV. The prophecies which were fulfilled in the birth of Christ. The prophet Isaiah has this remarkable prediction concerning the birth of a prince, of the Jewish nation, who was to set up a kingdom that should have no end. The character here given to this prince could only appertain to one who unites in himself the human and divine natures : " Unto us a child is born, unto us a son is given, and the government shall be upon his shoulder ; and his name shall be called Wonderful, Counsellor, the Mighty God, the Everlasting Father, the Prince of Peace." This description applies, with very great exactness, to Jesus of Nazareth, if we allow him to have been both divine and human ; and it applies to no other person that was ever born. Isaiah also predicts that he should also be born of a virgin, and that his name should be called Immanuel, which means *God with us.** Though there are some obscurities connected with this passage, yet it is evident that it could apply to no other person but Jesus Christ. No other person could properly be called " God with us." Moreover, it is said in the verse following, " Butter and honey shall he eat, that he may know to choose the evil from the good,"—i e. he shall be fed and nourished as other children are, till of sufficient age to discriminate between good and evil, when he shall choose the good and refuse the evil. This we find exactly fulfilled in the history of Christ ; and Matthew quotes this prophecy, as having received its accomplishment in the birth of Jesus. We find also, that he was

---

* Isa. vii, 14 ; ix, 6.

nourished in the same manner as other children; but, unlike them, when of sufficient age to discern between good and evil, he chose the good and refused the evil, while all other children choose the evil, and refuse the good. This shows that Christ was to be born without any stain of original corruption; and to this fact the apostle testifies, when he says he was made in all things like his brethren, and yet without sin. There is an allusion to this, also, in the first promise, where he is called the "seed of the woman," in distinction from the rest of mankind, showing that his birth was to be extraordinary, and out of the common course of nature.

The *place*, also, where Christ should be born, was predicted by the prophet Micah, that it should be in Bethlehem, the native town of David.* And it is remarkable how the Providence of God secured the fulfilment of this prophecy. His parents were residing in Nazareth, of Galilee. But the decree of Cæsar required that every one should go to the city of his fathers, where the records of the family were, which contained their genealogy, to be enrolled for the taxing. This illustrates the great truth, that the hand of God is in all the movements of kings, empires, and governments; and that while they think of nothing but the gratification of their own ambitious views, they are fulfilling grand designs of his Providence. So it is with sinners. God makes use of them, even while they are opposing his truth, to accomplish his will. And if they do not turn, and engage cheerfully in do-

---

* Micah v, 2.

ing his will, he will make use of them at last, to burn forever in hell, to the glory of his justice. Sinners are in God's hands ; and, willing or unwilling, he will make use of them to glorify himself.

V. The next class of predictions which I shall notice is, those that relate to the nation, tribe, and family, of whom Christ should come. When the Lord called Abraham, he intimated to him that the promised *seed* should be of his posterity ; and from among his children, Isaac, the child of promise, was selected as the progenitor of the Messiah. The promise was repeated to Isaac ; and between his two sons, the choice was made before their birth. Isaac was made, contrary to his own intention, to point out Jacob as the line of the promised seed. The promise was also renewed to Jacob at Penuel, where he saw the ladder reaching up to heaven, and repeatedly afterwards. Jacob points out Judah, among his children, as the head of the tribe of whom Christ was to come. To David, the Lord promised a perpetual throne and kingdom, which should endure forever. If this were to be understood literally, of the earthly kingdom of his family, it would not be true ; but understanding it of the Messiah, its fulfilment is now accomplishing in Jesus Christ. The prophets, Isaiah and Jeremiah, also predict the same thing ; and we find undisputed evidence, in the New Testament, that Christ came of the family of David, the tribe of Judah, the offspring of Jacob and Isaac, and the seed of Abraham, according to the promises.

VI. The *time* of Christ's coming is predicted. *Jacob* says, "The sceptre shall not depart from Judah, nor a lawgiver from between his feet, until Shiloh come."* *Sceptre* is here used as the emblem of authority. It is interpreted likewise here, as referring to the distinct tribeship. By the history of the Israelites, it will appear that the tribe of Judah very soon attained to pre-eminence over the rest of the tribes, having the kingly authority and superiority of numbers; till at length, after the captivity, the remnants of the other tribes became absorbed in the tribe of Judah, being called Jews, from the head of their tribe. And they continued to maintain their tribeship and government, under the posterity of Judah, till the coming of Jesus Christ. But the enrolment for taxing, under the Roman government, commenced at the birth of Christ. This taxing was a sign of subjection, as a Roman province; and a few years after, Herod, the last king of the Jews, (himself an Edomite) died, and Judea was parcelled out into several provinces, under Roman governors; and in a few years after the completion of Christ's ministry, the Jews were completely broken up, and dispersed to the four quarters of the earth, so that no tribeship, government, or authority remained.

There is a prophecy, also, in Haggai, which fixes the coming of Christ during the existence of the second temple,—the one erected after the destruction of Solomon's temple, and the return from captivity: "I will shake all nations, and the desire of

---

* Gen. xlix, 10.

PROPHECIES CONCERNING CHRIST. 197

all nations shall come: and I will fill this house with my glory, saith the Lord of hosts. The glory of this latter house shall be greater than of the former, saith the Lord of hosts: and in this place will I give peace, saith the Lord of hosts."* This was spoken to the Jews, with respect to the temple that was built after the return of the captivity. But this temple, according to the testimony of the same prophet, was nothing in the eyes of those who had seen its first glory; and Ezra informs us that it was so inferior, that those who had seen the first temple, and remembered its magnificence, wept when they saw this. So that this could not have been spoken literally of the temple itself. It is true, this temple was afterwards adorned and beautified by Herod the Great; yet the Shechinah, or visible glory of the Lord, which filled the temple of Solomon, never came into the second temple. So that the only explanation which can be given of this is, to refer it to the Messiah, who is called the Desire of all nations,—the great Deliverer, so long promised to the Jews, and desired by other nations, and in whom all the nations of the earth were to be blessed. In this sense, God did fill that house with his glory; and its glory was greater than the glory of the former; for Jesus Christ, who visited the second temple, was " One Greater than the temple" itself.

The coming of the Messiah is also fixed during the dominion of the Roman empire, by the Prophecy of Daniel. The image, which Nebuchadnezzar saw, represented the four universal monarchies, that of

---

* Hag. ii, 7.

Babylon, of the Medes and Persians, of the Greeks, and of the Romans. Nebuchadnezzar saw a stone cut out of the mountain without hands, which smote the image in his feet, and it was broken to pieces, and became like chaff before the wind; and the little stone became a great mountain, and filled the whole earth. Daniel, in his explanation of this dream, declares this little stone to be the kingdom of the Messiah; and as the feet which it smote represented the fourth kingdom,—the Roman empire, it agrees with the time when Jesus came.*

There is also another prophecy of Daniel, which fixes more definitely the time of Christ's coming.

---

* This prophecy has its fulfilment, in the establishment and propagation of Christianity The stone was cut out of the mountain without hands; that is, without the usual implements employed for such purposes So the kingdom of Christ arose, without any carnal weapons or instruments of power. The image which Nebuchadnezzar saw, represented the four universal monarchies, which were now existing in the last,—the feet of iron and clay, which represented the Roman empire. But Christianity smote this image in its feet. It was the gradual influence of Christianity, which undermined, and at length overturned the dominion of Pagan Rome, and finally the empire itself, which was " broken in pieces," a number of Christian states rising out of its ruins. This little stone has been extending,—it has long been a great mountain,—and it is destined finally to fill the whole earth. There are also a great number of other prophecies concerning the propagation and final and universal prevalence of Christianity, which either have been fulfilled, which are now fulfilling, or which are yet to be fulfilled, all of which furnish strong additional proof of the inspiration of the Scriptures, but their full elucidation would require a much larger space than could be given in this volume.

PROPHECIES CONCERNING CHRIST. 199

The angel Gabriel says to Daniel, " Seventy weeks are determined upon thy people and upon thy holy city, to finish the transgression, and to make an end of sins, and to make reconciliation for iniquity, and to bring in everlasting righteousness, and to seal up the vision and the prophecy, and to anoint the most holy. Know, therefore, and understand, that from the going forth of the commandment to restore and to build Jerusalem, unto Messiah the prince, shall be seven weeks, and three score and two weeks. And after threescore and two weeks shall Messiah be cut off, but not for himself: and the people of the prince that shall come, shall destroy the city and the sanctuary. And he shall confirm the covenant with many for one week, and in the midst of the week he shall cause the sacrifice and oblation to cease."

In prophetic language, each day is taken for a year. Thus God says to Ezekiel, in requiring him to lie in a certain position a certain number of days, for a sign to the people, " I have appointed thee each day for a year." It was common, also, among the Jews, to reckon weeks of years. The seventh was their Sabbatical year; and seven of these weeks of years brought them to their year of Jubilee. Daniel's seventy weeks, therefore, would be four hundred and ninety years. The only difficulty with respect to this period is, the fixing of the date of its commencement, there being four decrees for the return of the Jews. But whichever of these is adopted, the period of Christ's coming is pointed out with sufficient exactness. The following explanation of this period by

Dr. Kett, is the most satisfactory of any that I have met with :—

"The leading circumstances to be considered in examining the accomplishment of this prediction, are, the completion of the time specified, and the events connected with it. All agree that these seventy weeks are weeks of years, that is, every day in the week is reckoned as a year, which makes the whole number amount to four hundred and ninety years. This computation is not unexampled in profane authors, and is used elsewhere in Scripture. It is used in reckoning the years of the Jubilee,*—the time of sojourning in the wilderness,† and in the prophecy of Ezekiel.‡ These seventy weeks commence in the Jewish month Nisan, or March, in the seventh year of the reign of Artaxerxes Longimanus, King of Persia, in the year of the world 3547, as is clearly shown by many accurate chronologists, and proved at large by the learned Prideaux, in his Connexion of the History of the Old and New Testament with Profane History. This was the distinguished year and month in which Ezra, the leader of the Jews, obtained a commission for his return to Jerusalem, in order to restore the government of that city and the service of the temple. And the seventy weeks were completed in the month Nisan, in the year of the world 4037. This was the ever memorable year and month when Jesus Christ, the Messiah, closed his Divine mission, and suffered death upon the cross.

---

* Lev. xxv, 8. † Numb. xiv, 34. ‡ Ezek. iv, 5, 6.

" It is evident that various events are predicted by Daniel, in this remarkable prophecy. *The Messiah shall be cut off,—the people of the Prince shall come, shall destroy the city and the sanctuary,—desolations are determined, and the sacrifice and the oblation shall cease for the overspreading of abominations.*

" Now there are no occurrences in the Jewish history, to which these circumstances can be at all applied, except to the crucifixion of Christ,—the final destruction of the city and temple of Jerusalem, and the desolation of Judea by the Romans. But to those great events the words of the prophecy apply with such singular exactness, that they give a very energetic and lively description of them. And it may be farther observed, that this prophecy very plainly delineates the spiritual purposes of the gospel; for at the completion of this great epoch of the seventy weeks, it is determined *to make reconciliation for iniquity,—to bring in everlasting righteousness, and to seal up the vision and the prophecy,*—thus pointing out Christ, the Messiah, who died as the propitiatory sacrifice for the sins of the world,—rose again to certify that he had made atonement for sin, and established the promised 'kingdom of everlasting righteousness and life,'—and *sealed up the vision and the prophecy* by his final revelation of the Divine will to his beloved disciple St. John, the *last* of the prophets.

" Three different periods of time are included within the seventy weeks, and each of them is connected with an important event. The *seven weeks* to restore and rebuild Jerusalem,—the *three score and two weeks*, in addition to these seven weeks, after which the Messiah was to be cut off:—and *the midst of the week*, in which he should cause the sacrifice and oblation to cease. The first series of seven weeks, being forty-nine years, relates to the restoration of the Jews, and the rebuilding Jerusalem, begun by Ezra, and completed by Nehemiah. The opposition which the Jews, when returned from captivity, met with from the Samaritans, prolonged the sacred work exactly for that period of time; and the obstacles with which they had to contend, fully confirmed the words of the prophet, that *the wall should be built in troublous times*. The threescore and two weeks that succeeded, added to the foregoing seven, or in other words, four hundred and eighty-three years, bring the calculation of time down to the year 4739 of the Julian period, which was the exact year in which the gospel began to be announced to the world,—John the Baptist having been sent to prepare the Jews for its reception by his public ministry, which continued for the space of three years and a half. Its commencement at this period is accurately marked by the words of Christ, who said expressly, 'the law and the prophets were until John, since that time the kingdom of God is preached.'* And our Lord himself, in the midst of the week, *caused the sacrifice and oblation to cease*; for at that time, having completed the exercise of his divine mission in exactly the space of three years and a half, he fulfilled the great object of the ceremonial law, which was the type of atonement for sin by the sacrifice of himself upon the cross.

---

* Luke xvi, 16.

"So confident were the Jews, as to the precise application of the prophecy, that this saying is still extant in the Talmud, as the tradition of very ancient times. 'In Daniel is delivered to us the end of the Messiah;'—that is, the period at which he ought to come, as Jarchi, a celebrated doctor of the law, explains it. Nehumias, likewise a learned Rabbi, who lived fifty years before the Christian era, declared, 'that the time fixed by Daniel for the Messiah could not be more than fifty years before it was accomplished.' And, indeed, it is acknowledged by the Jews themselves, that the time when Jesus appeared, the Messiah was expected; and that the period, which Daniel had fixed, expired but a short time before the city and temple were destroyed by Titus,—before the customary sacrifices were abolished,—and before the Jewish government was overthrown.

"It is a very striking fact, in proof of the general belief of the Jewish nation respecting the time of the Messiah's appearance, that from the death of Herod the Great, when Judas of Galilee and Simon first assumed the title of kings and deliverers of the Jews, to the destruction of the temple, the Jewish history is filled with the names and actions of false Christs and false prophets, who deceived both the Jews and the Samaritans. None appeared *before* this period, and not more than one for five or six centuries *after* it.

"According as the reader shall reject or admit the hypothesis concerning the religion of the eastern nations, which many learned authors have labored to establish, he will suppose the general expectation which prevailed among the heathen nations to owe its origin to the dispersion of Daniel's prophecy by the Jews, or he will trace it to the patriarchal ages. The universality of this expectation would alone render it highly probable that the knowledge of prophecy confirmed and corrected tradition, rather than produced it. But if it be granted, and I see not how it can be denied, that the hope of a Redeemer was given in the very earliest times, and continued to exist throughout the world, though obscured and deformed by allegory and idolatry, probability rises almost into certainty."

With these facts before us, who will say that Daniel's seventy weeks failed to designate the time of Christ's coming?

VII. The next prediction which I shall notice is that of Moses, to the children of Israel :* "I will raise them up a prophet, from among their brethren, like unto thee." Stephen, in his address before the Sanhedrim,† applies this prophecy to Christ ; and it is manifest that there has never any other person to whom it would apply. God spake to Moses face to face ; but never to any other prophet, till Christ came, to whom he spake in an audible voice ; and who declared himself, that the Father showed him all things that He himself did.

VIII. The prophecies concerning the Spirit of God resting on the Messiah, were accomplished in Jesus Christ. The Psalmist, speaking of Christ, says, "God, thy God, hath anointed thee with the

---

* Deut. xviii, 15.   † Acts vii, 37.

oil of gladness, above thy fellows."* All other kings and priests were anointed with consecrated oil or perfume. But the Messiah was to be anointed with an oil above this ; and what could this be, unless it were spiritual ? Hence we find on the day of Christ's baptism, when he was initiated into his ministry, the Holy Ghost rested upon him, in the symbol of a dove ; which was an anointing infinitely above that of any other king or priest. The prophet Isaiah says, " There shall come forth a rod out of the stem of Jesse, and a branch shall grow out of his roots : and the Spirit of the Lord shall rest upon him, the spirit of wisdom and understanding, the spirit of counsel and might, the spirit of knowledge and of the fear of the Lord : and shall make him of quick understanding, in the fear of the Lord : and he shall not judge after the sight of his eyes."* This corresponds exactly with the accounts given of Jesus. John says, " God giveth not his Spirit by measure unto him ;" and if not by measure, it must be infinite in degree, which could not be said of any but an Infinite Being. It appears, also, from the accounts given of Jesus by the evangelists, that he was endowed with the spirit of wisdom and understanding above men, so that he was able to confound the most subtle of the Jewish doctors He was possessed, also, in an eminent degree, of the spirit of piety, which is what is meant by " the fear of the Lord." The character of Jesus Christ for *piety* is not sufficiently thought of. Besides those seasons of protracted communion with God, which he had in

---

* Ps. xlv, 7 ; Is. xi, 1–3.

solitary places, in the mountains and in the desert, he was habitually devout, to such a degree, that every word that he spake seemed to come burning from the throne of God. We also find him often engaged in prayer with his disciples; and this is spoken of in such a manner as to show that the practice was habitual. In one place, it is said, "it came to pass, as he was alone praying;" again it is said, "it came to pass as he was praying in a certain place." The incidental manner in which this is alluded to, in the narrative of other events, shows that it was his customary and common practice to pray with his disciples. We also find him in the act of prayer, in all the most eventful periods of his life. Thus he was praying when the Holy Ghost fell on him, at the time of his baptism. It was while engaged in prayer that the fashion of his countenance was changed, and he was transfigured on the holy mount. And it was while he was engaged in prayer that he sweat great drops of blood, falling down to the ground, for the ransom of his people. Nor was his piety less conspicuous in his general spirit than in his habits of devotion. His was a self-sacrificing spirit. His will was identified with the will of God. He had no will of his own, separate from the will of the Father. It was his meat and and drink to do the will of God. His compassion for sinners, also, was unbounded. His care for souls was most intense. He wept over sinners. Yea, he laid down his life for them. Such was the spirit of piety and habitual devotion, that a holy atmosphere surrounded him, which filled even his opposers with awe. And, according to the prophecy, he did not judge after the sight of his eyes ; for he discerned even the secret thoughts of men.

IX. The *works* of Jesus correspond with the predictions concerning the Messiah. Isaiah, speaking of the coming of the Messiah, says, " The eyes of the blind shall be opened, the ears of the deaf shall be unstopped : the lame man shall leap as an hart, and the tongue of the dumb shall sing."* Matthew, in describing the miracles of Jesus, says, " Great multitudes came unto him, having with them those that were lame, blind, dumb, maimed, and many others, and he healed them."

X. The *ministry* of Jesus corresponds with the predictions concerning the Messiah. The Psalmist, speaking in the name of Christ says, " I have preached righteousness in the great congregation : lo, I have not refrained my lips, O Lord, thou knowest "† Jesus preached righteousness in the great congregation, both in the temple, in the synagogues, and in the open air ; and let who would be present, rulers, priests, scribes, or Pharisees, he refrained not his lips. In Isaiah it is written, " The Spirit of the Lord God is upon me ; because the Lord hath anointed me to preach good tidings to the meek : he hath sent me to bind up the broken hearted, to proclaim liberty to the captives, and the opening of the prison to them that are bound ; to proclaim the acceptable year of the Lord ; to comfort all that mourn ; to appoint unto

---

* Is. xxxv, 5, 6.   † Ps. xl, 9.

them that mourn in Zion, the oil of joy for mourning, and the garment of praise for the spirit of heaviness."*
Jesus applied this prophecy to himself, in the synagogue of Nazareth, his native place; and it corresponds exactly both with the character of his own preaching, and the gospel which he left for his ministers to preach. The prophet says, "The Lord hath anointed me to preach good tidings to the meek." Jesus says, "Blessed are the meek, for they shall inherit the earth." Isaiah says, "He hath sent me to bind up the broken hearted." Jesus said to the broken-hearted sinner, who came to him, "Go in peace,—thy faith hath saved thee." Isaiah mentions, as one object of his coming, to "proclaim liberty to the captives, and the opening of the prison to them that are bound." He proclaimed liberty to the captives of Satan, and loosed them that were bound by him, while on earth; and he still proclaims in the gospel liberty to the captives of Satan, and looses those that are bound by the chains of sin. The prophet says he should come, "to proclaim the acceptable year of the Lord, and the day of vengeance of our God." The gospel of Jesus Christ proclaims that "Now is the accepted time, and now is the day of salvation." It also proclaims a day of vengeance,—when the vengeance of God will be executed with ten fold fury upon the rejecters of the gospel. The prophecy says, "To comfort all that mourn; to appoint unto them that mourn in Zion, to give unto them beauty for ashes, the oil of joy for mourning, the gar-

---

* Isa. lxi, 1.

ment of praise for the spirit of heaviness." Christ says, " Blessed are they that mourn, for they shall be comforted." And many now living can testify that he has given them beauty for ashes, the oil of joy for mourning, and the garment of praise for the spirit of heaviness.

XI. The conduct of Jesus, in regard to the applause of men, accords with the prediction of Isaiah, who says, " He shall not cry, nor lift up, nor cause his voice to be heard in the street."* Leaders in any exploit, in the East, or men who wish to raise a clamor or get up a party, bawl aloud to their companions as they go along the street. This appears to be what the prophet alludes to. But it was not so with Jesus. He never sought, but avoided the applause of men. How frequently did he charge those who had been healed by him to tell it to no man; evidently to prevent drawing after him a multitude, and collecting a party. When he discovered to his disciples, also, his true character as the Messiah; knowing the expectation of the Jews, that their Messiah would be a temporal deliverer, he charged them not to make it known, lest a party should be raised, to elevate him to the throne; and when such a party was raised, with the determination to take him by force, and make him a king, he departed into a desert place, to avoid them. So true it was, that he did not cry, nor lift up, nor cause his voice to be heard in the street.

---

* Isa. xlii, 2.

XII. The character of Christ, *as a sufferer*, corresponds with the predictions concerning him. Isaiah says, " His visage was so marred more than any man, and his form more than the sons of men."* " He is despised and rejected of men, a man of sorrows, and acquainted with grief : and we hid as it were our faces from him ; he was despised, and we esteemed him not." This agrees exactly with the accounts given of his sufferings, during the whole of his life. His early life was spent in poverty and hard labor. He suffered, in the commencement of his ministry, from the severest conflicts with the Tempter. And we may judge something of the sufferings of his holy soul from this source, by the pain experienced oftentimes by the sincere Christian, from the horrible suggestions of the Adversary. But this pain arises from the small degree of holiness possessed by the believer,—these wicked thoughts being so opposed to the new principle implanted in him by Divine grace. What, then, must have been the feelings of the holy Jesus, upon whose soul no spot of sin ever rested, to be enticed to tempt God, and to fall down and worship Satan, and accept of his usurped dominion over the earth ? He suffered, also, from fatigue, and hunger, and poverty, during his ministry. He performed his journeys through all the cities and villages, and through the desert countries on foot. Often he was hungry and weary ; yet at night he had not where to lay his head,— no place that he could call his home. Even the foxes and the birds of the air were better provided for than

---

* Isa. lii, 14 ; liii, 3.

the Lord of life and glory. He suffered, likewise, from grief. Jesus was a perfect *man*, as well as a divine person. The sensibilities of human nature must, therefore, have been with him most acute. He must have been tenderly alive to all those things which excite the tender and sympathetic emotions; and when these were wounded, his grief must have been most intense. What, then, must have been his feelings, when he looked abroad over suffering humanity; when he beheld all the ruins which sin has made in this fair and beautiful world; when he saw so many souls perishing; but especially, when all his efforts to save lost men, were looked upon with cold disdain, his motives traduced, his conduct viewed with suspicion, all his movements watched with an evil eye, his doctrines and works misrepresented, and he himself reviled, traduced, vilified, and persecuted, by the very beings he came to save? We have incidental allusions to his feelings in these circumstances. He was often moved with pity for the sufferings of the sick and infirm. His compassion was tenderly touched, when he saw the widow of Nain following her only son to the grave. He wept over the grave of his friend Lazarus. He was grieved, when he saw the hardness of men's hearts, on proclaiming to them the word of life. And we have reason to believe that "his visage was so marred" by these sufferings, as to produce the appearance of premature age; for when he spoke of Abraham's having seen his day, the Jews replied, "Thou art not yet fifty years old, and hast thou seen Abraham?" showing that they took him to be approaching the age of fifty years; whereas, he was but a little more than thirty. But all this was nothing, in comparison with the untold agonies which he suffered in the garden and on the cross ; when his soul was exceeding sorrowful, even unto death ; when he sweat great drops of blood, falling down to the ground ; when he cried out, " My God ! My God ! why hast thou forsaken me !" while breathing out his life, under the infinite weight of our sins, which were laid upon him. Surely he was a man of sorrows and acquainted with grief.

XIII. The character of Christ's enemies corresponds with that given them in prophecy. David says, " Why do the heathen rage, and the people imagine a vain thing ? The kings of the earth set themselves, and the rulers take counsel together, against the Lord, and against his anointed ?"* The apostles, in their prayer, in the fourth chapter of Acts, apply this to Jesus ; and the application is complete. Here is the rage of the heathen, in the cruel treatment, the contumely and abuse heaped upon him by the Roman soldiery. The people imagined a vain thing, when they thought to put an end to him and his work, by persuading the Roman government to crucify him. The kings of the earth,—Herod and Pontius Pilate, set themselves, and the rulers of the Jews took counsel against him.

XIV. The treatment which Jesus received from the people, corresponds exactly with the prophecies.

---

* Ps. ii, 1, 2.

David says, prophetically, speaking in the name of Christ, "I am a reproach of men, and despised of the people."* Isaiah says of the Messiah, "He is despised and rejected of men." When Jesus came into his own country, to preach the gospel, the people said, "Whence hath this man this wisdom, and these mighty works? Is not this the *carpenter's* son? Is not his mother called *Mary*? And his brethren James, and Joses, and Simon, and Judas? And his sisters, are they not all with us? Whence, then, hath this man all these things. And they were offended in him." According to the prophecy of David, they despised him, and reproached him with the meanness of his birth, and with his former occupation. The Scribes also reproached him, calling him a blasphemer; and others accused him of being intemperate, because he, in compassion, and for the purpose of doing them good, associated with publicans and sinners. He was hated, persecuted, and rejected, by his own people, whom he came to save. "He came unto his own, and his own received him not."

XV. The trial and condemnation of Jesus also accord with the predictions concerning the same. Isaiah says, "He was taken from prison and from judgment."† That is, he was not placed in custody, and allowed a reasonable time to prepare for trial, as was usual with those who were accused; but he was arrested, and immediately put upon his trial. And he was taken from just judgment, by being deprived

---

* Ps. xxii, and Isa. liii. † Isa. liii.

of a fair trial, false witnesses being allowed to testify against him ; and yet, when the judge pronounced him innocent, he was taken from this judgment, and delivered over to be crucified.

XVI. There is a very exact and striking agreement between the prediction and the event in regard to the manner in which Jesus was delivered up to his enemies. The prophet Zechariah, in a symbolical action, typifying Christ, said to the people, " If ye think good, give me my price ; and if not, forbear. So they weighed for my price thirty pieces of silver. And the Lord said unto me, cast it unto the potter : a goodly price that I was prized at of them. And I took the thirty pieces of silver, and cast them to the potter in the house of the Lord."* The manner in which this price is here spoken of, shows that it was regarded as an expression of contempt; and so the chief priests doubtless regarded it, for it was the price of a slave. The manner in which it was thrown back upon them, and given to the potter, agrees exactly with the event; for Judas went into the temple and cast down the thirty pieces of silver ; and the chief priests gave them for the potter's field. It was also predicted concerning Judas, that his days should be few, and another should take his office. Like Ahithophel, the traitorous counsellor of David, who appears to have been a type of Judas, he went and hanged himself ; and another person was appointed to take his office.

---

* Zech. xi, 12, 13.

XVII. The conduct of Christ's disciples, on the occasion of his being taken, was predicted by the prophet Zechariah : " Awake, O sword, against my shepherd, and against the man that is my fellow, saith the Lord of hosts : smite the shepherd, and the sheep shall be scattered."* Jesus, in the night on which he was betrayed, applied this prophecy to himself, and predicted its fulfilment : " All ye," said he to his disciples, " shall be offended because of me this night : for it is written, I will smite the shepherd, and the sheep of the flock shall be scattered abroad." And Mark records that, when Jesus was arrested, all his disciples forsook him and fled.

XVIII. Christ's conduct before Pilate was also predicted : Isaiah† says, " He was oppressed, and he was afflicted ; yet he opened not his mouth : he is brought as a lamb to the slaughter, and as a sheep before her shearers is dumb, so he opened not his mouth." When Jesus was accused by the chief priests and elders, before Pilate, he answered nothing. And when Pilate inquired of him, " Hearest thou not how many things they witness against thee ?" he made no answer. When he was brought before Herod, also, and questioned in many words, he answered him nothing.

XIX. The treatment of Christ on his trial and on the cross, was also predicted. The prophet Isaiah, speaking in the name of the Messiah, says, " I gave

---

* Zech. xiii, 7. † Isa. liii.

my back to the smiters, and my cheeks to them that plucked off the hair. I hid not my face from shame and spitting."* The prophet Micah says, "they shall smite the Judge of Israel with a rod upon his cheek."† David, speaking in the name of Christ, says, " All they that see me laugh me to scorn : they shoot out the lip, they shake the head, saying, He trusted on the Lord that he would deliver him, seeing he delighted in him."‡ And again, " They gave me gall for my meat ; and in my thirst they gave me vinegar to drink." All these were fulfilled most literally, and with surprising exactness, by the enemies of Jesus themselves. Matthew records, " Then did they spit in his face, and buffeted him ; and others smote him with the palms of their hands " The same evangelist records, also, that Jesus was scourged,—he gave his back to the smiters. They that passed by reviled him, wagging their heads. And the chief priests and elders mocked him, using the very words of the prophecy, saying, " He saved others, himself he cannot save. He trusted in God, let him deliver him now, if he will have him." Matthew records that they gave him vinegar to drink, mingled with gall ; and John, that when he cried out with thirst, they gave him vinegar to drink ; thus fulfilling the prediction of the Psalmist, " They gave gall for my meat ; and in my thirst, they gave me vinegar to drink." There is also an exact correspondence between the language of David, in the beginning of the twenty-second Psalm, spoken prophetically in the

---

* Isa. l, 6.   † Mi. v, 1.   ‡ Ps. xxii, 7 ; lxix, 21.

name of Christ, and that of Jesus on the cross, "My God! My God! Why hast thou forsaken me!" The death of the Messiah is also directly predicted by Isaiah and Daniel,—"he was cut off out of the land of the living,"—He poured out his soul unto death," —"Messiah shall be cut off." The piercing of his hands and feet was predicted by David, in the twenty-second Psalm,—also, the parting of his garments among his murderers, and casting lots for his vesture. Zechariah also speaks of his being pierced. The circumstances of his death and burial are likewise predicted by Isaiah. His crucifixion between the two thieves was a fulfilment of the prophecy of Isaiah, that he should be numbered with the transgressors. The prophet says, also, that " He made his grave with the wicked, and with the rich in his death; because he had done no violence, neither was any deceit in his mouth." It was customary for malefactors, not only to have an ignominious death, but also an ignominious burial; and this was, doubtless, the design of his enemies, when they secured his crucifixion between two malefactors; but " because he had done no violence," —because Pilate knew that he was innocent, he gave up his body to Joseph, that he might have an honorable burial; so that he was " with the rich in his death."

XX. The resurrection and ascension of Christ were also predicted. David, as the type of Christ, says, " Thou wilt not leave my soul in hell, (i. e. the grave), neither wilt thou suffer thine holy One to see corruption." This prediction is applied to this event, by the Apostle Peter, in his address on the day of Pentecost. And we learn from the answer of Martha to Christ, in regard to Lazarus, that it was the prevailing opinion among the Jews, that corruption took place with the dead before the fourth day ; so that if he saw no corruption, he must arise from the dead before that day. That he did rise on the third day, according to his own prediction, will appear clear from an examination of the accounts given by the evangelists. He was crucified the day before their Sabbath, which was our Friday ; and he arose from the dead on the morning of the first day of the week, which was the third day ; and reckoning the part of Friday and part of Monday as whole days, according to the custom of the Jews, we have three days that he was in the grave. His ascension was also foretold by David : " Thou hast ascended on high, thou hast led captivity captive." It was on the event of his resurrection, that Jesus rested the proof of his Messiahship. When the Jews required of him a sign, he replied, " destroy this temple," speaking of his own body, " and in three days I will raise it up." And on another occasion, he told them that there should no sign be given them but that of the prophet Jonah,— that as he was three days in the whale's belly, so the Son of man should be three days in the heart of the earth. And in a more open and explicit manner, he declared the same thing to his disciples. No impostor would have rested his claims on a foundation so certain of being overturned at his death. This proves the sincerity of Jesus ; and the event of his resurrection proves that, whatever his claims had been, they were just and true.

XXI. There remains but one class of predictions more to be noticed; and to this class I would call the special attention of all who are desirous of knowing the way of salvation. It is a matter of deep personal interest to you all. It is, as to the *object of Christ's death* And, in regard to this, there is a most exact agreement between prophets and apostles, and Jesus himself. Isaiah says, " Surely he hath borne our griefs, and carried our sorrows ; he was wounded for our transgressions, he was bruised for our iniquities : the chastisement of our peace was upon him, and with his stripes we are healed. All we like sheep have gone astray ; and the Lord hath laid on him the iniquity of us all. For the transgression of my people was he stricken. . . . Thou shalt make his soul an offering for sin. . . . He bare the sin of many." This is the prediction of Isaiah. With this agree the words of Jesus, "I lay down my life for the sheep ;" and of Peter, " His own self bare our sins, in his own body on the tree,"—" Christ hath suffered for sins, the just for the unjust, that he might bring us to God." Could any language be more explicit ? It would be impossible for us to use any language more expressive of the idea of one person standing in the place of another, and answering, by his own suffering, the just deserts of a guilty person. This is the great idea of atonement. Christ bore our griefs and carried our sorrows,—the griefs and sorrows which are the just reward of sin,—during the whole period of his humiliation. He was wounded for our transgressions, bruised for our iniquities, chastised for our breach of the peace of God's government, received stripes for our healing, and his soul was made an offering for our sin, when he was cruelly beaten and lacerated with thorns, and when he hung expiring on the cross.

PRACTICAL REMARKS.

1. The fulfilment of these prophecies, in the person of Jesus Christ, proves the Divine inspiration, both of the Old and New Testaments. It proves that of the Old, directly, in respect to those parts which contain these prophecies, and the whole, by the testimony of Christ, whose character, as the true Messiah, is established by their fulfilment This testimony I have repeatedly alluded to. It is contained in the text at the head of this chapter. And it is impossible to separate the fact that Jesus Christ is the true Messiah, the Saviour of the world, from that of the inspiration of the whole New Testament. They are identified; and the one must stand or fall with the other. The fulfilment of these prophecies, therefore, establishes the divine origin and authority of the Christian religion.

2. The predictions to which I have alluded, with the history accompanying them, show that the great design of the Bible is to reveal Christ, as the Saviour of the world. All the prophecies, promises, and types centre in him; and he is the *end* or *accomplish-*

ment of the Old Testament dispensation. But if, as some maintain, he was a mere teacher of religion, like any other prophet, apostle, or philosopher, he would be unworthy of such a place as he occupies in the revelation which God has made of himself. Whoever, therefore, rejects Christ, in his character of the Redeemer and Saviour of men, rejects the whole Bible, and the way of salvation therein revealed.

3. The whole gospel, as understood by evangelical Christians, is revealed in the prophecy of Daniel, which has been quoted. The objects of the seventy weeks, which the angel informed him were determined upon his people, were, first, to " finish the transgression, and to make an end of sins." These two expressions mean the same. It is a repetition, in a different form, of the same idea, after the manner of the Hebrew poets. It means the same as the declaration of the apostle, that Christ is the end of the law for righteousness, to every one that believeth; and the righteousness of the law is fulfilled in us, who walk not after the flesh, but after the spirit. Christ has finished the transgression and made an end of sin, to his people, in two respects,—he has destroyed its power to kill the soul, by removing the curse of the law, which is the strength of sin, having bared his own bosom to the curse, and received it in our stead. He has also made an end of sin, by breaking its power in the hearts of believers, and securing their ultimate, complete, and entire deliverance from it.

The second object specified in this prophecy is, to *make reconciliation* FOR *iniquity*. Here is the true idea of atonement. Those who reject the orthodox view of the atonement, maintain that Christ came, not to remove any difficulty in the way of God being reconciled to man, but to reconcile man to God. But the prophet says it is to *make reconciliation* FOR *iniquity*. And how has Christ made reconciliation *for* iniquity, if not by suffering in the place of the sinner? Hence Daniel says, " Messiah shall be *cut off*, but *not for himself;*" and if not for himself, for whom was it, but for the sins of his people, whom he has taken upon himself to save?

But another object was, to *bring in everlasting righteousness*. And Christ has brought in everlasting righteousness, by providing an everlasting righteousness for his people, and securing the righteousness and integrity of God's government, while he pardons sinners. In Christ, righteousness and peace have kissed each other. He has prepared the way for rendering those who believe in him righteous in the sight of God. He has completely and entirely fulfilled the law of God, as our surety, in our place, and thus wrought out for us a robe of righteousness, clean and white; and as our surety, also, he has borne the curse of the law for us, atoned for our sins, and completely justified us from their guilt. He has, also, made provision for cleansing us from the pollution of sin, so that we may have not only a judicial righteousness, to shield us from punishment, but a personal righteousness, to make us objects of complacency to Him, who is of " purer eyes than to behold iniquity."

Is not here a complete and perfect salvation? Is not this worthy of being revealed to patriarchs, kings, and prophets, for a succession of ages? Is it not a scheme which angels may well desire to look into ? No wonder that the hearts of the two disciples of Jesus burned within them, as they walked with him, on the way to Emmaus, while, beginning at Moses, and all the prophets, he expounded unto them the Scriptures concerning himself; showing that his sufferings and death were but fulfilling the Scriptures; and shall not our hearts burn within us, while we examine the same Scriptures? Will not the heart of every Christian wax warm, as he looks into these things, and discovers what his salvation has cost? And will not my readers leave all attempts at legal justification, and come and avail themselves fully of the everlasting righteousness which Christ has brought in?

4. This subject shows the amazing stupidity and guilt of those who live in the neglect of the gospel. The developement of this scheme to save lost men, was thought worthy of God to be made the subject of a revelation from heaven, continued at intervals, through a period of four thousand years. It occupied the attention of patriarchs, kings, prophets, and ministering spirits. It was the dread of Satan, who inspired his legions to oppose it. It is the object of wonder and adoring holy curiosity to the angels in heaven. And shall careless sinners be the only beings in the universe to be insensible to it? Ought they not rather to feel, of all others, the most deep and intense interest in it? You, who are placed here on a brief and uncertain probation,—who know that you must soon approach into the immediate presence of your Maker, to give up your account for transgressions without number; for sins immense, and for iniquities

infinite,—have you no interest in him, who has finished the transgression, made an end of sin, brought in everlasting righteousness, and made reconciliation for iniquity? Eternal love has been employed since the foundation of the world, in planning and executing this glorious scheme of redemption; and yet you do not feel interest enough in it to inquire whether it may be rendered available for the salvation of your own soul. O what amazing guilt, to despise such infinite love! Do you not, for your very indifference, deserve to be left to perish without the benefits of the salvation which you neglect and despise?

5. There is no salvation provided for those who reject Christ. The incorrigibly impenitent will not be cast off because the provisions of the gospel are not sufficient to save them, but because they will not avail themselves of those provisions. If you reject him, there remaineth no more sacrifice for sin,—there is no other provision made, and you must perish, and justly perish. If you go down to hell, after having received such offers of mercy as these, there is not a being in the universe that will pity you, or extend to you the least degree of sympathy. Even the devils may reproach you for rejecting offers which were never made to them.

6. The kingdom of Christ will triumph over all opposition. The little stone that was cut out of the mountain without hands, has already become a great mountain. It is destined to extend and fill the whole earth. Blessed are they whose feet rest firmly on this stone, as a sure foundation. But wo unto him that stands in the way of its progress; for "whosoever

shall fall on this stone shall be broken : but on whomsoever it shall fall, it will grind him to powder."

7. We learn from what has been said respecting the piety of Jesus, the standard of piety that is set before his people. The apostle Peter says he has left us an example, that we should follow in his steps ; and John says, " He that saith he abideth in him, ought himself also to walk, even as he walked." Now let us consider this, and see what it requires of us. In the first place, we must have the same general object in view which he had. And what was this ? He says it was his meat and drink to do the will of his Father. His will was absorbed in the Divine will. And when we speak of this, we mean his will *as a man* ; for he was a perfect man as well as perfect God ; and he had a perfect will ; but that will was in a state of perfect acquiescence in the will of God. To do the will of God was the highest purpose of his soul. And to imitate his example in this respect, is the very first principle of true piety. And how was this acted out ? In the first place, it was acted out in a zeal for the glory of God. His prayer, in the hour that he was troubled in spirit, was, " Father, glorify thy name." And the first petition in his last prayer with his disciples was, " Father,—glorify thy Son, *that thy Son may also glorify thee.*" This was the great idea that engaged his great mind,—the great emotion that filled his great heart. He felt for the honor of God and his law ; and therefore he came, as man's surety, to establish the authority of God's law,—to magnify and make it honorable. Here is a point on which, I fear, we have scarcely begun to feel in unison

with the spirit of our great Pattern. Our attention is directed to the condition of the impenitent; but we have not, it appears to me, begun to feel the dishonor that is done to God, by those who live in rebellion against his government. We look around us, and see sinners slumbering over the flames of hell; and we are stirred up somewhat in sympathy for them; but have we considered the fact that they are God's enemies? And has our zeal for his glory kindled up in our hearts a burning desire that they might return to their allegiance to him? And have we considered the fact, that this is an object of infinitely greater moment than their salvation? It is of infinitely greater importance that God should be obeyed, than that sinners should be saved. The eternal damnation of the whole human race would not be, in itself, so great an evil as that God should be disobeyed in a single instance; for God's authority,—God's honor as a moral governor, is of infinitely greater value than the honor, glory, or happiness of all created beings, forasmuch as he is infinitely greater than they all. And have we duly considered the dishonor which we bring upon God, when we backslide from him? Do we feel an adequate sense of the *guilt of backsliding* from God, and giving occasion for the enemies of God to blaspheme,—such as there would be, if we properly considered the example of Christ, of caring for the honor of God, as obligatory upon us? If we properly considered this subject, I think we should be abased before God, exceedingly below what we are. But, then, the professed followers of Christ, it seems to me, have not begun to come up to his spirit in sympathy for souls.

He wept over sinners,—from mere compassion for
them But this was not all that he did for them. He
led a life of toil and suffering, and endured a painful
death to save their souls. And his example, in this
very respect, is commended to us for our imitation.
The apostle John says, " Hereby perceive we the
love of God, because he laid down his life for us :
and we ought to lay down our lives for the brethren."
That is,—we should shrink from no pain or self-denial,
even to the laying down of our lives, if need be, to
save souls. How is it, Christian reader, with you ?
Have you wept in compassion for sinners ? Have
your souls been in agony for them, before the throne
of grace, as his soul was in the garden of Gethsem-
ane ? And have you shrunk back from no effort to
save them, because of the self-denial it required ? And
have you lived out the spirit of Christ ? Have you
shown the same spirit of devotion, which led him
so often to the mountain retreats for prayer ? Have
you ever got so near to God as he habitually lived, so
that you can often say in gratitude, with him, " Father,
I thank thee that thou has heard me. And *I know
that thou hearest me always.*" Can you come to God
in that spirit of loving, childlike confidence, intimate
fellowship and nearness of communion, which breathe
through his last prayer with his disciples, recorded in
the seventeenth chapter of John ? It was the devout
spirit of Christ, which gave his words such spirit and
life. And if we would carry with us habitually the
same spirit, our words would be " sharp arrows of the
Almighty, in the hearts of the king's enemies." Even
the very expression of our countenances,—the heav

enly radiance that would beam through them, would carry conviction to the heart of the sinner, and be a stronger testimony to the truth of Christianity, than all the arguments that the most learned men have been able to produce. Moreover, we are not only to live out the spirit of Christ, as it respects his zeal for the glory of God, his compassion for sinners, and his devotional habits, but in respect to the comparative estimate of temporal and eternal things. He was so constantly in communion with invisible things,—his thoughts and feelings were so habitually upon things unseen and eternal,—and he saw so distinctly the glories of heaven and the pains of hell; and so clearly perceived the unsatisfying nature, and the comparative insignificance of temporal things, that this world had no hold upon his affections. If the world could see us living so, they would believe there was a reality in religion. And if we would allure them to seek the pearl of great price, we must show, by our general conduct and spirit, that we possess that pearl ourselves,—that we have an object of pursuit infinitely above theirs. But if they see us driving as eagerly after the world as they do themselves; as much engrossed in its cares and pursuits; and as ready to drive a hard bargain as they; how can we make them believe this? I commend to you, especially, the study of the spirit of Christ. Hold up before your minds, as a pattern, the spirit of his piety. And do not think it is too high to be imitated by us. Of course, I speak not of the *degree* of his piety, as though it were to be expected that any of his followers were to possess this spirit in the same degree that he did. But I speak of the *kind*; and the word of God expressly declares that, if we have not this spirit, *in some degree*, if we do not in some measure sympathize with him, in the objects which he pursued, in the emotions which he felt, and the spirit which he manifested, we cannot be his disciples. When we speak of the piety of Christ, we speak of him *as a man*, and whatever he did, *as a man*, fulfilling the relations of a man to his Creator, he did *for our imitation*. Let us then study the *character of his piety*, *as a character to be imitated*; and strive, as we behold the glory of God shining through it, to be changed into the same image, from glory to glory.

8. Finally. Christ is presented in the subject we have been contemplating, as an object of love. There is one view of Christ which I think we are not sufficiently accustomed to contemplate. That is, his embodying the divine image in a perfect human form. When we attempt to contemplate God as an invisible Spirit, it is difficult for us to get any realizing apprehension of his holy nature. But, then, all our ideas of human nature are formed from the acquaintance which we have had with it in its ruins. But when man was first created, he was one of the most lovely beings in the universe. He was fashioned after the image of God. He embodied that image in a human form. There are some remains of the fall, which appear beautiful and lovely The natural affections, sympathies, and sensibilities of human nature are of themselves lovely; and if sanctified and made holy, every one of them would be so lovely as to call out towards them the affections of holy beings. Now we

are to contemplate Jesus Christ as a *perfect man*. The ruins of the fall are not seen in him. All the natural sensibilities, sympathies, and affections of human nature appear in him, purified from every thing base, sensual, or selfish. Here is a man capable of disinterested love and friendship. Here is a man, keenly alive to every benevolent emotion, in whom no spot appears. When we look around upon our friends and acquaintances, we see many lovely persons; but our contemplation of their characters is always disturbed with some defect,—some dark spot,—some shade, which intrudes in the way of the outgoings of our love. But fix now your eye on that friend you love the most; and suppose all these dark shades banished,—every imperfection removed,—benevolence glowing in every feature of his countenance,—love running through all his actions,—selfishness entirely removed from his soul,—all his powers of mind perfectly developed,—all the affections of his soul pure and heavenly; and then, to this perfect man add the mysterious union of the Divine Nature, and this Being acting out his benevolent sympathy in laying down his life for his enemies, and we have the Lord Jesus Christ,—the Son of God,—" God manifest in the flesh." And can we gaze upon such a character as this, without admiration and delight?—without having our souls drawn out towards him in holy affection? And will not this affection and delight rise into rapture, when we contemplate this Being as *our* Saviour? And shall we wonder that the dying saint, catching a glimpse of such a character, should be ravished with the sight, and call out in broken accents *to others* to behold the *beauty* of Christ ?* And though yet in the flesh, can we not get so near to him as to behold his beauty, and be ravished with the sight, and " rejoice with joy unspeakable and full of glory ?"

---

* Miss Caroline Richards, a lovely youth of fifteen, who died in Roxbury, Mass., a few months ago, having maintained a credible Christian profession for five years, when her speech was nearly gone, called to her mother, and said, in broken accents, " *Beauty,—beauty,—beauty* ," and, on being interrogated as to what she saw so beautiful, replied, " CHRIST."

CHAPTER VI.

Fourth Pillar, continued.—*Types of the Old Testament.*

Romans xv, 4.

"Whatsoever things were written aforetime were written for our learning, that we, through patience and comfort of the Scriptures, might have hope."

Some are disposed to undervalue the Old Testament. They say Christ came to introduce a *new* law or *new* covenant; and that therefore he has abrogated the *old*. But Christ teaches no such thing. On the contrary, he says he came not to destroy the law or the prophets, but to fulfil; and that not one jot or one tittle shall pass from the law, till all be fulfilled. The only part of the Old Testament which is done away in Christ, is the ceremonial observances, which have their accomplishment in him. The substance having come, we have no longer any need of the shadow. Yet the record of these shadows, according to the declaration of the apostle in the text, was written for our instruction; and if it was written for our instruction, it is our duty to study it, that we may understand what is the voice of God, which speaks to us through these representations of things fulfilled in Christ. It is easy for the spiritual mind to perceive why God has given us a record of the manner in which Christ and his gospel were represented to the ancient saints. These representations furnish most striking illustrations of the object of Christ's work, and of the nature of the plan of salvation revealed in the gospel. It is with this view that I enter upon the consideration of the Types of the Old Testament dispensation. And if those who are desirous of knowing the way of salvation, will give diligent heed to the instruction contained in these types, they will see the glory of Christ's gospel, and its perfect adaptedness to their wants.

A *Type* is a representation of some person, thing, or event, (which, at the time it is given, is yet to come,) by some other person, thing, or event, which bears a resemblance to it. But in order to constitute a *type*, it is not only necessary that there should be in it a resemblance to the thing typified, but that it should have been *designed* to represent it. The old writers, by overlooking this, may have given way to some fanciful interpretations; yet it appears to me that modern commentators have gone to a contrary extreme, in maintaining that nothing is to be considered as typical, except where there is an express declaration of its typical character in Scripture. Where such declarations occur they are incidental, and with no special design to teach this particular thing; and how do we know that there may not be many other types, to which no such incidental allusion has been made,—are we to suppose that God has given instruction in the form of types, which he never intended should be available to his people in any age? Moreover, these allusions are mostly in the New Testament; and are we to suppose that all the instruction given in these types was designedly sealed up from the very persons to whom they were of old especially given? Many of these allusions, also, are explained by modern commentators as mere illustrations or accommodations. But I cannot forbear the remark, in this place, that if some of the old writers fell into a *fanciful* mode of interpreting the Scriptures, some of our modern expositors have fallen into a *Germanizing* mode, certainly no less disastrous to the cause of truth. They use an infidel's pruning-hook upon the tree of life. It need not be a matter of wonder, then, if they should cut off some of its branches, on whose luscious fruits the saints of old used to regale themselves with fond delight. I have, however, confined myself chiefly, in the following pages, to those types, the typical character of which is taught in Scripture. I have not attempted to consider *all* the types, but only a specimen of such as are most easily understood, and most strikingly illustrative of the way of salvation. It therefore seemed to suit my purpose better to make the selection chiefly from those concerning the typical character of which there is no dispute. My object is three-fold:—(1.) To awaken attention to this most interesting branch of divine revelation, by presenting a specimen of the instruction to be obtained from it; (2.) To illustrate the way of salvation, and show the agreement between the Messiah revealed in the New

Testament, with the *typical*, as well as *prophetic* representations concerning him, in the Old; and (4.) To show, in the fulfilment of these types, the inspiration of the Scriptures; on which I shall remark more in full at the close. In the comparison of a *type* with its *antitype*, or the object represented by it, it is important to bear in mind that a type always falls short of its antitype. This must always be the case, when an infinite object is represented; because it must be shadowed forth by finite things.

With these preliminary remarks, I proceed to consider some of the types of the Old Testament, by which the way of salvation was shadowed forth to the ancient saints:—

I. The first type of Christ was the *first man*, Adam. That Adam was a type of Christ, we learn from the declaration of Paul, in the fifth chapter of Romans; where he calls him the "figure of him that was to come." The typical resemblances between Adam and Christ are three.

1. *Dominion.* Adam was created with dominion over all things in this world. All things on earth were put under him. He was made a little lower than the angels, yet crowned with glory and honor above all the creatures upon earth. So Christ, in his incarnation and humiliation, was made a little lower than the angels, yet crowned with glory and honor, and all things in the mediatorial kingdom put in subjection under him.

2. Adam is the *natural head* of his race, and Christ is the *spiritual head* of the church. Paul says

God gave him to be head over all things to the church; and represents him as bearing the same relation to the church which the head does to the body.

3. There is another resemblance, which divines call *representation*. The old covenant of works, they say, which was made with Adam, was made with him as the representative of his race. This covenant was the continuance, in a state of holiness and felicity, on condition of perfect obedience; with the threatening of death for disobedience. And in this covenant Adam was put upon trial, not for himself only, but in a certain sense for his posterity also. By his fall, he involved them all in the consequences of his own transgression. So also Christ, in his mediatorial character, stands in the new covenant, which is the covenant of grace, in the same relation to his people which Adam stood to his posterity. The covenant of grace was made with Christ, as the head, representative, or surety of his people. He has undertaken for them, and in their behalf, to do for them what Adam failed to do,—to live a life of perfect obedience; and not this only, but to repair the breach which has been made in the first covenant, by sin. He was made a little lower than the angels, that he might taste death for every man. This representative character of Adam and Christ, is explicitly declared in the fifth chapter of Romans, and in the fifteenth chapter of first Corinthians:—" As by one man sin entered the world, and death by sin; and so death passed upon all men, for that all have sinned." " Death reigned from Adam to Moses, even over them that had not sinned after the similitude of Adam's transgression,

who is the figure of him that was to come." " Through the offence of one many be dead ; much more, the grace of God, and the gift by grace, which is by one man, Jesus Christ, hath abounded unto many." " By the offence of one, judgment came upon all men to condemnation ; even so, by the righteousness of one, the free gift came upon all men unto justification of life. For as by one man's disobedience many were made sinners, so by the obedience of one shall many be made righteous." " As in Adam all die, so in Christ shall all be made alive." These passages are sufficient to show that there was a sense in which Adam stood on trial for his natural seed, and Christ for his spiritual seed. And here is the idea of suretyship, or the substitution of one for another, in the eye of God's law, on which rests the whole scheme of the atonement.

II. The second typical representation of Christ is found in the worship of God, through the medium of bloody sacrifices. The apostle Paul, in his epistle to the Hebrews, discusses this subject at length, and shows that these sacrifices were designed as a typical representation of the great sacrifice which Christ made, once for all, when he offerered up his own body upon the cross. And he explains the reason why bloody sacrifices were appointed,—because, " without shedding of blood there is no remission ;" and the reason of this is, that the penalty of transgression was death ; and no expiation could be made for sin without the death of the victim offered, and this required the shedding of blood, because the life was in the blood.

Yet these victims could avail nothing for the forgiveness of sin, except as they pointed forward to the great sacrifice which the Saviour was to make.

The first account which we have of these sacrifices is, the offerings of Cain and Abel. But it is fair to infer, that this act of theirs was not performed merely at the instigation of their own minds; especially as it agrees with the worship which was afterwards formally instituted, and declared to be typical of the promised Saviour. It is evident, then, that a revelation must have been made to our first parents, immediately after the fall, informing them of this medium of renewing the communion with God, which they lost in the fall. And this is corroborated by the fact, that God made them clothing of the skins of beasts. They had not yet received the grant of animal food, which was not given till after the flood; and it is not probable that permission would have been given them to kill animals merely for the sake of their skins. It is, therefore, an easy and fair inference, that these were the skins of beasts slain in sacrifice. There is also another point of deep interest in regard to this I cannot wholly divest myself of the idea that there was a typical meaning in this very matter of clothing; though there does not seem to be sufficient authority for declaring this positively. But we may use it as an illustration; and as such it is very striking. The first effect of the transgression was a conviction of sin, manifested by a sense of shame. And their first effort to hide their shame, was made on the same principle that awakened sinners attempt to get clear of the curse of the law. It was by their own works,—they sewed or platted fig leaves together, and attempted to cover themselves with them,—an apt and striking illustration of the miserable garments of self-righteousness, in which convicted sinners attempt to hide their naked exposure to God's wrath. But God made them coats of skins; and so he has furnished for those who will receive it, a garment that will perfectly cover and hide them from his wrath.

We find here, also, an explanation of the difference between the sacrifices of Cain and of Abel. Paul says, "By faith Abel offered a more excellent sacrifice than Cain." But how was it by *faith* ? Evidently that he *believed* in the promised Saviour,—he felt his need of something to atone for his sins; and therefore he brought the *bloody sacrifice*, which had been instituted by God as a type to point forward to the great sacrifice. But Cain was self-righteous. He did not feel his need of a Saviour. He thought, as many do now, that he could come before God in his own name, without the intervention of a Mediator, and be accepted. And so he brought an offering of the fruits of the earth,—a sacrifice without blood,—a mere thank-offering. But he was disappointed. God did not accept his offering.

Nothing is more plainly taught in the Scriptures, than that the bloody sacrifices of the Old Testament were designed to represent the great atoning sacrifice of Christ. It is in allusion to this that Isaiah says, "He shall make his soul an offering for sin." Paul, likewise, in allusion to the same thing, says in his epistle to the Hebrews, "Almost all things are by the law purged with blood; and without shedding of blood there is no remission. It was, therefore, necessary that the pattern of things in the heavens should be purified with these ; but the heavenly things themselves, with better sacrifices than these. For Christ is not entered into the holy places made with hands, which are figures of the true , but into heaven itself, now to appear in the presence of God for us ; nor yet that he should offer himself often, as the high priest entereth into the holy place every year with the blood of others ; for then must he often have suffered since the foundation of the world : but now once in the end of the world hath he appeared, to put away sin by the sacrifice of himself. Christ was once offered to bear the sins of many." This is illustrated in the most striking manner, by the services of the day of atonement. This was a solemn service, which occurred once a year. On that day there were two victims selected, one for a sin-offering and the other for a scapegoat. The first was slain, and his blood sprinkled within the vail, by the priest, to make atonement for himself and the people. Then the sins of the people were, in a formal manner, laid over upon the head of the live goat. The priest laid his hands upon the goat's head, and confessed over him all the iniquities of the people, and put them upon the head of the goat ; which was sent away, to bear upon him all their iniquities unto a land not inhabited. This represents Christ bearing our sins ; and to this, doubtless, Peter alludes, when he says, " He bare our sins in his own body on the tree " Then the body of the goat that had been slain, and also of a bullock, which had been previously offered in a similar manner for a sin-offering, were both burned outside of the camp. So the apostle tells us Jesus suffered without the camp. The offering of incense represents the intercession of Christ before God ; and the sprinkling of the blood at the time of incense, shows that it was in consequence of his having shed his blood for us, that he is enabled to intercede for us effectually, now that he sits on the right hand of God, who is seated on a mercy-seat,— all this being represented, as the apostle tells us, by the " Holy places made with hands, which are the figures of the true."

The same thing was represented, in a very touching manner, by the sacrifice of Abraham. Isaac was the child of promise ; and as such, a type of Christ, as we learn from the third chapter of Galatians, where Paul declares that the *Seed*, to whom God referred in his promises to Abraham, was Christ ; and Christ is typified in this very thing,—Isaac, being the child of promise, and born out of the usual course of nature, as Christ was. Abraham's freely offering up his son, at the command of God, notwithstanding his strong affection for him, as the child of promise, seems to be a representation of that wonderful act of God, in giving his only-begotten and well-beloved Son to die for us,—offering him up freely for our sakes ; and the passive submission of Isaac, represents the conduct of Christ, in offering up himself voluntarily, as a sacrifice for our sins. The resurrection of Christ, also, is prefigured by the deliverance of Isaac from death, as we learn by the apostle, who says that Abraham received Isaac from the dead *in a figure*. There is a striking coincidence, also, in the place of this offering, and the manner in which the victims went to it. It was Mount Moriah on which Isaac was offered. It was Mount Moriah on which the temple stood, near which Christ was crucified. Isaac went up to the place, bearing the wood for the burnt-offering; and Christ went to the place bearing the wood of the cross. But at the close of the scene the figure is changed; and Isaac, who was doomed to die, is made to represent the sinner condemned to death, while the ram represents Christ; and as Isaac was saved from death, by having the ram substituted in his place, so believers are saved from the death to which they are doomed for their sins, by having the sufferings and death of Christ substituted for theirs.

III. I shall notice but one more of the types in this chapter; and that is *Noah's Ark*. We learn the typical character of this, from the apostle Peter, who says, "Christ hath once suffered for sins, the just for the unjust, that he might bring us to God, being put to death in the flesh, but quickened by the Spirit: by which also he went and preached unto the spirits in prison; which sometime were disobedient, when once the long-suffering of God waited in the days of Noah, while the Ark was preparing, wherein few, that is, eight souls, were saved by water, the like figure whereunto even baptism doth also now save us (not the putting away the filth of the flesh, but the answer of a good conscience toward God,) by the resurrection of Jesus Christ." This does not mean that Jesus went into hell, and preached to the spirits that were confined in prison there; but that while the Ark was preparing, he preached by Noah to the spirits that were in prison at the time Peter wrote his epistle. And baptism is here put for the thing signified by it,—being really and truly baptized into Christ. Let us, then, look at the resemblances. A flood of water was coming, to drown the whole world. The Ark was prepared, as a place of security for all who entered it. But there is a more dreadful storm approaching, when the Lord Jesus shall be revealed from heaven, in flaming fire, taking vengeance on them that know not God. But Christ will be an Ark of Safety to all who are *in him*; and as the Lord shut Noah in, and secured him from the storm and the flood, so he will keep by his mighty power unto salvation, all who enter into the true Ark. It is probable, also, that the flood was intended as a type of the last day, when this world shall be on fire, and the elements shall melt with fervent heat, and the world, and all that is therein, shall be burnt up. Then there will be a mighty and overwhelming destruction to all, except those who have taken refuge in Christ, the Ark of Safety.

PRACTICAL REMARKS.

1. We learn from this subject the great principle on which the whole scheme of the gospel is founded. It is that of representation, suretyship, substitution. Christ, as the surety, representative, or head of his people, has undertaken to accomplish all that is necessary to secure their complete, perfect, and final salva-

tion. He stands responsible for them, to the justice of God. Does that justice claim their everlasting destruction? He has bared his own bosom to the stern requirements of justice; and by the union of the divine nature with the human, he has given a sufficient value to his sufferings to atone for the sins of the whole world. Does the law still demand perfect obedience? That obedience he rendered in the days of his flesh, his divinity also giving it an infinite value, so that by virtue of their union with him, all his people have the benefits of a perfect righteousness. Nor is this all. He has not only satisfied the demands of law and justice for his people; but he has provided for their complete redemption from the power of sin and Satan, and their eternal glorification. He has led captivity captive; he has conquered the great Adversary, and swallowed up death in victory. And their union with him entitles them to share with him, in the inheritance of all things. He, being the Eternal Son of God, is heir of all things; hence he says, "All things which the Father hath are mine:" and Paul says that those who have received the spirit of adoption are joint heirs with Christ. In view of the same truth,—our union with Christ, our spiritual head,—he says in another place, "all things are your's, and ye are Christ's, and Christ is God's."

What could be presented to the mind of an inquirer, bowed down under a sense of guilt, more exactly suited to his case? Do you feel the wrath of God abiding on you? Trust yourself in the hands of your great Surety, who will stand up in your place, and be responsible for you. He will stand between you and the wrath of God—the demands of eternal justice—and it will have no force upon you, because it has spent itself upon him. His hands, his feet, his temples, and his side, testify that he has paid the debt. But, do you still feel that the law has claims upon you for positive obedience—for a perfect righteousness, as well as for satisfaction for your disobedience? He stands up as your representative. His righteousness is perfect and complete. And your union with him, if you come to him, entitles you to all the benefits of his perfect righteousness. He stands in your place. He has entered into a covenant of grace with the Father, from eternity, to have, by virtue of his own obedience and sufferings, all who come to him. What more can you want? Only believe. But there is the difficulty,—you will not believe. Notwithstanding all the assurances he has given, you will not believe. You will not take him for a whole Saviour, but must needs insist on having some righteousness of your own wherein to trust, in addition to his. You are going about to establish your own righteousness,—sewing together your wretched figleaf aprons, which can never hide your naked soul from the wrath of God. You must have a better covering,—one provided by God himself.

2. We learn from this subject the true idea of atonement. From all the bloody sacrifices of the Old Testament, it appears that the great idea of expiation or atonement for sin, is in the death of a *substituted victim*,—a victim substituted in the place of the sinner. And that nothing short of death is sufficient, is evident from the declaration that, "without shed-

ding of blood there is no remission." But the victim must be of sufficient value to take the place of the sinner; and this is true of the great offering in which all others centre. We have here also an illustration of the act of faith by which the sinner becomes personally interested in the great atonement. The priest, in behalf of the people, laid his hands upon the head of the scapegoat, and confessed over it the sins of the people, and by an act of faith in the word of God, which appointed this observance, transferred the sins of the people to the head of the victim. So we are to confess our sins before God, and by an act of faith, behold them transferred to the head of the great victim, on whom the Lord hath laid the iniquity of us all. By which, however, we are not to understand that the moral turpitude of the believer's sins is transferred to Christ; but only that they are transferred to him in the same sense that a debt is transferred to the surety, —he becomes responsible to God for them, and relieves us of the curse of the law, which otherwise would rest upon us in consequence of our transgression.

3. We learn from this subject that there can be no acceptable worship, except such as is presented in the name of Christ, in view of the great atonement which he has made for sin. Cain offered to the Lord similar worship to that offered by all disbelievers in the atonement of Christ. He felt no need of expiation for sin; and he treated the idea of atonement with the same contempt with which it is now treated in many congregations of professed worshippers. Cain was not an avowed infidel. He believed in worship-

ping God. But he was self-righteous. He had no sense of sin, and felt no need of an atonement. But Abel was a believer in the atonement. He presented a bloody offering. His offering was accepted, while Cain's was rejected. These two men represent the two great classes into which mankind have always been divided,—believers and unbelievers. As Cain persecuted Abel, so have his seed always persecuted the seed of Abel. Even among us, those self-righteous moralists, who feel no need of being saved from their sins, will vex and harass the true believer, with ridicule and opposition, even while the profession of extreme liberality is on his lips. This is *liberal Christianity*,—and it is the same kind of liberality which Cain exercised towards Abel,—a liberality of hatred, on account of the truths believed and professed by the true children of God.

4. The example of Abraham exhibits a practical exhibition of what is meant by forsaking all for Christ. This is the term of discipleship. "Whosover he be of you," says the Saviour, "that forsaketh not all that he hath, cannot be my disciple" The meaning of this, as illustrated in the conduct of Abraham, is, that we must make such an entire consecration of every thing to Christ and to God, that we shall be ready, with the same promptness, to give it up at his call. Isaac was very dear to Abraham. He was the consummation of all his hopes, for which he had been, for more than twenty years, a wanderer in a strange land. He had many severe trials of his faith before; but now God called for his beloved Isaac. And did he hesitate? Not a moment. He went deliberately to

work to obey this command, as though it were a long-settled point with him, that whatever the Lord should order must be acquiesced in as a matter of course. How is it, Christian reader ? Have you no beloved Isaac, which you are withholding from God, or permitting to come between him and your affections ? God may find it necessary to call upon you to sacrifice your Isaac ; yet if you freely give him up to God, he may permit you still to enjoy him, as he did Abraham. He may give him to you, as life from the dead. But has he come to any of you, and taken away your Isaac ? Remember that the trial of your faith, being much more precious than of gold that perisheth, may thereby be found unto praise, and honor, and glory, at the appearing of Jesus Christ.

5. This subject gives us an exhibition of the *love of God*, which is adapted to melt and subdue our hearts. Who can describe or imagine the emotions of Abraham's bosom, when God said to him, "Take now thy son, thine *only* son Isaac, and get thee into the land of Moriah, and offer him there for a burnt-offering !" Yet Jesus Christ was God's only-begotten and well-beloved Son ; and he freely offered him up for us ; and that while we were yet sinners,—yes, "God commendeth his love to us, in that while we were yet sinners, Christ died for us !" O how should this affect our hearts ; and how deeply ungrateful are they, who will neither be moved by this love, nor accept of Jesus Christ as their Saviour ! With what infinite abhorrence must God look upon those who neglect, slight, or despise such a manifestation of his love ! Yet every impenitent sinner does thus slight, or neg-

lect, or despise this infinite love of God. Yes, even those that are partially awakened, will not suffer their hearts to be melted and subdued with this love. Yet they complain that they cannot feel that they are sinners. Some of them make the most frivolous excuses imaginable for slighting eternal love. Some think if such and such a companion would love God, they would love him too. But this is setting up their friendship with a mortal worm above the friendship of the infinite God! Others are afraid of being ridiculed by their companions, if they come out and make a suitable return for such infinite love. But it is better to bear the ridicule and scorn of a wicked companion, than to be an object of scorn and derision of the whole universe in the day of judgment; for of them that are ashamed of Christ now, he will be ashamed then; and God will laugh at their calamity, and mock when their fear cometh. In that day his offers of mercy will be clean gone forever, and in his anger he will shut up his tender mercies forever.

6. Finally, this subject furnishes occasion for exhortation to sinners to flee to the Ark of Safety. The long-suffering of God is waiting for you, impenitent reader, as it waited for the old world in the days of Noah. Now God is waiting to be gracious. He bids you flee to Christ, the true Ark, before the storm of wrath approaches, which is to overwhelm you in despair and eternal destruction. If you take refuge in him, you will be secure in the day of God's awful visitation. To you it may be very near. You will soon have to pass through the deep waters of death. But if Christ is your Ark, you will pass over in safety.

Soon, also, "the Lord will come with fire, and with his chariots like a whirlwind, to render his anger with fury, and his rebukes with flames of fire." But if you are in Christ, the true Ark, when you pass through the waters, he will be with you; and through the rivers, they shall not overflow you; when you pass through the fire, you shall not be burnt; neither shall the flame kindle upon you; for the Lord your God, the Holy One of Israel, shall be your Saviour.

CHAPTER VII.

FOURTH PILLAR, concluded.—*Types of the Old Testament, continued.*

IV. THE next type which I shall consider is *Melchizedek*. The fact of the typical character of Melchizedek is explicitly declared by Paul, in his epistle to the Hebrews. Who Melchizedek was is not certain. Commentators have advanced various opinions on the subject; but the most probable one is, that he was a pious king, of one of the tribes of the Canaanites. This is the conclusion to which any one would naturally come, by reading the account given of him in Genesis. Yet, as a type of Christ, he was greater than Abraham, for Abraham paid him tithes; and it is probable that God had revealed to him Melchizedek's typical character, so that these tithes were paid to him, with faith in his great Antitype. The resemblances between Melchizedek and Christ are, that they both united in themselves the offices of priest and king; Melchizedek was king of Salem, which is King of Peace, and Christ is the Prince of Peace, because it is through him alone that peace is proclaimed on earth,—in him righteousness and peace meet together; they both hold their priesthood by the same tenure, receiving it not from hereditary descent, as the sons of Aaron did, so that, in this respect they were without father and mother,—both received their priestly office directly from God, and it was not to descend to their posterity, but to remain in themselves, unchangeable and perpetual. This contradicts the Popish idea of the descent of Christ's priesthood to his ministers, and represents him as still exercising the priest's office before God, making intercession for his people. It is, therefore, profane for any man to call himself, or permit himself to be called, a *priest*. We have no priest but Christ. His ministers are only his servants, ambassadors whom he has sent out to invite people to the gospel feast.

V. The next type we notice is, the two sons of Abraham, representing, in allegory, or type, the children of the two covenants. The covenant of works, made first with Adam, and given in full on Mount Sinai, is represented by Hagar, who was a bondwoman, and whose children were born into bondage. It is to be observed, that *Hagar* is the Arabic name for *Mount Sinai*. The Jews, though children of Abraham after the flesh, were yet in bondage to the law, which was given upon Mount Sinai. They sought justification by the law; but it only brought them into bondage; for they could have no justification by it, unless they fulfilled it perfectly. This applies equally to those who now seek justification by their own works. All who are in a natural state are born after the flesh, as Ishmael was; and they are in bondage to the law, and under its wrath and curse, because they have not kept it ; and if they continue in this state, they will be finally cast out, as Ishmael was. But the covenant of grace is represented by Sarah, who was a freewoman, and whose children, therefore, were born free. Her son, Isaac, was not born after the flesh, but by promise, out of the ordinary course of nature. So the true children of Abraham, under the covenant of grace, are " born not of blood, nor of the will of the flesh, nor of the will of man, but of God." And by virtue of this new and heavenly birth, they are the children of Abraham, and heirs according to the promise ; and they are delivered from the curse of the law, through the covenant of grace, whereby Christ has redeemed them from the curse of the law, being made a curse for them.

VI. *Moses was a type of Christ.* The Lord said unto Moses, concerning the children of Israel, " I will raise them up a prophet, from among their brethren, like unto thee, and will put my words into his mouth ; and he shall speak unto them all the words that I shall command him." This, Stephen applies to Christ, in his address before the Sanhedrim, at the time of his martyrdom ; and no other prophet has ever appeared, " like unto Moses, to whom the Lord spake face to face," excepting Jesus Christ. The typical resemblances between Moses and Christ are these :—They were both saved in infancy, from the persecution of cruel kings ; they were both, in early life, before the commencement of their ministry, employed in secular and laborious pursuits ; they both rejected the temptation to worldly greatness, to do the will of God ; they resembled each other in character, both being meek and faithful ; Moses delivered the children of Israel from Egyptian bondage, as Christ delivers his people from the bondage of sin and Satan ; they were both maltreated and rejected by their own people, whom they came to save ; they both united in one person the offices of prophet, priest, and lawgiver ; the Lord spake to them both with an audible voice, and face to face ; they were both transfigured : Moses, when his face shone as the face of an angel, and Jesus, while at prayer on the Mount of transfiguration, " when the fashion of his countenance was altered, and his raiment was white and glistering ;" and they both exercised the office of Mediator between God and man. Moses stood between the people as the medium of communication between them and God, as Christ does now.

VII. The vail which Moses put over his face, when he spoke to the people, after going into the tabernacle before God, Paul informs us, represented the comparative obscurity of the Old Testament dispensation. The people could not look steadfastly in Moses' face, because it shone, as it were, the face of an angel. This vail, the apostle said, still remained upon the hearts of the Jews, when the law was read ; for they could not steadfastly look to the end of that which was abolished. But this vail, he says, is done away in Christ. We can look upon him as our Mediator, without being dazzled with the brightness of his countenance ; and in him all obscurity is taken away from the method of salvation.

VIII. The redemption of the children of Israel out of Egypt, and their whole journey through the wilderness, appear to be typical of Christ's redemption of his people from the bondage of sin and Satan, and of the Christian life; while the land of Canaan, with the entrance of the children of Israel into it, was typical of heaven, and the final entrance of the people of God into that blessed abode. This will appear from the following considerations:—(1.) The passover was evidently typical of the application of the blood of redemption to believers. Paul expressly declares this; and it most evidently had its accomplishment in Christ; and this was the last of the means used to deliver them from bondage, as application to the blood of Christ is the last means by which the sinner is brought out of bondage. (2.) Paul declares that the passage of the Red Sea, under the cloud, was typical of baptism, which is the door into the Christian church, and entered near the commencement of the Christian race. Their pilgrimage through the desert must, therefore, represent the Christian pilgrimage through this world, which, in regard to spiritual things, very much resembles that desert land through which they passed. (3.) Paul declares expressly that certain things which happened to them, in their progress through the wilderness, happened to them for examples or types; he also declares that the manna and the miraculous supply of water in the wilderness, represented the spiritual meat which Christ has provided for his people; and Christ himself asserts the same thing in his discourse to the Jews, recorded by the evangelist John. So that it is a fair inference, that this journey was intended to represent the Christian life. And it is clear from what Paul says, in the fourth and eleventh chapters of Hebrews, that Canaan was a type of heaven. He represents some as having failed of that rest, as typical of others that will fail of entering the heavenly rest. He also represents the patriarchs, while sojourning in the land of promise, as seeking a better country, that is, an heavenly. The same thing, also, is to be inferred from the fact, that Canaan, like the heavenly rest, is a land of promise. And if the deliverance of the children of Israel from Egypt, and their journey through the wilderness, are typical of the commencement and progress of the Christian life, then all the events connected with them must be typical of things connected with Christian experience. All the ceremonial law, also, which was given during the journey through the wilderness, was typical of Christ and the gospel. They were, the apostle says, "shadows of good things to come." This gives the narrative of these events a double interest to the minds of Christians. But it is necessary to guard against carrying these typical resemblances too far; for a type never comes fully up to the antitype, and there are generally some parts of it which do not apply at all to the thing signified by it. Moreover there is often more than one thing signified by the same type, so that some things necessary to carry out the one, will not apply to the other. Here is evidently not only a type of the redemption of individual Christians, with their personal experience; but also of the church of God, taken collectively, all under one and the same figure. This mingling of figures is very common in the Scriptures, with reference to this very thing. Thus the *kingdom of God* is a figure, which Christ and the apostles apply often in the same expression, to represent both the church at large and the kingdom which Christ sets up in the heart of the believer.

IX. David was a type of Christ. This we learn by the application of the sixteenth Psalm to Christ, by Peter on the day of Pentecost; together with the similar application of other passages in the Psalms to Christ, where David was speaking in the first person. I have not space here to trace the resemblances between David and Christ; and refer to it only for the purpose of saying that it explains many things in the Psalms, where David speaks in the first person, which could not apply to himself. This is important to be borne in mind in reading the Psalms. It relieves all the difficulty felt by many on reading those Psalms in which David prays for the destruction of his enemies. These enemies are the enemies of the church; and their destruction, for the salvation of the church, was a laudable object of desire.

X. The burial and resurrection of Christ, according to his own testimony, was typified in the prophet Jonah.

XI. We have reason to believe that the polluting effects of sin were typified by the loathsome disease of leprosy. This disease polluted and corrupted the whole body, even while the person lived; and it seems to be referred to in Isaiah's description of the sins of the Jewish nation, which forcibly describes the state of the unregenerate heart : " The whole head is sick, and the whole heart faint. From the soul of the foot, even unto the head, there is no soundness in it, but wounds, and bruises, and putrefying sores." The ceremony of cleansing the leper, also, is evidently designed as a type of the cleansing of the soul from both the pollution and guilt of sin by the blood of Christ. The priest took two birds, and killed one of them, and dipped the other in its blood, and let it go free. This represents the sinner set free from the sentence of death by the death of Christ. The priest, then, with a branch of hyssop, sprinkled the leper with the blood, and pronounced him clean. This appears to represent baptism, which signifies the application of the blood of Christ by faith to the heart of the Christian, producing inward purification ; as the apostle says, "purifying our hearts by faith." This seems to be alluded to by David, when he says, " Purge me with hyssop and I shall be clean," &c., and by the apostle John, when he says, " The blood of Jesus Christ cleanseth from all sin."

PRACTICAL REMARKS.

1. We learn from this subject why so many Christians live in slavish fear, and are all their lifetime subject to bondage ; and why the awakened sinner so frequently remains for a long time in a state of distress, with protracted convictions, instead of coming

out into the liberty of the gospel. Oftentimes the Christian, when he has been betrayed into sin,—when he has felt or done wrong, seeks peace of conscience by resolving to reform. But this gives him no relief. This is going to Mount Sinai, which gendereth to bondage. It is seeking justification by the law. And all who seek justification by the law, are the children of the bondwoman. This does not relieve his conscience, and he goes on, burdened with guilt and trembling with fear, groping on in the dark, and going still farther from God. It is, doubtless, this servile spirit of bondage, which often leads young converts to backslide from God. But instead of this, we should go to Mount Sion, and behold the cross of Jesus Christ. There is no terror there. The cross speaks peace to the troubled soul. Here we find not the spirit of bondage, but the spirit of adoption, whereby we cry, " Abba, Father." So it is with the awakened sinner,—if he would go to Mount Sion, as soon as he beheld the cross his burden would fall off, and he would be delivered from the terrible bondage under which he groans. But he goes to Mount Sinai; and that thunders terror in his ears. He goes about to amend his ways,—to do better, with the hope of preparing himself to be converted; but all this only brings him still deeper into bondage. But if he would come at once to the cross, he might obtain immediate pardon and peace. No sinner was ever sent empty away from Mount Sion, where he had been to get a sight of the cross. Beware, awakened sinner. " What saith the Scripture? Cast out the bondwoman and her son: for the son of the bondwoman shall not be heir with the son of the free woman." If you continue in this state you will be cast out like Ishmael. No one will enter the promised inheritance in this way. You must give up your self-righteousness, and seek adoption into the family of God as an heir of promise, through the grace of God in Christ, or you will certainly be cast out. Nor will it be any advantage to you, in this case, that you have been baptized, and brought under the covenant. Ishmael was the natural son of Abraham, circumcised and brought under the covenant. Yet he was cast out. Here, also, is a solemn warning to mockers. Ishmael, the son of the bondwoman, mocked Isaac, the child of promise; and he was cast out of his father's house. So now, the sons of bondage, who mock at the heirs of promise, will be cast out of the house of our Heavenly Father, into outer darkness, where shall be wailing and gnashing of teeth.

2. We learn from this subject that there is no salvation by Moses. He could lead the children of Israel only to Jordan. It required another person,—*Joshua*, whose name signifies a Saviour; and who seems to have been a type of the risen and triumphant Saviour, —it required him to introduce them into the promised land. So the law, which was given by Moses, cannot bring us to the heavenly Canaan,—it can do no more than to bring us to Christ. This shows why so many, who are awakened and convicted of sin, never come to any thing. They go no further than Moses leads them; and with the unbelieving Israelites, they will fall in the wilderness. Moses is their leader, and he cannot carry them over Jordan. Convicted sin-

ner! you must leave Moses, and fly to Christ, or you are lost! No matter how deep your conviction. The law can do nothing for you but to convict and condemn. And no doubt multitudes are now in hell, who have been under deeper convictions than you. Take warning by the Israelites who fell in the wilderness, and flee to Christ. He, like Joshua, will give you rest.

3. We learn from this subject the necessity of a Mediator between God and man. Moses was a type of Christ, in his character of Mediator. The people were taught the necessity of a Mediator, in an impressive manner, as they stood before Mount Sinai. They saw the thunderings, and the lightnings, and the noise of the trumpet, and the mountain smoking: and they removed and stood afar off. And they said unto Moses, speak thou with us, and we will hear; but let not God speak with us, lest we die. And so terrible was the sight that even Moses said, I exceedingly fear and quake. They saw that they were sinners, and that they "could not endure that which was commanded," nor stand before a God of infinite holiness, who is a consuming fire to the wicked. But what was the glory of Sinai, compared with the unveiled glories of the blessed and only Potentate, the King of kings and Lord of lords, who only hath immortality, as it appears in that light which no man can approach unto? And, if the children of Israel, God's chosen people, could not endure the glory of Sinai, which was but a figure of the glory that shall be revealed, without some one to stand between them and God, can you, O presumptuous man, stand up in your own confidence,

before that throne from which the earth and heaven shall flee away? A single ray of glory, from that burning throne, shining into your heart, would discover such hidden iniquity and vile pollution there, that you would call to the mountains and the rocks to fall on you, and hide you from the face of Him that sitteth upon the throne. However good or amiable you may appear to yourself now, you will then see your need of a days-man, to stand between you and God. Hear what God himself says to you: "Can thine heart endure, or can thine hands be strong, in the day that I shall deal with you?" If you come up before God without a Mediator, God will deal with YOU; but, if you go there in the name of Christ, with him as your Mediator, God will not deal with you, but with Christ; who will take your place, and answer for you, as the advocate answers before the court for the criminal, or the surety for the debtor.

4. We learn from this subject why it is so difficult for impenitent sinners to understand the way of salvation. All impenitent persons are in a similar state to that of the unbelieving Jews, who rejected Christ. However much they may assent to the truths of Christianity, they do continue in their hearts to reject the Saviour, and seek justification by the works of the law. Is it not so, impenitent reader? Do you not feel in your heart, that, after all, you are about as good as the generality of Christians, and, therefore, you will stand as good a chance as they? This might, perhaps, to some extent be true, as to outward conduct, if they relied upon this for salvation. But they have long since renounced all dependence

upon their own works, and fled for refuge to Jesus Christ; and now, their good works are performed with far different motives from yours. Now it is true of you, as it was of the unbelieving Jews, that this veil is upon your heart. Your minds are blinded. You perceive not the things of the Spirit, because your hearts are carnal, and they are spiritually discerned. You are looking at the ministration of death, which was written and graven in stone; and you cannot perceive the glory of the ministration of the Spirit. But that speaks nothing but condemnation and death; while the ministration of the Spirit reveals life and peace, through faith in Jesus Christ; which is infinitely more glorious than the ministration of death.

5. We learn from this subject the condition of sinners. It is here represented in a figure, by the hard bondage of the Israelites. Sinners are represented in the Bible as being under the power of Satan, carried captive by him at his will; and as being the servants of sin, yielding themselves to its dominion. This is a hard service. The way of transgressors is hard. The yoke of Satan is a galling yoke; and, like Egyptian bondage, it is growing worse and worse, the longer they continue in it. The demands of sin are greater and greater, while its promises of reward are all delusive, and continually receding, like the promises of liberty, which Pharaoh held out to his bondmen. Nor will Satan any more easily render up his dominion over sinners, than Pharoah did over his. Indeed, the whole history of the dealings of God with the children of Israel in Egypt, furnishes a striking illustration of the dealings of God with the awakened

sinner; and their conduct, and that of Pharaoh, illustrate the feelings of sinners under the awakenings of God's spirit, and the schemes of Satan, for retaining them in his service. When Moses and Aaron came to the people, and told them that God had come to deliver them from their bondage, they were glad, and bowed their heads and worshipped. But all this was selfish,—they had no regard to God in it, but only desired to be freed from bondage; and so when Pharaoh increased the rigor of their bondage, and they saw difficulties in their way, they began to be vexed, and to murmur against God, and to be angry with his servants. So it is with sinners. When first awakened, they think they are willing to serve God, and are pleased with the idea of having the consolations of religion, and of being saved. But as soon as Satan discovers that they are beginning to think of leaving his service, he rages and storms as Pharaoh did, and increases their burdens,—stirring up all the evil dispositions and malevolent feelings of their hearts, so that they are overwhelmed with sore distress; and their hearts often rise in opposition to God, and to those who have been instrumental of awakening them. But when the power of their convictions is strong upon them, Satan changes his course, as Pharaoh did, and allows them to promise that they will go and serve the Lord; but this he only makes a pretext for keeping them in his service. And so he goes on, putting one excuse after another into their mouths. One plague after another came upon Pharaoh, and every time he would promise to let the people go; but then, every time, there was a holding back of something.

At first, he would let them go, only they must not go very far away; then he would let them go, but they must not take their little ones; and again they might go with their little ones, but they must leave their cattle behind. All these things were devices to retain the people in his service; but God would make no compromise. He must have their whole service. So with sinners. Satan would retain them in his service, and so he persuades them to reserve this thing or that, which they are not willing to give up; and to resort to this or that expedient for delay. One would be willing to serve the Lord, if this or that young companion would go; but he has more regard for his associates in the hard bondage of sin and Satan, than he has for God. He would rather go down to hell and serve Satan forever, along with his companions, than to break away from them and serve God alone. Others are not ready. God has called too soon. They have this or that pleasure to seek first; or there is something, they imagine, in their circumstances, which, in their view, renders it inconvenient or impossible for them to go yet. Some young people think they have not yet had their fill of pleasure; or they are ambitious of accomplishing something which they regard as essential to their future distinction in society; or they find some other expedient for delay. They are in love with the pleasures of Egypt; and they have not yet made up their minds whether they will leave the service of Satan; yet while they linger, God may seal them over to eternal condemnation. Others, in the prime of life, have yet something to accomplish for themselves, before they are ready to go out of Egypt. They would get a competence,—they have a farm to pay for,—or this or that object to accomplish, before they are ready. They would delay a little longer; and so it will presently come to pass that, when they cry out of their hard bondage, with bitter tears, God will say to them, "Because I have called, and ye refused; I have stretched out my hand, and no man regarded; but ye have set at naught all my counsel, and would none of my reproof; I also will laugh at your calamity, and mock when your fear cometh. When your fear cometh as desolation, and your destruction cometh as a whirlwind; when distress and anguish cometh upon you; then shall they call upon me, but I will not answer; they shall seek me early, but they shall not find me." It is a fearful thing to trifle with the strivings of the Holy Spirit. If you now choose your own ways, then God will choose your delusions, because, when he called to you, none did answer, and when he spake, none did hear.

6. This subject furnishes a very striking illustration of Christian experience. When the children of Israel had escaped from Egypt, and passed the Red Sea, they were full of joy, and lifted up their united voice in a song of praise to God. But they knew nothing of the way that was before them. They probably anticipated a speedy entrance into the promised land. So the young convert, when he has just escaped from the bondage of Satan, is full of joy and wonder, and lifts up his voice in praise. And this is well. God gives him a foretaste of heavenly joys, to prepare him to encounter the conflict that is before

him. But of this conflict he knows nothing. He anticipates the same calm, serene, uninterrupted enjoyment, which he experiences in the freshness of his first love. It is well that the trials to come are hid from him, that he may gather strength for the conflict. But it was only three days after the children of Israel were rejoicing and singing the praises of God, on account of their deliverance, when they began to murmur for want of water. So with the young Christian. While all is calm and peaceful, he knows not the evil that yet remains in his heart; but when crosses and trials come, remaining corruptions rebel, and he finds his heart frets against the providences of God. The same thing is repeatedly illustrated, by similar conduct, on the part of the children of Israel, when brought into straits. There are, also, awful examples of backsliding. The children of Israel, even in sight of Mount Sinai, turned back to the worship of the gods of Egypt; and often they sighed for the pleasures of the land which they had left. And how often do young converts, even in sight of the altar where they pledged themselves, and of the emblems of the dying love of the Saviour, go back to their idols, and hanker after the pleasures of sin. Whether such are truly converted, or not, I do not pretend to determine; but many do thus backslide, who are afterwards recovered to a more devoted life, as Aaron and the tribe of Levi were; but probably the greater part of backsliders will fall in the wilderness, as the greater part of those did, who bowed down to the golden calf. Yet how dreadful the sin of a leading man or a minister, as Aaron was, who backslides, and leads a multitude along with him, many of whom will not return when he returns. There are, also, solemn warnings against *unbelief*. But for this sin, the children of Israel might have entered the promised land in about two years; but to cure them of this sin, they were driven about in the wilderness forty years. And but for this sin, Christians might, doubtless, come into a state of elevated and permanent enjoyment of God, with a constant foretaste of the heavenly Canaan, without being tossed and driven about in a dry and barren land for many years, as it appears most of them are, to cure the plague of their hearts. There are many more points of resemblance between the journey of the children of Israel and the experience of Christians, which I leave the reader to trace out, by comparing them with his own experience. I leave the point with this remark :—That there does not appear to have been any necessity for the children of Israel to have encountered the evils which they did in the wilderness. If they had gone forward in the same spirit which they began, trusting in God for every emergency, submitting to him, and rejoicing in his holy providences towards them, it is altogether probable, that, after a short and easy passage through the wilderness, they would have gained possession of Canaan without difficulty. But it was their sins which created all the difficulty. So with the Christian. There is no necessity for his backsliding. There is no necessity for his walking in darkness. If he would but trust in God, looking continually to Jesus, he might go on his way rejoicing and hoping firm unto the end. There were some among the children of Israel who did not backslide. Caleb and Joshua kept on an even course of obedience, and never departed from God; and they became pillars in the church, and were richly rewarded in the land of Canaan. O that there were many such in the churches of our day!

7. This subject furnishes two valuable illustrations of the nature and necessity of faith in Christ, in the Passover and the brazen serpent, both of which are typical, as appears both from their connection with the great typical events already mentioned, and from the allusions made to them by Christ and the apostle Paul. The paschal lamb represented the sacrifice of Christ. The victim selected was a lamb, the emblem of innocence, to show that he was to suffer the just for the unjust; it was to be roasted and eaten whole, to show, perhaps, that Christ is to be taken as a whole and complete Saviour, and that we are to rely upon him alone for salvation; and not a bone of it was to be broken, to point to the same thing in the death of Christ. But the blood of the lamb was to be sprinkled upon the door-posts, as a sign to the destroying angel, to pass over those houses. Now it would have been of no avail for any family that the Passover was slain, if they had not sprinkled the blood on the door-posts. The destroying angel would have entered in and performed his work of death. So with sinners: it will be of no avail to them that Christ has died to atone for their sins. There must be an application of his blood by faith. It required faith in God's appointed means, to induce the children of Israel to sprinkle the blood of the Passover on their

doors; and it requires faith in the way of salvation which he has now appointed, to render it available for the salvation of any. If any had presumed on the goodness of God, and said, "Surely, God is too good to send his destroying angel into my house, to kill my first-born," and so had neglected the appointed means of preservation, would his house have been saved? So now, if any one presumes to be wiser than God, and to say, "Surely, God is too good to punish any of us forever in hell," and so neglects the blood of sprinkling, will God pass over him in the day of vengeance?

So of the brazen serpent. The people were bitten with fiery flying serpents, whose sting, like the sting of sin, was certain death. Multitudes around, were falling into the grave under the influence of the venomous poison, as multitudes now are dropping into the bottomless pit under the sting of sin. The brazen serpent, an emblem of Christ on the cross, was raised up in sight of all the people. Their sin was unbelief; and to look upon the brazen serpent required faith in God's word; but if they would not look, they must die. There was no remedy. So with sinners. Their great sin is unbelief. The act of faith required of them, is, to look to Christ on the cross,—to look at him in his humiliation and exaltation,—suffering, bleeding, dying, rising, ascended on high,—and trust in his almighty power to save. It was no great thing required of the dying Israelite,—it was only "look and live,"—it is no great thing that is required of you, dying sinner,—only "look and live." But refuse to look and live, and you must certainly die,—for ever die.

8. This subject teaches the dreadful nature of unbelief, and with what awful abhorrence God regards it. It was unbelief, or want of confidence in the word of God, which brought those dreadful plagues upon the children of Israel in the wilderness, and shut a whole generation out of the promised land, leaving their carcasses in the wilderness. This is a solemn warning to us. It is unbelief, or want of confidence in God's promises, which keeps the church so low. It is unbelief, O impenitent reader, which will destroy your soul. God says, though he is gracious and merciful, long-suffering, and abundant in goodness and truth, he will by no means clear the guilty, but will punish them with everlasting destruction from the presence of God, and the glory of his power. But you say, "No; I do not believe it,—God is too good to punish men forever in hell." The reason you think so is, that you have no adequate views of the evil of sin. This one sin of unbelief is enough to shut you out of heaven forever. Would you have a man in your house that would not believe your word? No; and God will not have you in his house, if you believe not his word; for the "fearful and the unbelieving," as well as the "abominable and murderers," "shall have their part in the lake which burneth with fire and brimstone: which is the second death." There is no mansion in our Father's house for unbelievers,— there is no place there for those who make our Father a liar!

CONCLUSION.

In the foregoing pages, I have shown that the *Plenary Inspiration of the Holy Scriptures*, rests on four strong and massy pillars. The first is, the adaptedness of the system of religion which they reveal, to the circumstances and wants of men. This, I think, I have proved beyond question; and, also, that there is no other system of religion which answers this end. But this falls to the ground the moment the Plenary Inspiration of the Scriptures is given up. For those who regard the Scriptures at best as but partially inspired, invariably give up or deny what is essential to the grand system there revealed. Therefore, this pillar, which supports the Plenary Inspiration of the Scriptures, likewise supports the Evangelical System, in distinction from Socinianism, or Unitarianism, Universalism, and kindred errors. None of these have any claim, on the score of adaptedness, to the wants of man. They are mere caricatures of Christianity; and they by no means form this pillar of which I speak. If they were put under the *Plenary Inspiration of the Bible*, they would be like a marred and broken column. They would not support it. They do not even profess to rest upon it, but reject it, as the only means of their own support. But evangelical Christianity is the system taught in the Bible, understood in its plain and obvious import; and what this system has done, and what it is capable of doing for mankind, show that it must be of God.

CONCLUSION. 273

The Second Pillar is entirely different in its nature from the first. It is composed of the *evidence of fact*. It is a mere question of *fact*, not of opinion. And I think no fact, which depends on the testimony of credible witnesses, sustained by circumstantial evidence, is more clearly and fully established, than that the Scriptures of the Old and New Testaments are the infallible word of God, containing a perfect standard of truth and duty. This has been abundantly shown in the foregoing pages; though but a small part of the evidence has been exhibited. Yet if this is impartially examined, on the common principles of evidence, the witnesses will be found unimpeachable, their testimony consistent and fair, and every link in the chain of circumstances perfect and entire. This pillar cannot be shaken.

The Third Pillar is a marvellous one To the eye of the unbeliever, it is nothing but an ill-shapen mass of ruins, which does not at all support the edifice. On the contrary, in his view, it appears certain that the building must fall, *because* it is supported by such a pillar. But to the believer, it is a column of massive strength and stupendous grandeur; and the more he examines it, the more he discovers the perfection of its parts and the beauty of its architecture. The unbeliever argues, from the nature of the things taught in the Bible, that it cannot be from God. He beholds in it nought but a mass of " contradictions and absurdities ;" while the believer is not only convinced in his understanding, but feels in his heart, that the things taught in the Scriptures must be a revelation from God. This strange fact is accounted for in this same book; and this is a further evidence of its divine origin: "The natural man," says the Bible, "receiveth not the things of the Spirit of God: for they are foolishness unto him: neither can he know them, because they are spiritually discerned."

Lead a blind man up before a piece of splendid architecture, and he cannot discern its beauty. So lead a natural man to contemplate the spiritual things revealed in the Bible, and he cannot see their beauty, because he has no spiritual discernment. But multitudes who reject the Bible on this very ground,—on account of what it teaches,—never carefully look into it with what discernment they have, to see what it does teach. They condemn it without examination. This is prejudice and injustice in the highest degree. But it is true of most of the champions of infidelity, who have written against the Scriptures. An English gentleman, in conversation with Thomas Paine, some time after the publication of his "Age of Reason," found him deplorably ignorant of the Scriptures, and drew out from him the confession, that he had never carefully studied them. And the assertions of those pretended *Christians*, who come out at this day against the Plenary Inspiration of the Scriptures, show that they have never given the Bible a thorough, impartial, and candid examination, in order to know what it does teach.

The Fourth Pillar is a column constructed of four pieces, most curiously wrought together, and so placed, that every one who examines it must see that it is impossible for the edifice which it supports, to fall. The two branches of prophecy, one relating to

CONCLUSION. 275

the Jews, and the other to the rest of mankind, agree so perfectly with history, as to demonstrate the fact, that the prophecy must have been given by inspiration. And, then, the twofold predictions of the Messiah, contained in the prophecies and types, delivered generations before he came, and all so perfectly fulfilled in the person of Jesus Christ, show beyond contradiction, both that these prophecies and types must have been given by inspiration, and that Jesus Christ must be a divine person.

In view of all this array of testimony, I cannot but admire and adore the condescension of the blessed God, that he has been pleased, in so diversified and conclusive a manner, to attest his revelation; adapting the evidence to the constitution of different minds. With what astonishment, then, must the angels look upon the stupidity and blindness of men, when they see this revelation rejected by such multitudes of the human race! And how aggravated must be the sin of *unbelief*, when committed against such testimony! Who can doubt that the Bible is rejected, not from want of evidence, but because the truths which it reveals are hated? And no wonder that the sin of *unbelief* is ranked among the most enormous crimes, and punished accordingly. Rejecters of the Bible are not merely *mistaken;* but they are *criminal*. It is not an *error* only, but a *sin*, to reject the Bible. And it is a great and aggravated sin in the sight of God. It casts contempt upon him, and openly sets his authority at defiance. It is sinning presumptuously,—a sin which, by the law of Moses, was punished with death: " But the soul that doeth aught

presumptuously,—the same *reproacheth* the Lord; and that soul shall be cut *off from his people.*"*
YET THERE ARE MEN AMONG US, STANDING IN PULPITS CONSECRATED BY OUR FATHERS TO THE PROCLAMATION OF THE WORD OF GOD, AS CONTAINED IN THE HOLY SCRIPTURES, AND ACKNOWLEDGED BY A DELUDED PEOPLE AS CHRISTIAN MINISTERS, WHO PROCLAIM FROM THESE PULPITS THAT THE BIBLE IS NOT THE WORD OF GOD!

---

* Numb. xv., 30.

APPENDIX.

A.

FACTS SHOWING THE ANTIQUITY AND AUTHENTICITY OF THE BIBLE.

In the foregoing pages it has been shown that the authenticity and truth of the Holy Scriptures cannot be separated from their inspiration If they are *true*, they must be inspired, because they lay claim to direct inspiration; and many of the facts stated are of a miraculous nature; so that if the Scriptures were not given by inspiration, it will follow that they are full of falsehood and imposture Any facts, therefore, which go to prove the truth of the statements contained in the Bible, go just as far to prove its inspiration. I have, therefore, collected in this note a number of interesting facts of this nature, in a condensed form, which my plan did not admit of being brought into the body of the work Some of these will be of use in the study of the introductory lesson of volume V, of my " Scripture Questions " It is hoped, however, that these brief statements will not prevent a more extended examination of the subject, by such as have the means of making it ; but the rather operate as an incitement to inquiry and research.

I. ANTIQUITY OF THE OLD TESTAMENT.

Among all the books in the world, not one is to be found that comes within the reach of the writings of Moses in point of antiquity. They stand alone, without any record to cope or compare with them. The Bible may well be said to contain the only history of our race. There is no authentic profane history of higher antiquity than about the conclusion of the canon of the Old Testament. Nehemiah, the last of the sacred historians, was contemporary with Herodotus, the father of profane history. The high antiquity of these Scriptures is proved beyond question, by three facts. (1) All the books of the Old Testament, except Job and those professedly written after the Babylonish captivity, were written in pure Hebrew, which ceased to be a spoken language after that period. These books, therefore, must have been written before the Babylonish captivity. Job is a mixture of Arabic and Hebrew, just what might have been expected from the scene having been laid in Arabia, the remainder are a mixture of Hebrew and Chaldee, which fixes their date in the generation of the captivity. (2) It is an undeniable fact that the Old Testament was translated into Greek more than two centuries and a half before the Christian era, during the reign and by the order of Ptolymy Philadelphus, king of Egypt. (3) The Old Testament was translated into Chaldee, and commented on by Jewish writers, before the Christian era. All these facts together show the Old Testament Scriptures to be books of high antiquity.

II. GENUINENESS OF THE BOOKS OF THE OLD TESTAMENT.

The genuineness of the Pentateuch was acknowledged by Porphyry and Julian, two of the most bitter of Pagan writers. The impossibility of the corruption of the text, within several centuries before the Christian era, will appear from the fact of its being in the possession both of the Jews and Samaritans, who were at bitter enmity against each other, and the Samaritan Penteteuch has come down to us, and is found to agree with the Hebrew. The same may be said, also, of the Greek and Chaldaic versions; which furnished a guard against interpolation. Nor could the text of the Old Testament have been corrupted since the Christian era; because the original Hebrew has been in the hands of both Jews

APPENDIX 279

and Christians, who would operate as a guard upon each other. And the impossibility of its interpolation before the period first spoken of, will appear from the extreme care taken to preserve the exact integrity of the text. "With a strictness the most punctilious, and a zeal the most persevering, it has in past ages been a practice among the Jews to number how often each Hebrew letter recurred in each and every book, or how often in the beginning, middle, and end of a word, and every varied mode was tried by which the fidelity of a manuscript could be ascertained. On the discovery of the slightest error, whatever the previous labor, the parchment was committed to the flames. A perfect copy of the Scriptures was often the work of years."

III. FACTS CORROBORATIVE OF THE SCRIPTURE NARRATIVES.

"The heathens had a tradition among them, concerning the primeval chaos whence the world arose, and the production of all things by the efficiency of a Supreme Mind, which bears so close a resemblance to the Mosaic account of the creation, as proves that they all originated from one source, while the striking contrast between the unadorned simplicity of the one, and the allegorical turgidity of the other, accurately distinguishes the inspired narratives from the distorted tradition. This remark applies particularly to the Chaldeans, Egyptians, Phœnicians, Hindoos, Chinese, Etruscans, Greeks, and Americans"*

The following extract from the learned Grotius, is invaluable.

"The nations which most rigidly retained ancient customs reckoned time by nights, darkness having originally preceded light, as Thales taught from the ancients. The remembrance of the completion of the work of creation on the seventh day was preserved by the honor in which the seventh day was held, not only among the Greeks and Italians, as we learn from Josephus, Philo, Tibullus, Clemens Alexandrinus, and Lucian (and, as is manifest, among the Hebrews,) but also among the Celts and Indians, by all of

---

* Horne

whom time was divided by weeks, as Philostratus, Dion Cassius, and Justin Martyr inform us, and as the most ancient names of the days do show. From the Egyptians we learn that man's life at the beginning was simple or innocent, and that his body was naked; hence the golden age of the poets, which, according to Strabo, was celebrated by the Indians. Maimonides remarked that the history of Adam, of Eve, of the tree, and of the serpent, existed in his time among the idolatious Indians; and witnesses likewise of our own age testify that the same tradition exists among the inhabitants of Peru and of the Philippine islands, who derived their origin from India, that the name of Adam is found among the Brahmins, and that the Siamese reckon 6000 years since the creation of the world. Berosus, in his history of the Chaldeans, Manetho, in that of the Egyptians, Hæstiæus, Hecatæus, Halbanicus in their histories of Greece, and Hesiod among the poets, have related that the life of those who were descended of the first men extended to nearly a thousand years, which is the less incredible, as the histories of a great many nations, and especially Pausanias and Philostratos among the Greeks, and Pliny among the Romans, relate that the bodies of men in ancient times were much larger, as was found by opening the tombs. Catullus, following many of the Greek writers, relates that divine visions appeared to man before the frequency and enormity of his offences secluded him from converse with the Deity and his angels. The savage life of the giants, mentioned by Moses, is almost every where spoken of by the Greek writers, and some of the Roman. Concerning the deluge, it is to be remarked, that the traditions of all nations, even of those which were long unknown, and have been recently discovered, terminate in its history, whence also all that time was called unknown by Varro. And what we read in the poets, mystified by the license of fable, the most ancient writers had related truly, *i. e*, agreeably to Moses, viz, Berosus among the Chaldeans, Abydinus among the Assyrians, who, like Plutarch among the Greeks, mentions the sending forth of the dove, and Lucian, who says that at Hierapolis of Syria there existed a very ancient history both of the ark, and of chosen men and other living creatures having thereby been preserved. At Molo, also, and at Nicholaus Damascenus, the same account prevailed, the latter of which had

APPENDIX. 281

the name of ark, as Apollodorus also relates in the history of Deucalion. Many Spaniards likewise testify that in parts of America, Cuba, Mechoana, Nicaragua, the remembrance of the deluge, of the preservation of animals, and of the crow and pigeon, is still preserved, and of the deluge itself, in that part now called Golden Castile, and Pliny's remark that Joppa was built before the flood, informs us of a part of the world which was then inhabited. The place where the ark rested after the flood, on the Gordyæan mountains, is pointed to by the constant tradition of the Armenians, from age to age, till the present day. Japhet, primogenitor of the Europeans, and from him Ior, or, as it was formerly pronounced, Javon of the Greeks, also Hammon of the Africans, are names to be found in the writings of Moses, and others are traced by Josephus and other writers in the names of nations and places. Which of the poets does not mention the attempt to climb the heavens? The burning of Sodom is recorded by Diodorus Siculus, Strabo, Tacitus, Pliny, and Solenius. Herodotus, Diodorus, Strabo, and Philo Biblius bear testimony to the very ancient custom of circumcision, which was practised among the descendants of Abraham, not the Hebrews only, but also the Idumeans, Ishmaelites, and others. The history of Abraham, Isaac, Jacob, and Joseph, in accordance with that of Moses, formerly existed in Philo Biblius, taken from Sanchoniathon in Berosus, Hecatæus, Damascenus, Artaphanus, Eupolimus, Demetrius, and partly in the very ancient writers of the Orphic songs, and something is still extant in Justin, taken from Trogus Pompeius. In almost all these there is also a history of Moses and his actions. For the Orphic songs expressly mention that he was drawn out of the water, and the two tables were given him from God. To these we may add Polemon, and not a few things relating to the departure out of Egypt, from the Egyptian writers Manetho, Lysimachus, and Chæremon. Nor can it appear credible to any prudent man, that Moses, to whom both the Egyptians and many other nations, as the Idumeans, Arabians, and Phœnicians, were hostile, would have dared to speak openly of the origin of the world and of the most ancient events, which could be refuted either by former writings, or was opposed to the ancient and popular belief, or that he would have published what happened in his own time, which many alive could have disproved.

Diodorus Siculus, Strabo, Pliny, also Tacitus, and after them Dionysius Longinus (on the Sublime) all speak of Moses. Besides the Talmuds, Pliny and Apoleius mention also Jamnes and Mambres, who resisted Moses in Egypt. Many things are found in the Pythagorean writings about the rites given by Moses, and also some things in other writers. Strabo and Justin, out of Trogus, particularly bear witness to the religion and justice of the ancient Jews, &c."

Eupolemus and Dius mention many remarkable circumstances of David and Solomon, agreeing with the Old Testament history; and Herodotus has a remarkable passage, evidently referring to the destruction of the Assyrians, in the reign of Hezekiah, in which he mentions Sennacherib by name. There is, likewise, a general correspondence between sacred and profane history, even in regard to things mentioned incidentally *

The following statement is taken from "Keith's Demonstration of the Truth of Christianity."

"In respect to the creation of the world from a state of chaos, and the formation of man from the clay or dust of the earth, though alike antecedent to all human testimony, the concurrence of the Scriptural narrative with that which had come down from the earliest ages is such that Ovid, recounting it, seems to be the paraphrast of Moses. Long prior to the most ancient of records, the great events which involved the destiny of our race were necessarily such as could not but be transmitted, though in a faint and fabulous form, from generation to generation. And the golden age, in which holiness and happiness prevailed, denotes the primeval innocence and bliss, when all things were good as God created them. The garden of the Hesperides, bearing golden apples, is a picture of the garden of Eden, where grew every tree that is pleasant to the sight; while the serpent that is reputed to have guarded them, together with the prevalence of serpent-worship throughout the world, is too faithful a testimony that there was a serpent there. Testimonies to the same fact may be drawn from the New World as from the Old. 'It is quite notorious that serpent-wor-

---

* Horne.

ship was the great characteristic of Mexican mythology If the serpent symbol at Palenque, conveys a strong indication of Tultican affinity with Syria, there are numerous others of a still more convincing nature Dupaix exhibits a silver medal, found in one of the sepulchral monuments, which indeed points to the source of the whole Ophitic (serpent) worship A man and woman are represented in a garden with a serpent near them This is obviously a picture record of the first pair in Eden, the serpent, and the fall ' Pandora's box, on the opening of which, by the hand of a woman, all evils spread throughout the world, is a significant emblem of the origin of evil , while hope, at the bottom, was as significant a symbol of the prophetic promise, that, by the seed of the woman, evil would finally be destroyed.

" The memory of the deluge was not lost by any nation from the one extremity of the globe to the other ; and in proof that the tradition was maintained through many ages, evidence of the same fact has been borne in modern times from China, Hindostan, the islands of the Pacific, Mexico, and Peru, which concurs with the testimony, remote in time as in place, which Chaldea, Egypt, Persia, Greece, and Rome anciently supplied ' The people of Mechoacan have preserved a tradition, according to which Coxcox, whom they called Tezpi, embarked in a spacious *acalli*, with his wife and children, many animals and grain, the preservation of which was dear to the human race When the Great Spirit commanded the waters to retire, Tezpi sent forth from his bark a vu'ture. The bird, nourished by dead flesh, did not return, on account of the great number of carcasses which were scattered upon the newly-dried earth. Tezpi sent out other birds, of which the humming-bird alone returned, bearing in its beak a branch covered with leaves After which Tezpi, seeing that the soil began to be covered with new verdure, left his bark near the mountain of Colhuacan ' ' Everywhere,' adds Humboldt, ' the traces of a common origin, the opinions concerning cosmogony, and the primitive traditions of nations, present a striking analogy even in minute circumstances. Does not the humming-bird of Tezpi call to mind the dove of Noah, that of Deucalion, and the birds, according to Berosus, which Xisutrus sent forth from the ark, to try if the waters had subsided, and if as yet he could erect altars to the gods of Chaldea"—*Humboldt, Vues des Cordilleres*, p 227. The raven no less than the dove, and the order no less than the name, the first, the ravenous bird not returning, the second, forever afterward the bird of peace, re-appearing and re-entering, identify each narrative as that of the selfsame fact with a speciality of circumstances which sober reason cannot misinterpret or mistrust And the leafy twig in the bill of a little bird needs but to be traditionally brought back again from the extremity of the globe, where, without the possibility of being transplanted anew, it had flourished for many ages, in order to prove, at last, as fresh a testimony, to the old world and to the new, of the truth of the fact, as at first it was a sure token to the inmates of the ark that they should soon tread on the renovated earth How, but as coming from the only surviving family of man, could the tradition have been preserved simple and uncorrupted, in the midst of the remotest regions so long undiscovered. One half of the world was unknown unto the other, but the twig that a bird did bear was remembered by both, nor was the leaf forgotten It survived like the ark in a deluged world, and it alone may show that faith may bud again where afore it was blasted "

A traveller, named Du Pratz, inquired of a priest of one of the western tribes of North American Indians, respecting their views of the creation The priest replied that God kneaded some clay, and made it into a little man, and when he had examined it, and found it well formed, he blew upon it, and it was filled with life and activity One of the chiefs of the *Sauks* told Major Marston that they believed the Great Spirit first created two men out of the dirt of the earth, but finding that these alone would not answer his purpose, he took a *rib* from each, and made two women, and that all the human race came from these four He said they were all of one nation till they behaved so badly that the Great Spirit came among them, and talked different languages to them, so that they separated, and formed different nations An old Indian in Ohio informed Dr Beatty that they had an old tradition that the waters once overflowed all the land, and drowned all the people then living, except a few, who made a *great canoe*, and were saved in it. He said, also, that a long time ago, the people went to build a high place ; but while they were building it they lost

APPENDIX. 285

their language, and could not understand each other. The Indians also have a tradition that the first woman had two sons, and that the elder killed the younger. The Mandans have a ceremony, in which they have a kind of curb, six feet across and ten feet high, which they call the *great canoe*, and which is evidently designed to represent Noah's ark. In this ceremony they have some edged tools, to represent the tools with which the ark was made, which, in the end, they throw into the water.

Here we discover traditions of the creation, the story of Cain and Abel, the deluge, and the building of Babel, and division of languages, which can be accounted for on no other supposition than the truth of the Mosaic narrative.

Another species of corroborative testimony to the truth of the Scripture narratives, is, the existing monuments of facts therein recorded. The following statement is extracted from Keith:—

" The prophetic fate of the sons of Noah is visible to this hour, the very names of several of the earliest nations,—such as the Canaanites, Assyrians, Elymœites, Lydians, Medes, and Hebrews,—corroborate to the letter the historical facts recorded by Moses, that Canaan, Ashur, Elam, Lud, Madai, and Eber were justly numbered among the descendants of Noah, by whom the nations were divided in the earth after the flood. ' The period of seven days, by far the most permanent division of time, and the most ancient monument of astronomical knowledge, was used by the Brahmins in India with the same denominations employed by us, and was alike found in the calendars of the Jews, Egyptians, Arabs, and Assyrians. It has survived the fall of empires, and has existed among all successive generations, a proof of their common origin.' While the destruction of Sodom, synchronical with the call of Abraham, did not pass unnoticed by ancient writers, the Dead Sea, a bituminous lake, unlike to any other, is a striking corroboration of the recorded judgment on the cities of the *plain*, which its waters have since filled, and the recent and remarkable discovery, that the Jordan, before its course was stayed, passed through the plain, and flowed into the Red Sea, is strikingly illustrative of the Scriptural narrative, as Colonel Leake, the learned editor of Burckhardt's work, has observed ; and that fact has since been amply elucidated by the scientific Leon Laborde, and the evidence is set before us by a chart of the channel, or of the valley through which the Jordan flowed, and which still retains its name, El Ghor, where the Jordan once flowed, as where it still flows on.

"And while the alleged want of a contemporary history is thus newly supplied, a still more recent discovery presents a contemporary picture, coeval with the birth of Moses, and copied by Rosselini and Wilkinson, which may be said to be a commentary on the first chapter of Exodus, and to set the Israelites before our eyes actually engaged in the hard bondage of mortar and brick as Moses describes them. The Egyptian taskmaster is set over them with a rod in his hand, the diversity of color as well as of their countenances, distinguish the oppressed Hebrew slaves, and the whole process of their labor is seen till the tale of bricks may be counted. 'Their countenances are as perfectly Jewish,' according to the Literary Gazette, 'as those of any old clothesmen from St Mary Axe, who now perambulate the streets of London. Neither Lawrence nor Jackson could have painted more real Jews, the features so changeless and so peculiar to that people. And then their occupation, the several portions of the process of brick-making, their limbs bespattered with the mud, and their Egyptian taskmasters with the scourge superintending their labor. The whole seems to us to be a clear and decisive evidence, not only of the captivity, but of the actual circumstances related in the history of Moses. The Egyptians in the original are painted in the usual red, the Israelites of a sallow color, and when we reflect that, throughout all the other subjects figured in these sepulchres of Beni-Hassan, the utmost regard is paid to individuality, and even to minute accessories, we cannot imagine a reason to induce us to question the truth and application of this remarkable discovery.' 'Rosselini's last livraison of illustrations brings those Jews before our eyes who were captives in Egypt under the eighteenth dynasty, and previous to the Exodus. Independently of other evidence drawn from the phonetic language to prove that they are Jews, no cursory reader who glances at their lineaments or persons will for a moment doubt their identity. These Jews are employed under the dynasty of the very kings contemporary with Moses, in the specific act of slavery, which he and Manetho both describe, viz, making bricks and working in the quarries. An Egyptian taskmaster superintends the work, and the bricks, according to their delineation, are precisely those which are found in walls constructed of bricks, the date of which is assignable to the era in question.' *The Egyptians set over them taskmasters to afflict them with their burdens, and made their lives bitter with hard bondage, in mortar and in brick, and in all manner of service in the field.**

"The temporary triumph of the Egyptians over the Jews, in a subsequent age, has also, in that land of their enemies, a striking memorial. Shishak, or Sheshouk, king of Egypt, is represented in another of Champollion's drawings 'as dragging the chiefs of above thirty conquered nations to the feet of the idols of Thebes.' One of these is represented in hieroglyphic characters, as *Joudaha Malek*, the *king of Judah* And in the chronicles of the kings of Judah we read that Rehoboam (the son of Solomon) forsook the law of the Lord, and all Israel with him And in the fifth year of King Rehoboam, Shishak, king of Egypt, came up against Jerusalem, and took the fenced cities of Judah, and came to Jerusalem. Then came Shemaiah the prophet to Rehoboam and to the princes of Judah that were gathered together to Jerusalem because of Shishak, and said unto them, Thus saith the Lord, Ye have forsaken me, and therefore have I also left you *in the hands of Shishak.* So Shishak, king of Egypt, came up against Jerusalem, and took away the treasures of the house of the Lord, and the treasures of the king's house he carried away also the shields of gold which Solomon had made "† Rehoboam, the king of Judah, is still to be seen, as for a time he was left, according to the word of the prophet, *in the hand of Shishak*, king of Egypt.

"The history of the Jews needs not any other concurring evidence to show that their prophetic fate was portrayed by Moses as faithfully as a painter could depict their visage While he is thus set forth as the prophet of the Highest, it may be mentioned, as Grotius and others have shown, that Pagan writers, in ancient times, failed not to pay some tribute of respect to the legislator of Israel. As a writer, he was deemed worthy by Longinus of honorable mention in his treatise on the Sublime As the promulgator

---

* Exodus i, 11, 14.   † 1 Kings xvi, 26. 2 Chron xii, 1–9

of a new religion, wholly divested of idolatry, Strabo describes him as abandoning Egypt, followed by those who worshipped God alone, and planting his people and his faith in that land of which Jerusalem was afterward the capital. The name of the desert, *El Tih*, or the *wandering*, is yet a testimony of the wanderings of the Israelites. And in reference to the history of Moses, Laborde, who partly traversed the same route, states that the Bible is so concise and so precisely true, that it is only by a close attention to each word that all its merit can be discovered. The tomb of Aaron, on the summit of Mount Hor, is one of the most conspicuous objects in the land of Edom, and, surrounded as it is by many an evidence of prophetic truth, still bears testimony to the death and burying-place of the first high-priest of Israel. Aaron died there on the top of the mount. Though, till within these very few years, unheard of and unknown, and situated in the midst of the land of the enemies of Israel, though for many ages possessed by the wild Arabs, neither of Israelitish nor of Christian faith, yet there, on the top of Mount Hor, where he died, is the tomb of Aaron, a memorial on the spot."

The name of *Peleg* was given, according to the Mosaic account, because that, in his days, the earth was divided among the families of the sons of Noah,* and it is ascertained, by modern discoveries, that the origin of primitive kingdoms is traced to a common era, and identified with the life-time of Peleg. To the same period, also, the Mosaic account assigns the building of Babel, and the diversity of tongues is to be traced to the period of the division of the family of man into distinct nations.

The prophetic name given to Abram, is also a standing witness to the truth of the Mosaic history. "Thy name shall be called Abraham, for a father of many nations have I made thee."† *Abraham*, in Hebrew, signifies *the father of a multitude*. And "to whom," says Keith, "since his days, can the name so appropriately pertain, as to him whose descendants peopled Palestine, Edom, and Arabia; and whom the Arabs, with their multitude of tribes, and the Israelites, dispersed throughout the eart

---

* Gen x, 25–32 † Gen x, 25–32

both alike still numbered by millions, have claimed, for more than a hundred generations, as their common father? And whose prophetic name yet awaits its full significancy, till all the families of the earth shall be blessed in his seed, and all nations shall call that man the father of the faithful." The same is true, also, of the name of Sarah.

The name *Ishmael,—the Lord shall hear*, still existing in the numerous tribes of wandering Arabs, who claim him as their father, testifies to the fact recorded Gen. xvi, 7-13, and to this is added the well of *Beer-lahai-roi*, which still exists, a monument of the fact which gave its name, which signifies *the well of him that liveth and seeth me.*

The name *Beer-sheba, the well of the oath*, yet marks the place where the covenant was made between Abraham and Abimelech,* and bears witness to the transaction recorded by Moses.

The same thing might be traced through all the names of cities and places in the Holy Land. These names were generally significant of some event narrated by the sacred writers; yet it is the united testimony of travellers, and a fact beyond dispute, that these places still retain their original Hebrew names, or a corruption which can easily be traced to the original; and this even where nothing but ruins remain to point out the spot. Rev. Eli Smith, of the Syrian mission, says these facts are so obvious that even infidel travellers, who never read the Bible at home, find a Bible an indispensable companion of their travels in the Holy Land. Taken in connection with the signification of these names, and the events narrated in the Bible, these monuments furnish a lasting memorial of the truth of the sacred histories.

The right of circumcision, now practised by all the descendants of Abraham, furnishes a standing witness of the narrative given by Moses, of the covenant made with Abraham. And so the passover, which is now celebrated in the four quarters of the earth, still bears witness to the deliverance of the Israelites from the bondage of Egypt.

Rev. Eli Smith states that, as he was travelling in the region where the battle was fought by Joshua, in behalf of the Gibeonites,

---

* Gen xxi 27-32

at about the same period of the moon and time of day, he was filled with wonder at beholding the sun standing directly over Gibeon, and the moon over the valley of Ajalon; thus furnishing a standing evidence of the miracle, wrought by Joshua, when he said, "Sun, stand thou still upon Gibeon; and thou moon, in the valley of Ajalon." This fact is also corroborated by a passage in the Chinese history, which "speaks of Yao, their king, declaring that in his reign the sun stood so long above the horizon that it was feared that the world would have been set on fire; and fixes the reign of Yao at a given date, which corresponds with the age of Joshua."* The same event is also corroborated by the fable of Ovid, who tells us that a day was once lost, and that the earth was in great danger from the intense heat of an unusual sun; and this fable is connected with the name of a Canaanitish prince.* Mr. Smith likewise states that he and his companion, Dr. Robinson, on their visit to Mount Sinai, ascended the very place where the law was given; which is an abrupt and precipitous mountain, rising so suddenly from the plain below as forcibly to remind him of "the mount that might be touched;" and that the plain below rises in the form of an amphitheatre, and is extensive enough that the thousands of Israel might have stood upon it in plain view of the Holy Mount. He was, he said, very forcibly impressed with the idea that the place was made on purpose for the delivery of the law; and now it stands a living monument of the reality of that awful transaction.

The discoveries of science, in *geometry* and *astronomy*, corroborate the Mosaic account of the creation, and show that these subjects must have been fully understood by the Mind which indited that account. This is a subject, however, which cannot be condensed into the limits of a paragraph. It is worthy of being studied; and it is adverted to here, chiefly for the purpose of calling attention to it, as an interesting and profitable matter to be studied.

---

* Nelson.

THE NEW TESTAMENT.

AGREEMENT OF THE WRITERS OF PROFANE HISTORY WITH THE FACTS RELATED IN THE NEW TESTAMENT.

The following is condensed from Horne's Introduction to the Study of the Holy Scriptures —

1. From the New Testament we learn that Jesus was born at Bethlehem of Judea, in the days of Herod the king, and during the reign of Augustus. Josephus states that a prince of the name of Herod reigned over all Judea for thirty-seven years, even to the reign of Augustus. The character given to this Herod in the Scriptures agrees with that given to him in profane history; and also the division of his territories among his three sons Josephus speaks of Archelaus reigning in Judea, whom he represents as cruel and tyrannical. This corroborates the testimony of Matthew, who says, that when Joseph heard that Archelaus did reign in Judea, in the room of his father Herod, he was afraid to go thither, and turned aside into the parts of Gallilee, which were under the jurisdiction of Herod Antipas.

Luke relates, Acts xii, 1–3, that Herod the king stretched forth his hand to vex certain of the church, and that he killed James, the brother of John, with the sword, and because he saw that it pleased the Jews, he proceeded further to take Peter also. Josephus informs us that this Herod was grandson of Herod the Great, whom the favor of Caligula and Claudius had raised to royal dignity. He was exceedingly zealous for the institutions and customs of the Jews ; which accounts for his putting James to death, and causing Peter to be apprehended There is a wonderful agreement between the accounts of this king's death, as given by Luke and Josephus. Luke says, "Upon a set day, Herod, arrayed in royal apparel, sat upon his throne, and made an oration unto them. And the people gave a shout, saying, 'It is the voice of a god, and not of a man.' And immediately the angel of the Lord smote him, because he gave not God the glory. And he was eaten of worms, and gave up the ghost." Josephus says that Herod came into the theatre, early in the morning, dressed in a robe or garment made wholly of silver, of most wonderful workmanship; and that the reflection of the rays of the rising sun from the silver, gave him a majestic and awful appearance. In a short time his flatterers exclaimed, one from one place and one from another, that he was a god, and they entreated him to be propitious to them, saying, "Hitherto we have reverenced thee as a man, but henceforth we acknowledge that thou art exalted above mortal nature." Immediately after, Josephus says, he was seized with pains in his bowels, extremely violent, and was carried to his palace, where he was worn out by the excruciating pain in his bowels And Josephus assigns substantially the same cause as that given by Luke —" Because the king had neither reproved his flatterers, nor rejected their impious adulation "

The character of Felix, as given by Luke, also agrees with that given him by Josephus and Tacitus. So also, the character of Gallio, as indicated by his conduct during the riot at Corinth, agrees with that given him by his brother Seneca, the celebrated philosopher, who represents him as a man of sweet and gentle disposition, and of much generosity and virtue. Luke says Gallio was deputy,—in the original *proconsul*,—of Achaia, and history informs us that, at that time, proconsuls were sent into this country.

2. There is an agreement between the New Testament histories and profane writers in regard to the sects, morals, and customs of the Jews. It appears from Josephus that the Jews, under the Romans, enjoyed the free exercise of their religion, with the power of accusing and prosecuting, but not of putting any man to death. This explains their answer to Pilate, when he told them to take Jesus and crucify him,—they said, *It is not lawful for us to put any man to death.*

The accounts given by the evangelists of the sects of Pharisees, Sadducees, and Herodians, as well as of the depravity of the Jewish nation in the time of Christ, and of the hatred between the Samaritans and Jews, are all confirmed by Josephus So, also, the Roman mode of treating prisoners and crucifying criminals, as mentioned in the New Testament, is corroborated by the testi-

APPENDIX. 293

mony of Cicero, Plutarch, and other writers, who have incidentally mentioned it. The famine in the reign of Claudius, mentioned Acts xi, 28, is also mentioned by Josephus

From the accounts given of the Acts of the Apostles, by Luke, it appears that there were synagogues of Jews in all the places where they preached ; and from the writings of Philo, Josephus, and others, it appears that the Jews were dispersed into many countries before the destruction of Jerusalem

When Paul was brought before the chief Captain, Acts xxi, 38, that officer asked him, " Art thou not that Egyptian, which before these days madest an uproar, and leddest out into the wilderness four thousand men that were murderers ?" Josephus has recorded at length the transaction here incidentally mentioned. During the government of Felix, which was the time alluded to by Luke, an Egyptian, who pretended to be a prophet, led into the wilderness several thousand men, and marched against Jerusalem, promising that the walls should fall down at his command Felix went out against him, and dispersed his followers The chief Captain calls him, " *That Egyptian ;*" and Josephus calls him *the Egyptian,* and *the Egyptian and false prophet*

3. There is a perfect accuracy in the incidental allusions of the apostles to the character and pursuits of heathen nations Paul says, *The Greeks seek after wisdom ;* which is notoriously their character, as described in profane history. Luke, in giving an account of Paul's visit to Athens, speaks of that city as " wholly given to idolatry " The Athenians, according to profane history, adopted the gods of all nations, and crowded into their capital all the divinities of the known world. Their streets were so encumbered with statues, that it was said to be easier, at Athens, to find a god than a man. So, also, the account given of the character of the Athenians —" All the Athenians and strangers which were in their city, spent their time in nothing else but to tell or hear some new thing " Demosthenes describes them as loitering about, and inquiring in places of public resort, if there be any news ?

Paul complains that among the Cretans there were " many unruly and vain talkers and deceivers," &c., and he quotes from one of their own poets, " The Cretans are always liars, evil-beasts, slow-bellies," and adds, " which witness is true." This exactly

25*

agrees with history. From the time of Homer, the island of Crete was regarded as the scene of fiction. Many authors affirm that its inhabitants were infamous for their violation of truth, and at length their falsehood became so notorious, that to *cretise*, or imitate the Cretans, was a proverbial expression among the ancients for lying.

4. Testimonies furnished by adversaries to the name and faith of Christ, further corroborate the New Testament narratives.

The following passage from Josephus is so remarkable, that its genuineness has been doubted; but Horne maintains, in a long argument, that it is genuine,—that it agrees with the context,—and that it could not have been interpolated. Josephus says, after relating a sedition of the Jews against Pontius Pilate, which the latter quelled,—" Now there was, about this time, Jesus, a wise man, if it be lawful to call him a man; for he performed many wonderful works. He was a teacher of such men as received the truth with pleasure. He drew over to him many of the Jews, and also many of the Gentiles. *This was the Christ*. And when Pilate, at the instigation of the principal men among us, had condemned him to the cross, those who had loved him from the first, did not cease to adhere to him For he appeared to them alive again on the third day, the divine prophets having foretold these and ten thousand other wonderful things concerning him. And the tribe or sect of Christians so named from him, subsists to this time "

The Jewish Talmuds, also, admit the main facts respecting the birth of Christ, his journey into Egypt, &c, and also that he performed many miracles; but they impute them to magic arts.

It was customary for the governors of provinces to send to the emperor accounts of remarkable transactions, which occurred in the places where they resided, which were preserved as the *acts* of their respective governments. Pilate sent such a work to Rome, which was called *Acta Pilata*. Eusebius says, " Our Saviour's resurrection being much talked of, Pilate informed the emperor of it, as likewise of his miracles, of which he had heard; and that, being raised up, after he had been put to death, he was already believed by many to be a God These accounts were deposited among the archives of the empire; and the Christian writers, in

APPENDIX. 295

their apologies, often appealed to the *Acts of Pilate*, to prove the truth of what they asserted. Tiberius Cæsar even proposed to the Senate to have the name of Jesus enrolled among the Roman gods. The main facts respecting Christ, as narrated by the evangelists, are attested by heathen writers, especially Tacitus and Celsus.

The miraculous darkness, mentioned by the evangelists as covering the earth at the time of Christ's death, with the great earthquake, are mentioned and recognized as facts by Celsus, a most bitter opposer of Christianity. Tertullian, also, in his apology, expressly refers his adversaries to this darkness, as a known and admitted fact.

In addition to the foregoing, there is another species of corroborative testimony, derived from ancient coins, medals, and inscriptions, which establishes many facts incidentally alluded to in the Bible. But a bare allusion to some of these inscriptions and repesensations is all that can be given here. A coin struck at Apamea, in the reign of Philip the elder, has on it a representation of Noah's Ark,—a man and woman passing out of it, and two persons remaining inside,—a dove fluttering over it, with an olive leaf in her mouth,—and another bird perched on the roof,—and on one side of the Ark is the word *NOE*, in Greek characters. Facts respecting Egypt, alluded to in the narrative of Moses, are confirmed by representations contained in the tombs and other ruins in that country, some of them very striking. The account of the war carried on by Pharaoh-necho, against the Jews and Babylonians, related in the second book of Chronicles, and confirmed by Herodotus, the historian, is corroborated by a sculpture in the tomb of the son of that king, representing three different sets of prisoners in a triumphal procession, who are evidently Jews, Ethiopians, and Persians. In Acts xiii, 7, the Roman governor of Cyprus is called a proconsul; and on a coin which was struck in the reign of Claudius Cæsar, is inscribed the same title which Luke gives to Sergius Paulus, proving that the country was then under the government of proconsuls. There is also a coin, which confirms what Luke says of Philippi, (Acts xvi, 11, 12,) that it was the chief of that part of

Macedonia, and a colony. In the fourteenth verse of the same chapter, we read of Lydia, a dealer in purple from Thyatira; and among the ruins of that place there is an inscription made by a corporation of dyers, by which it appears that the business of dying purple was carried on at that place. The triumphal arch, erected in Rome, by Titus, to commemorate his victories in Palestine, still exists, an undeniable proof of the histories of the destruction of Jerusalem, and the dissolution of the Jewish state, which show the fulfilment of Christ's predictions. There are, also, medals of Judea vanquished, struck by the order of Titus, one of which furnishes an extraordinary fulfilment of Isaiah's prediction, delivered at least eight hundred years before —"She being desolate, shall sit upon the ground."* On this medal, the conquered country is represented under the emblem of a desolate female, sitting under a tree. This, also, agrees with what Jeremiah says, in Lamentations "How doth the city *sit* solitary! How is she become as a widow!"

These are only a specimen of a great many similar facts, of which any one may satisfy himself by examination.

The foregoing facts furnish circumstantial evidence of the truth of the sacred volume, of the strongest kind. They prove that these books were written in the age to which they are ascribed; and also, that whenever the writers have alluded to existing facts, their statements are perfectly and minutely accurate. This establishes the credibility of the authors; and if they are proved to be correct in all particulars concerning which we have concurrent testimony, they are entitled to credit in regard to every thing else. But if all their statements are true, they must have been inspired, so that what they wrote is the word of God; for this they assert. Moreover, all the traditions which have been mentioned, as agreeing in the main with the accounts of the sacred writers, are so far mixed with fable, as to point to the sacred records for the true account. These things certainly prove that the Bible is not a forgery; but that it was written by honest and credible men, at the time it professes to have been written. And no one can give it a careful perusal, with this belief concerning it, without coming to to the conclusion that it is a revelation from God.

---

* Isaiah iii, 26.

B.

INSPIRATION.

The following definition of inspiration, with the Scripture proofs referred to, is more full than that given in the body of the work It is a just and clear explanation of the *theory of inspiration*, so far as it is proper to theorise on the subject It is by the Rev. John Brown, of Haddington.

"In what manner the influence, by which the penmen of the Scriptures were directed, affected them, we pretend not fully to explain It is enough for us to know, that thereby they were infallibly guided and determined to declare what they did not formerly know ; to conceive properly of what they had formerly known, and to express their subject in terms absolutely just in themselves, and calculated to convey the truths represented to others. But so far we may conclude, that, while the penmen exercised their own reason and judgment; Ps. xlv, 1 ; Mark xii, 36 ; Luke i, 3, Acts i, 1, 1 Peter i, 11, the Holy Ghost (1) Effectually stirred them up to write, 2 Peter i, 21, (2) Appointed to each his proper share or subject correspondent with his natural talents, and the necessities of the church in his time ; 2 Peter i, 21 ; Mat. xxv. 15; (3) Enlightened their minds, and gave them a duly distinct view of the truths which they were to deliver ; Jer. i, 11–16, and xiii, 9–14, Ezek. iv, 4–8 ; Dan x, 1, 14 ; and ix, 22–27, and viii, 15–19, and xii, 8 ; Amos vii, 7, 8 ; and viii, 2 ; Zech. i, 19, 21 ; and iv, 11–14 ; and v, 6 ; 1 Peter i, 10, 11 ; Eph. iii, 3, 4, John xvi, 13. Perhaps this illumination was given all at once to Paul, when caught up to the third heaven, but was bestowed gradually on the other apostles ; Mark iv, 34 ; Luke xxiv, 17, 45 ; John xx, 22 ; Acts ii, 4 ; and x, 9–15, 28, 34 ; (4) He strengthened and refreshed their memories to recollect whatever they had seen or heard, which he judged proper to be inserted in their writings ; John xiv, 26, Luke i, 3 ; Jer. xxxi, 3 ; (5) Amidst a multitude of facts, he directed them to write precisely what was proper for the edification of the church, and neither more nor less ;

John xx, 30, 31 ; and xxi, 25 ; Rom. xv, 4 ; 1 Cor. x, 6-11 ; Rom. iv, 23, 24 ; (6) He excited in their minds such images and ideas as had been treasured up in their memories, and directed them to other ends and purposes than themselves would ever have done of their own accord. Thus, under inspiration, Amos draws his figures from herds, flocks, and fields , Paul makes use of his classical learning ; Amos i-ix ; Acts xvii, 28 ; 1 Cor. xv, 33 ; Titus i, 12 ; (7) He immediately suggested and imprinted on their minds such things as could not be known by reason, observation or information, but were matters of pure revelation ; Isa. xlvi, 9, 10 ; xli, 22, 23 ; and xlv, 21 ; whether they respected doctrines, 1 Tim. iii, 16 ; or facts past or future, Gen. i, ii, iii ; Lev. xxvi, &c. (8) He so superintended every particular writer, as to render him infallible in his matter, words, and arrangement ; and, by his superintending influence, made them all in connection so write, as to render the whole Scripture, at any given period, a sufficient infallible rule to direct men to true holiness and everlasting happiness ; Deut. viii, 4 , Ps. xix, 7-11 ; cxix and i, 2 ; John v, 39 ; Mat. xxii, 29 ; Luke xvi, 29, 31 ; Rom. xv, 4 , 2 Tim. iii, 15-17 ; 2 Peter i, 19. Many of the sentences recorded in Scripture are not inspired in themselves, being the words of Satan or of wicked men ; but the Scripture report relative to these expressions is directed by divine inspiration. That our books of the Old and New Testament, the APOCRAPHAL TRACTS being excluded from both, are of an INFALLIBLE and DIVINE original, is thus evident.''

www.ingramcontent.com/pod-product-compliance
Lightning Source LLC
Chambersburg PA
CBHW071958220426
43662CB00009B/1175